SMITHSONIAN CONTRIBUTIONS TO ANTHROPOLOGY

VOLUME 6

Rocafuerte Painted (red and black-on-white) square basin of Form 14, painted in Technique 2. The unusual double snake motif is executed in low relief on the rim and in painting on the interior. This vessel was assembled from sherds in the sample from N–P–2, Cut 1 and Broadside A (U.S. National Museum).

Archeological Investigations on the Rio Napo, Eastern Ecuador

Clifford Evans and Betty J. Meggers

SMITHSONIAN INSTITUTION PRESS

Washington 1968

A Publication of the

SMITHSONIAN INSTITUTION

United States National Museum

LIBRARY OF CONGRESS 67–60067

UNITED STATES GOVERNMENT PRINTING OFFICE, WASHINGTON, 1968

For sale by the Superintendent of Documents, U.S. Government Printing Office
Washington, D.C. 20402 - Price $4.50

Preface

The eastern slopes of the Andes attracted our attention in 1950, when it became probable that the Marajoara Phase on the island of Marajó at the mouth of the Amazon was derived from northwestern South America. Our first opportunity to investigate the possibilities for archeological fieldwork came when we were in Guayaquil, Ecuador, in 1954 and met Coronel Jorge V. Gortoire, who had served for a period as commandant of the Ecuadorian Army Post at Tiputini. Conversation with him reawakened our latent interest in the area, and we began to make specific plans. In October 1956, having been awarded Grant No. 2012 from the Penrose Fund by the American Philosophical Society and granted official detail by the Smithsonian Institution, we returned to Ecuador to undertake the fieldwork.

Through the courtesy of Coronel Rafael Andrade Ochoa, at that time Commander-general of the Fuerza Aerea Ecuatoriana, we received authorization to fly from Quito to Tiputini in an Ecuadorian Air Force DC–3 transport plane. However, almost daily rains maintained the airstrip in unsuitable condition for landing and after several weeks of waiting in Quito for the weather to break, we gave up and arranged to fly by commercial airline in a Junkers Tri-Motor to Shell-Mera and then in a single engine Norseman to Tena. A day on horseback brought us to Latas, where we secured a dugout canoe manned by Quechua-speaking Indians to take us downriver. Although the trip was longer and more difficult than it would have been by air, it gave us invaluable first-hand experience with conditions along the Rio Napo (pls. 1–5). We were able to follow our hourly progress on U.S. Air Force Preliminary Base Map 950A (Scale 1:500,000), which perfectly reproduced every bend and island. By the afternoon of the fifth day, when we arrived at Tiputini, we were well prepared to appreciate the comments of Orellana's men, who preceded us by 415 years.

When we stepped on shore at Tiputini, the military post that was to be our base of operations, we were delighted to discover not only that there was an archeological site on the spot, but that the pottery included incised and excised techniques of decoration diagnostic of the Marajoara Phase, although only painted vessels had been previously reported from the Rio Napo. With the cooperation of army personnel and local residents, we were able to investigate a number of sites particularly along the portion of the river between Tiputini and the mouth of the Rio Yasuní, which marks the boundary between Ecuador and Peru. We also checked the lower Rio Tiputini. During our stay, the river was unusually low, and extensive sand bars reduced the channel in places to a slender meandering stream (pl. 4b). Giant trees temporarily resting on beaches (pl. 3b) attested to the force of the current at other times of the year, lending credence to descriptions by Orellana's companions (see pp. 106-107), who had the misfortune to encounter higher water than we did.

At the conclusion of the survey, we had accumulated several tons of specimens and were sufficiently familiar with the river to look forward to returning to Quito by air. As was the case in October, intermittent rain kept the airstrip soft, but we were prepared to wait as long as necessary this time, since going by river would have taken at least two weeks. An Ecuadorian Air Force DC–3 finally came on December 15, and two hours after takeoff we were in Quito—by every standard of comparison, another world.

We left behind us in the Province of Napo-Pastaza many friends never to be seen again, and memories still fresh as we write this ten years later. Sr. José Bernardo Crespo Pando made us his guests while we worked at Nueva Armenia, and allowed us to use his home as a base from which to visit nearby sites. Philosopher, businessman, and astute observer of the world from afar, he was an invaluable promoter of our cause as well as an entertaining host. Several pleasant days were also spent at the home of Sr. José Rafael Urvina on the Rio Tiputini, where we received all possible cooperation and courtesy. Other land owners who granted us permission to work on their property and to whom we offer our thanks are Sr. Juan Francisco Buitrón (Hacienda San Juan, Cotacocha), Sr. Osvaldo Bijarini Aridi (Florencia), and Sr. Alfonso Antonio Cox Vega (Bello Horizonte). Sr. Pedro Jarrín, at that time Jefe Político of the Junta del Cantón Aguarico, kindly allowed us to dig a few holes in the main street of Nuevo Rocafuerte.

Since we were unable to arrange for a trip to the Rio Aguarico, we are particularly indebted to Rene Alberto Hinoyosa Carrera, then a second lieutenant stationed at Tiputini, who collected sherds for us from Cabo Minacho on the Rio Güepí and Pañacocha on the Rio Cuyabeno (fig. 3). Other young officers at Tiputini, who provided us not only with various kinds of assistance but also with pleasant companionship, include Soloman Hernandez V., Augustín Carvalho V., Raul Costales, and Fausto Bustamonte. We are indebted to the commandant at that time, then Major J. Gonzalo Ramos Sevilla, for permitting us to use Tiputini as our base, and providing us with quarters and other kinds of help.

During our negotiations to enter the Oriente by air, we were aided in numerous ways by Jorge V. Gortaire V., then a colonel and director of the Colegio Militar "Eloy Alfaro" in Quito. Other kinds of help and guidance were provided by Enrique Martinez Q., manager of the Compañía General de Comercio y Mandato in Quito, and his assistant Francisco Punina Y. To these and other military and governmental officials whose names escape us after a decade, we wish to express our appreciation for the many favors, large and small, that we have not forgotten, and which helped to make our visit memorable as well as scientifically fruitful.

Finally, we wish to record our indebtedness to the late Emilio Estrada, who while teasing us for persisting in our "whim" to go to the Rio Napo, exercised his considerable influence to help us secure the necessary permissions from military authorities. Although his interventions were often unobtrusive, it is probable that they were instrumental in making it possible for us to carry out the work described in the present report.

Other obligations have been incurred during efforts to work out the affiliations of Rio Napo archeological complexes. Our ability to trace the downriver movement of the Polychrome Horizon Style (fig. 68) stems from permission granted by the Ethnographical Museum in Göteborg, Sweden, to take detailed notes and photographs during the summer of 1960 of sherd samples collected in the 1920's by Curt Nimuendajú. This museum work was supported financially by Grant No. 2664 from the Penrose Fund of the American Philosophical Society. Peter Paul Hilbert, who is responsible for what little stratigraphic information is available from the middle and upper Amazon, has again generously made available unpublished data. Donald Lathrap, whose chronological sequence in eastern Peru is one of the rare reliable reference points, has kindly allowed us to consult his unpublished doctoral dissertation at Harvard University, which supplements data secured by examination of the collections from his 1956 fieldwork. We wish also to record our appreciation to the American Museum of Natural History, the Museum of the American Indian (Heye Foundation), the Brooklyn Museum, the Museum of Primitive Art, the

Peabody Museum of Archaeology and Ethnology (Harvard University), the Musée de l'Homme (Paris), the Museu Paraense Emilio Goeldi (Belem), the Museu Paulista (São Paulo), the Instituto Geográfico e Histórico do Amazonas (Manaus), the Museo Víctor Emilio Estrada (Guayaquil), the Museo Arqueológico del Banco Central del Ecuador (Quito), and the Casa de la Cultura Ecuatoriana (Quito), all of which have granted us permission to examine and photograph specimens or have provided us with photographs for publication. Several Napo Phase anthropomorphic urns have passed into the hands of private collectors, who have allowed us to include them in our illustrations. To Thomas P. Flannery, Alan C. Lapiner, Jay C. Leff and Howard S. Strouth, we take this opportunity to offer public thanks.

Carbon-14 dates have been furnished by the Smithsonian Institution and the University of Pennsylvania. We are indebted to the Creole Foundation for a grant to assist in obtaining the first series of dates from the latter laboratory.

In conclusion, it is a pleasure to record once again our indebtedness to members of the Smithsonian Office of Anthropology Processing Lab staff, especially Willie Mae Pelham and Robert C. Jenkins, for their careful preparation of the sherd collections for study. George Robert Lewis, scientific illustrator in the Smithsonian Office of Anthropology, has produced his customarily excellent drawings from badly eroded pottery, poor illustrations in published sources or photographs, as well as the maps and diagrams. We apologize for delaying so many years to provide them with captions. The plates owe their clarity to the high quality enlargements furnished by the staff of the Smithsonian Institution Museum of Natural History Photo Lab. The manuscript was efficiently typed by Anne M. Lewis, Smithsonian Office of Anthropology.

For scholars interested in consulting the illustrated material, some clarification of the symbols and legends may be useful. All specimens not otherwise credited are in the United States National Museum, where a large type collection of sherds has been deposited. Specimens in other collections are so identified, and addition of the word "courtesy" indicates that the photographs were supplied by the individual or institution named. A key has been employed in figures showing rim profiles, permitting rapid recognition of association between form and presence or absence of red slip or decoration, explained in each caption. The relative frequency of rims, shown in black, white, or hachure, approximates the relative popularity of the form with each type of surface treatment.

CE
BJM

Smithsonian Institution
Washington, D.C.
December 13, 1966

POSTSCRIPT

After leaving our hands in mid-December of 1966, this manuscript pursued a devious route through reviewers and editors, and was finally ready for press in late May of 1967. By that time, however, all publication funds had been committed and typesetting had to be delayed until the beginning of the next fiscal period. On July 12, 1967, a messenger from the Government Printing Office (GPO) picked up the nine assorted packages containing our edited text, figures, charts, tables, and plates; two packages containing an edited manuscript and illustrations from another department; and eight skids loaded with cartons of surplus publications for condemnation and destruction. On August 16,

1967, our editor phoned the GPO to inquire the date that galley proof might be expected (having been advised that typesetting would take about six weeks), and learned to her dismay that the manuscript and accompanying packages in question had not been received. A thorough inquiry on the part of persons in all agencies involved over a period of several weeks finally reconstructed the incredible series of events that resulted in the two manuscripts and their illustrative materials accompanying the condemnation material through spot checks and transfers from one vehicle to another to a waste paper salvage company and thence to the city dump, where they were presumably burned (not being suitable for salvage as waste paper). A carbon of the unedited text, original draft copies of maps, diagrams and tables, and a miscellaneous group of photographic enlargements of individual negatives were the only things remaining in our office. The most heartbreaking aspect of the loss was the destruction of the original drawings, which had consumed more than a year of painstaking labor on the part of Scientific Illustrator George Robert Lewis.

In the reconstitution of illustrative material, we have had the cooperation of the entire Smithsonian Institution on a priority basis, a concession that we deeply appreciate. To shorten the time required to reproduce the figures, we also have had the assistance of Scientific Illustrator Marcia Bakry, who has redrawn all the maps and rim profile diagrams. George Robert Lewis has recreated most of the line drawings of specimens; a few have been eliminated because of insufficient time. We wish to record our gratitude to both of these individuals for tackling the job conscientiously and rapidly, and producing results that are as good as or better than the first attempts. The Museum of Natural History Photographic Laboratory has provided quality service with close to "polaroid" speed in reprinting to specific scale, contrast, and tone the numerous negatives from which the final plates were again assembled and remounted. Joan Horn of the Smithsonian Institution Press, who fortunately saved all her editorial notes, has accorded us priority treatment and tackled the job with her usual enthusiasm, fervor, and accuracy the second time around. Anders Richter, Director of the Smithsonian Institution Press, and the staff of the Government Printing Office have collaborated to assure that publication time was as brief as possible. To these and other individuals who have sympathized with our predicament and resupplied lost illustrations, we extend our heartfelt thanks. To our contemporary colleagues at the Smithsonian Institution who may be fearful for the fate of their manuscripts, we offer the observation that the rate of frequency for this type of occurrence appears to be only once every hundred years.

CE
BJM

February 29, 1968

Contents

Tables

TEXT

APPENDIX

Illustrations

FIGURES

PLATES

Archeological Investigations on the Rio Napo, Eastern Ecuador

Geographical Description

The eastern Ecuadorian lowlands are a vast level carpet of tropical rain forest drained by myriad rivers and streams that merge one by one to form major tributaries of the Amazon (fig. 1). Their nearly adjacent, generally parallel courses dissect the terrain when the water level is low, and spill over the intervening land when it is high, so that ". . . one can not travel because of the great amount of water and the marshes and creeks that there are there" (Pizarro, *in* Heaton, 1934, p. 250). In 1541, this was "a great uninhabited region" (op. cit., p. 247), transversed by Pizarro and Orellana and their forces with hardship and privation, and the archeological record indicates that along the banks of the Rio Napo at least this label was applicable during long intervals in prehistoric times.

The eastern face of the Andes is abrupt in Ecuador, and the rivers cascade in narrow ribbons down steepwalled canyons. At Tena, only 90 kilometers east of Latacunga in the central highlands, the elevation drops to 512 meters. Between these towns the eastern cordillera rises above 4000 meters and snow-capped Cotopaxi, 75 kilometers northwest of Tena, reaches 5897 meters. The eastern slope is clothed in dense vegetation, the product of warmth and moisture. Rainfall records over a 7–8 year period at Tena show an average of 218.4 millimeters in January (the dryest month) and 502.9 millimeters in June (the wettest month), with a yearly average of 3810.0 millimeters. Although there is fluctuation over a 24-hour period, average monthly temperature is nearly constant. Records at Tena for a 4–5 year period show averages of 22.3°C for the coldest month (July) and 23.9°C for the warmest month (November), with an annual average of 23.3°C (Ferdon, 1950, pp. 69, 75).

Daily temperature fluctuation is considerable, however, as a few observations made during our stay at Tiputini clearly show. From a 6 a.m. low of 21.7°C, the temperature may rise to 27.7°C at 10 a.m., 30.0°C at midday, 31.7°C at 2 p.m., falling to 26.7°C at 8 p.m. On a rainy day, the midday reading may be only 25.5°C, rising to 26.7°C at 2 p.m. and falling back to 25.8°C at 5:30 p.m. These are shade records; one experiment in the sun pushed the maximum to 47.2°C. In human terms, there is great variation in sensation of heat at the same temperature depending on the strength of the breeze and the presence or absence of sun or rain. Although 21.7°C was the lowest reading we achieved, our most vivid memories are of being chilly rather than too hot.

October, November, and December are generally the dryest months, but rain can be expected any day of the year. Showers are briefer in this "dry season," and the lessened precipitation is reflected in the lowering of the rivers. The Napo in December of 1956 was filled with large sandbars between which the water meandered in narrow channels (pl. 1*a*). Since even the dryest month receives more rain than falls in many other parts of the world over a whole year, vegetation remains lush and green.

The fauna is Amazonian and includes a variety of birds and mammals suitable for sustenance of man, although wildlife is rarely seen by a modern traveler. Orellana's expedition was furnished with "meats, partridges, turkeys and fish of many sorts" (Carvajal, *in* Heaton, 1934, p. 175) and something called "monkey-cat" (op. cit., p. 411) by Indians living near the mouth of the Rio Curaray. Peccary, agoutis, and monkeys are still caught and eaten in the area. Of cultivated plants, the Spaniards were offered "maize and yuca and sweet potatoes and

1

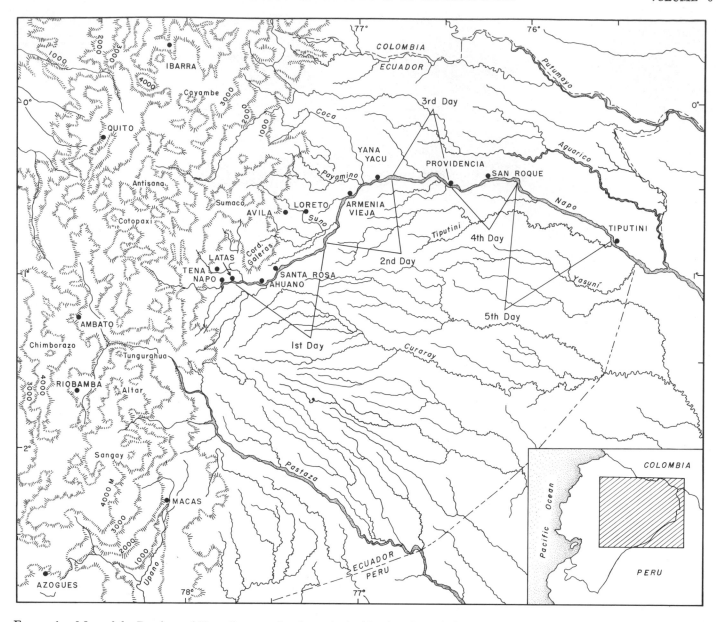

FIGURE 1.—Map of the Province of Napo-Pastaza, showing principal landmarks and distances covered during descent of the Rio Napo.

other food products" (Ortiguera, *in* Heaton, 1934, p. 314) raised in slash and burn clearings (pl. 1*b*).

A more vivid impression of the stretch of river between Latas (pl. 2*a*) and Tiputini as it appeared during five days of November is provided by observations from the journal kept during our trip. The daily distance traversed (fig. 1) provides a scale against which the progress of Orellana's expedition can be measured (see pp. 106-107).

NOVEMBER 9—FIRST DAY: The river between Latas and the Rio Misahualli has rock outcrops. The current was strong and we floated most of the way. The paddlers don't work much, but we seemed to be travelling at a good pace. Following the map (fig. 1), we saw nothing at Vargas Torres. Farther down

there was a settlement with a church and several houses near where Ahuano is shown on the map. Passed there at 1 p.m. For the next 2 hours, we could see the Cordilleira Galeras to the north and west (15 km. from the Napo). Along the river were small steep-sided hills, sometimes sliced through making sheer 15 meter cliffs with strata of large pebbles like on the present beaches. Between the hills were low areas and sandbars covered with tall fan-leafed cane. During the afternoon, the land became generally lower, with wide sandbars often covered with large rounded pebbles and littered with whole trees left by the last high water (pl. 2*b*, 3*b*). Down here the river seems to rise less than they said it did at Latas, but it is hard to tell how much from the appearance of the vegetation. It is not a smooth flowing river, but full of eddies, back washes, and turbulent areas. When we cross one of the latter, it sounds as though the bottom of the boat was being sand blasted.

Stopped at 2:30 p.m. for 20 minutes at the settlement of some gold panners near where Santa Rosa is shown on the map. It was a low bank and must flood in June. The paddlers swapped oranges for some corn meal cakes and one-quarter of a roasted monkey. The sun came out hot and bright and we were glad it had been shady before. The river is so wide, 500–1000 meters, that there is a lot of reflection and it doesn't take long to sunburn. There are innumerable islands and other places that become islands in high water. This is the widest river we have travelled on—it makes the Essequibo in British Guiana look like a creek. It must be fantastic in the rainy season when it overflows the present banks.

Except near Ahuano, we passed no settlement all day and only 3 or 4 times did we see a house being lived in. The land is too low or too steep for agriculture and the river is too rough with turbulence to be very good fishing. A few kapok trees, some purple flowered vines, otherwise the usual palm and evergreen vegetation. Very few birds. Beautiful blue sky and white clouds, white tree trunks, green leaves.

When we stopped it was 6 p.m. and almost dark. There was a wide bar on the left bank and we had to walk several hundred meters back to where there was a grove of trees to hang the hammocks. Slow sprinkle off and on throughout the night.

NOVEMBER 10—SECOND DAY: Awoke at 5:30 a.m. as the sun was rising and got away at 6:05 a.m. The morning was sunny and the river had dropped about a meter so the current was less swift. Passed the mouth of the Suno on the left at 8:05 a.m. and got caught in the cross waters until the men had sense enough to get farther out in the Napo. These river tributaries are difficult to detect because their mouths look like those of branches of the Napo coming from around islands. The places shown on the map above and below the Suno no longer exist. The islands are larger, the banks are generally low and by noon we had passed out of the area of pebbly sandbars. In the vicinity of the Suno we could see a range of mountains to the northwest, including the cone of the volcano Sumaco (pl. 3a) with clouds hanging below the peaks (50 km. from the Napo). About 11:15 a.m. we passed the 300 meter contour line. Passed Armenia Vieja at 11:35 a.m. The river has slowed down considerably and by 2 p.m. the men were having to paddle. It is remarkable that the water flows at all when one thinks that it drops less than 300 meters in 3218 kilometers, under 15 centimeters per 1.6 kilometers.

At 1 p.m. we stopped at the mouth of a small creek entering from the left bank above the Payamino to dynamite fish. One of the men cut a stick of dynamite into thirds, wrapped one-third in a leaf, tied a pebble to the bundle to make it sink, added the fuse and cap, borrowed our matches and headed up the bank. We waited with 2 men in the boat below the mouth. They threw in a few hunks of clay and then the charge. Two men dived in immediately and started grabbing fish so fast they had to hold some of them in their mouths. One started drifting downstream and our men took after it, wasting a lot of energy because they didn't catch it. Loaded the catch (half a dozen large fish and a few more small ones) and continued with only a half hour lost. Stopped at 1:40 p.m. at the mouth of the Payamino for 15 minutes while the men borrowed a pan from the residents to cook some of the fish for lunch. High bank, no sherds.

Passed the mouth of the Coca at 2:30 p.m. and found one farm on the upstream side with some cows. The Coca has its mouth divided by an island. Below, the Napo is wider with banks from 1–6 meters high showing signs of erosion during the last high water. Most abundant wild life is butterflies, several of which flitted around the boat, as well as some large bees. A few more birds than yesterday—half a dozen white herons, one blue egret, a tree full of paraquets, oriole nests, a couple of kingfishers. A few can be heard singing in the forest.

A high, 6-meter bank appeared on the left at 4 p.m. and was occupied by the most extensive settlement we have seen since the village of Napo. The Indians said it was Yana Yacu. There was a school near the bank and a motor launch at the dock. Stopped at 5:05 p.m. on a sandbar on the left bank and started looking for a place to sleep. The trees were farther from the shore than last night and separated from the beach by a shallow lagoon. Judging from its dampness, this bar was mostly under water yesterday. The Indians started cutting bamboo from among the driftwood and putting poles in the ground to support our waterproof nylon tarps as a tent. The poles seemed secure so we started to cook supper as it was getting dark. All was well until 3 a.m. when we had a shower. Then from 4:30 a.m. until dawn we were not sure we would escape catastrophe. A strong wind rippled and ballooned the tarps and we discovered that several places were not well tied. The rain blew in from the north end and sprinkled in from the east, but fortunately not enough to get us really wet. The rain was accompanied by lightning and thunder until dawn.

NOVEMBER 11—THIRD DAY: Cooked coffee and oatmeal at 6 a.m. as the rain beat steadily down. The area beneath the tarp was invaded by termites, which were dispatched with DDT. Inquired at 7 a.m. if we went or waited, and the men said wait.

9 a.m.—clouds beginning to break. Spent the past 3 hours absorbing the atmosphere of rain on the Napo and contemplating the view to the west, upriver, with trees increasingly gray with distance, dull gray sky, eroded and polished tree trunk and driftwood immediately beside the tent, sandbar continuing beyond and also on the other shore—a dismal and dreary scene. No one living for miles around; nothing but sand, low cane, and trees. Howling monkeys in the distance. We are learning why no one lived here. This is the dry season too! We feel for Orellana in 1541 without nylon tarps and primus stoves, but remembering the cold rainy highlands, perhaps he didn't find it much different—maybe better since it is warmer here.

10 a.m.—Stopped raining so broke camp and left. Sprinkled for a couple of hours. Passed the mouth of the Jivino at 2:20 p.m. and arrived at Providencia at 6:10 p.m. just after sunset. The river is very capricious now. The sandbars change form constantly and are very extensive in this area. Out in the middle of a stretch a kilometer and a half wide it is so shallow our dugout cannot get across. We had to back off once this afternoon. As a result of having to zigzag, we make less distance than we otherwise could. In the current we make good time.

NOVEMBER 12—FOURTH DAY: Didn't get away until 7:40 a.m. It was clear when we left but clouds began to build up during the morning, some white, others black. Protection from the sun was welcome. A couple of light showers. Came to San Roque at 1:00 p.m. and had a hard time getting to the house because of a large sandbar in front. Left at 2:10 p.m., the sky cloudy and the breeze cool. More detours around sandbars not yet above water. We are told this is the best time to travel. Next month when the water is lower, it flows swiftly through a narrow channel and is dangerous. In June when it is high, it is a menace, very wide, full of foam, and carrying along debris from twigs to huge trees.

We can follow our progress well with the U.S. Air Force 1:500,000 Preliminary Base Map #950A, although a few of the islands seem to have changed since the air photos were taken in 1943. Came to a high red bank at 4:15 p.m. with half a dozen abandoned houses, which we deduce to be an abandoned oil camp at the beginning of the trail to the Aguarico. Decided to stop, remembering two nights ago when we traveled another hour below Yana Yacu and got caught on a sandbar in the rain. First mosquitoes came out at dusk so had to dig out the nets.

NOVEMBER 13—FIFTH DAY: About 5 a.m. it started to sprinkle and we were afraid we were stuck for most of the day. However, it stopped and the boys said we had to get started if we would make Tiputini tonight. Shoved off at 5:40 a.m. Pushed along all day with one stop to dynamite fish (no luck), one for the men to bum some food (half a smoked agouti with head, and 6 small bananas) and one to cut cane for poles to be used on their return trip. Banks 1–3 meters high, houses separated by long uninhabited stretches from 1 to 2 hours apart. Channel broken by many large islands but the river has fewer bends so we are making faster progress on the map (fig. 1). Trees not dense, shores fringed with cane growing in strips 100–200 meters long; 3 main leaf types: fan-leafed, banana-leafed, and asparagus-leafed. More trees with brown and gray trunks, less than half are white. Occasional hanging vines with red, pink, or white flowers. Clouds building up all day to the east but dissolving with no rain. Thunder in the distance also. Eroded treetrunks and branches of temporarily stationary driftwood protrude, especially near the banks. This river is very dirty. The surface has fine sticks and the water is so heavily laden with silt that a cupful has a brownish tint.

Were pleasantly surprised to round a bend and see Tiputini in the distance. Looked like a city compared with other settlements along the river. Pulled in at 5:15 p.m.

In climate and topography, eastern Ecuador is part of a zone extending up to an elevation of about 600 meters along the eastern Andes for about 8 degrees north and south of the equator (Tosi, 1960, p. 236). In this region, the silt-laden rivers overflow annually inundating most of the countryside. Because silt deposition is heaviest in the riverbed and along the margins, the larger rivers gradually increase their elevation and build up bordering dikes. The amount of alluvium deposited decreases with increasing distance from the river channel, producing a decline in elevation. As a consequence, the annual fall of the rivers (pl. 4) is not accompanied by drying of the hinterland, where drainage is impeded by impermeability of the soil and lack of access to all but the small and less elevated streams. Evaporation is slow and extensive areas remain mucky or inundated throughout the year. Only the dikes remain permanently above water or rapidly emerge as the water goes down.

To these disadvantageous factors is added limited soil fertility. The situation has been summarized as follows by Tosi (1960, pp. 243–244; translated from Spanish):

. . . The climax soil of this formation, which is not common and does not occupy extensive areas, is so called Low-Humic Latosol ("latosol húmico dulce"), the product of the cumulative effect of climate and natural vegetation on the basic rocks of

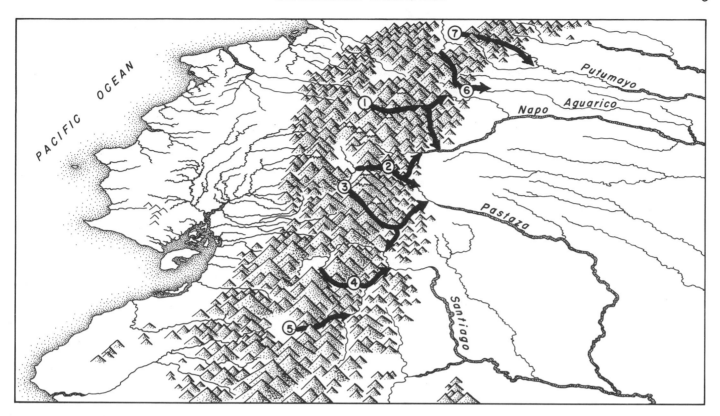

FIGURE 2.—Principal routes of communication between the highland basins and the eastern lowlands of Ecuador.

igneous or metamorphic origin and moderate slope. The pH of 5.0 to 6.5 indicates a certain degree of natural fertility under forest cover and a good capacity for maintained or even increased productivity with fertilization and other special agricultural techniques . . . . More extensive geographically and much more common is a complex of residual soils derived from ancient marine, lake or alluvial sediments, which were already very deficient in certain basic minerals at the time of their deposition . . . .

In part, this degree of senility . . . is due to the absence of relief and of slope of the land: the rhythm of its geological erosion is not and has not been as rapid as the rhythm of the influence of atmospheric phenomena on the subsoil or of the removal of bases from the upper horizons. This is the enigma: the most level residual soils and those consequently best suited for mechanized cultivation are among those of lowest natural fertility. The majority are useless for permanent cultivation even with abundant and frequent fertilization because of their very low capacity for alteration and the toxicity of the iron and aluminum they contain . . . .

These lands are clearly of little or no value for development of an agricultural or pastoral economy. Beneath the exuberant and dense natural forest cover exists a very delicate ecological equilibrium. If this primary equilibrium is interrupted by cutting, burning, open cultivation or pasturing, the inevitable result is loss of the already limited natural fertility of these soils, which leads to their rapid abandonment.

Although the limited potentiality of the eastern lowlands has inhibited construction of modern roads, numerous ancient trails provide communication with the highlands (Wolf, 1933, pp. 225–226; Porras, 1961, pp. 113–117). The two most travelled routes are that from Quito to Papallacta and Baeza, with a northern branch leading to the Rio Coca and a southern one to Tena and the Rio Napo (fig. 2–1), and that from Ambato via Baños and Mera to Puyo and the Rio Pastaza or the Rio Napo (fig. 2–2). Other trails lead from the Riobamba basin to Macas on the Rio Upano or to the Rio Pastaza (fig. 2–3); from the Cuenca basin to the Rio Santiago (fig. 2–4); and from the Loja basin to the Rio Zamora (fig. 2–5). Two more routes originate in southern Colombia: one from Tulcán to the headwaters of the Rio Aguarico (fig. 2–6), and the other from the Pasto region of the Rio Putumayo (fig. 2–7). Other trails link rivers either at the edge of the foothills or where their courses run in closest proximity. Once in the lowlands, abundance of navigable rivers, the flatness of the terrain and the uniformity of environment facilitate movement in almost any direction (pl. 5).

Human settlement of the easten Ecuadorian lowlands cannot be understood except in the context of the topography, climate, natural resources, and agricultural potential of the region. Combining limited subsistence possibilities with almost unlimited flexibility of riverine movement, the environment not only channeled but in large measure has determined the character of the archeological record along the Rio Napo.

No evidence of preceramic inhabitants has been reported, and in view of the nature of the terrain and vegetation, it is doubtful that remains can be found if preserved. Four pottery-making phases have been recognized, each of independent origin, and all but the last apparently of relatively short duration in the area. These will be described separately in detail, preliminary to a reconstruction of the prehistory of this segment of eastern lowland Ecuador.

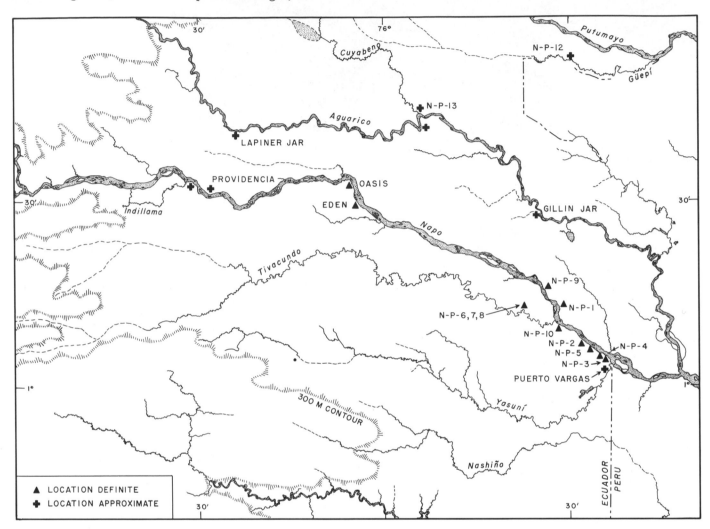

FIGURE 3.—Rio Napo and its tributaries, showing the location of archeological sites and isolated finds.

The Yasuní Phase

DESCRIPTION OF SITES AND EXCAVATIONS

Two habitation sites of the Yasuní Phase were encountered in close proximity on the right bank of the Rio Napo about 3 kilometers below the mouth of the Rio Tiputini (fig. 3). Neither provided sufficient depth for stratigraphic excavation.

N–P–10: Puerto Miranda Hill

A small grass covered hill rises 16 meters above the low water level on the right bank of the Rio Napo. The summit is relatively level, and the slope precip-

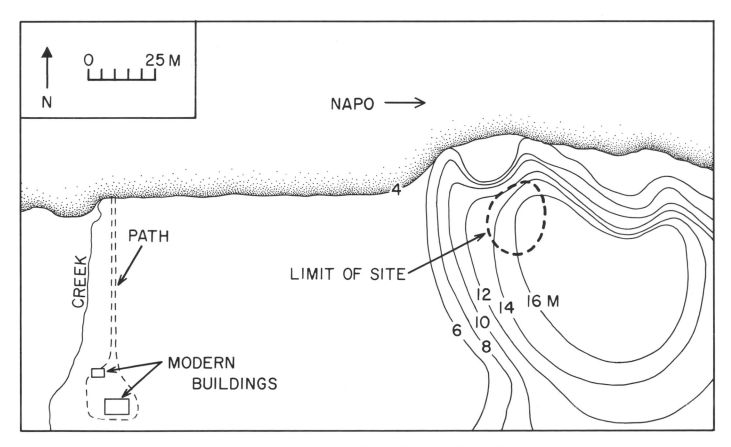

FIGURE 4.—Sketch map of the Yasuní Phase site of N–P–10.

itous only on the north side, where the river has exercised its cutting action (pl. 3c, 6a). A small creek drains into the river about 120 meters upstream, and the surface from here eastward and over the hill has been cleared of its natural forest for pasture.

A small habitation site is located on the northwest portion of the summit and probably formerly extended into the area now lost by erosion (fig. 4). Sherds occur over an approximately circular area 18 meters in diameter to a depth of 20–30 cm., beneath a sterile zone 5 cm. thick occupied by dense grass roots. Soil in the habitation zone was grayish brown, in contrast to the reddish color of the sterile clay. Small rounded pebbles were frequent, the larger ones broken. Sherds were abundant but small and very badly eroded. The hardness of the soil and shallowness of the deposit made stratigraphic testing impossible and the majority of the sherd collection came from a 2 by 1 meter area along the exposed margin facing the river. Four sherds were encountered near a modern house beside the creek on the level land to the west.

N–P–11: Puerto Miranda Bank

The artificial grassland extends for about half a kilometer along the bank of the Rio Napo upstream from the creek west of N–P–10 (fig. 3). The elevation of the almost vertical bank (pl. 6b) rises gradually from 4 meters above low water level in the vicinity of the creek to 6 meters at the vicinity of the site, toward the western part of the clearing. Testing in the area of highest elevation revealed sherds for a distance of about 145 meters along the bank and 15 meters inland. The existence of a number at the water's edge, fallen from the upper edge of the bank, suggests that part of the site had been lost by erosion. The refuse deposit extended to a depth of 25–30 cm., with sherds sparse in the upper 10 cm. Soil was brownish gray sandy clay. The sherd sample was collected from the summit as well as the river bank.

Data from Other Investigations

No other sites or artifacts attributable to Yasuní Phase origin have been reported from the Rio Napo or its tributaries.

ANALYSIS OF MATERIALS

Stone Artifacts

Close examination of rocks from Yasuní Phase sites revealed the majority to be either concretions naturally present in the soil or small waterworn pebbles. Only four showed traces of shaping for use.

Abrader

FIGURE 5

A thin rectanguloid piece of coarse quartzite with metamorphosed surfaces has edges apparently rounded by use. One surface is slightly concave and the other correspondingly convex. Length is 5.5 cm., width 4.2 cm., thickness 1.2 cm. From Site N–P–10.

Ax Fragments

FIGURE 6

A piece of quartzite has been shaped by percussion into what appears to be the butt of an ax. Outline is not symmetrical. The sides are slightly concave and have been smoothed to facilitate hafting. The implement is broken immediately below this region. Cross-section is roughly ovoid. Surfaces are extremely uneven and there is no evidence of pecking or polishing. Width at the lower end of the notches is 5.2 cm., thickness 2.0 cm. Existing length is 4.2 cm. From Site N–P–11.

A spall of metamorphosed tuffaceous sandstone has a smooth to polished surface suggesting that it may have come from an ax. However, this identification remains tentative since no other polished axes have

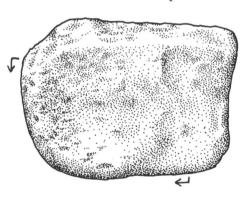

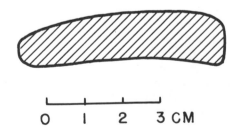

FIGURE 5.—Yasuní Phase stone abrader. Worn edge is between arrows.

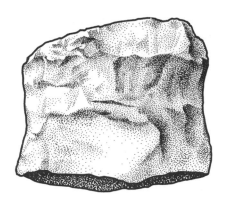

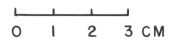

FIGURE 6.—Yasuní Phase ax fragment.

been collected from Yasuní Phase sites. From Site N–P–10.

Hammerstone

A waterworn pebble of sandstone conglomerate shows slight battering on one end. It is 3.0 by 3.0 by 2.5 cm. From Site N–P–10.

Ceramic Classification

The pottery types of the Yasuní Phase are based on classification of 1365 sherds from N–P–10 and 35 rim and diagnostic body sherds from N–P–11. Both samples are badly eroded, typically removing both surfaces and any decoration that might have been applied to them. Consequently, the 4-percent occurrence of decorated sherds probably is an inaccurately low representation of the original frequency.

Yasuní Phase pottery is now brittle, crumbly and soft, all characteristics for which erosion seems largely responsible. Many sherds have been "dissolved" down to the core, producing an abnormally thin wall (a factor that has been taken into consideration in measurement of body wall thickness). Only deeply incised or punctated decoration and modeling remain visible under these circumstances. Extreme erosion also causes rounding of broken edges, making

intentional lobing difficult to distinguish at times from nature's handiwork.

Two plain types have been recognized on the basis of temper: Miranda Plain tempered with sand, and Yasuní Plain tempered with ash. The small number of decorated sherds includes six distinct techniques, each of them represented by very few examples. Such small samples would normally be treated as "unclassified decorated," but in this case ease of reference and the probability that the techniques represented were more frequent than surviving evidence implies have served to justify the recognition of six decorated pottery types. Decoration, apparently applied to a plain surface, is by incision, punctation, zoned hachure, a row of nicks, and simple adornos. A few sherds show traces of red wash or slip. The majority of lobed and nicked rims have been included in the plain types in the absence of other evidence of decoration. However, many, if not all, may belong to vessels originally additionally ornamented by incision or zoned hachure on the walls.

No complete or restorable vessels exist for the Yasuní Phase. All forms have been reconstructed from evidence provided by rim, body, and base sherds, including orientation, contour, and diameter. Although all are treated as circular, some fragments exhibit a degree of flatness suggestive of ovoid form. Diameters at the large end of the size range may represent such cases, and may thus be misleading. The presence of square vessels seems improbable in the absence of sherds from corners, which are abundant in Napo Phase pottery where square vessels are common.

Pottery type descriptions have been arranged in alphabetical order, following descriptions of vessel shape characteristics. Provenience and frequency of both pottery types and vessel shapes are given on Appendix tables 1 and 2.

Reconstructed Vessel Forms

Common Forms

1. Shallow bowl or platter (fig. 7–1):
   Rim: Profiles are unstandardized. The principal variants are interior thickening to produce a broad, level or slightly insloping surface or, less commonly, upturned 1.0–1.5 cm. below the lip. Some of the latter appear to have a horizontal incision on the exterior about 5 mm. below the lip. Exterior rim diameter 22–48 cm.; majority 28–40 cm.
   Lip: Tapered or rounded.
   Body wall thickness: 5–10 mm.
   Base: Probably rounded or slightly flattened.
2. Rounded bowl (fig. 7–2):
   Rim: Direct, outslanting at an angle between 50 and

70 degrees. Rim diameter varies between 8–36 cm.; majority 24–36 cm.

Lip: Tapered, rounded, or flattened.

Body wall thickness: 5–7 mm.

Base: Probably rounded or slightly flattened.

3. Small rounded bowl with slightly everted rim (fig. 7–3):

Rim: Sharply everted 0.5–1.0 cm. below the lip and typically slightly thickened on the interior at the region of eversion, producing a flat horizontal or slightly insloping top. Interior rim diameter 6–20 cm.; majority 6–8 cm.

Lip: Tapered or rounded; occasionally undulating.

Body wall thickness: 2.0–3.5 mm.

Base: Probably rounded.

4. Large rounded bowl with slightly everted rim (fig. 7–4):

Rim: Everted and thickened 1–2 cm. below the lip, producing a trianguloid profile. Rim top is flat and level or outsloping. Interior rim diameter 18–34 cm.; majority 28–32 cm.

Lip: Rounded or rarely, flattened; occasionally embellished with notches or miniature lobes.

Body wall thickness: 3.0–8.5 mm.

Base: Probably rounded or slightly flattened.

5. Large bowl with short vertical wall (fig. 7–5):

Rim: Outsloping walls turn upward 1.5–3.0 cm. below the lip producing a rounded shoulder, above which the wall is usually thickened. Slight to pronounced eversion occurs about 1 cm. below the lip, often combined with interior thickness producing a flat, usually horizontal top. Interior rim diameter: 14–38 cm.; majority 26–36 cm.

Lip: Rounded

Body wall thickness: 4.5–7.5 mm.

Base: Rounded or flattened.

6. Large, deep, carinated bowl with trianguloid rim (fig. 8–6):

Rim: Slightly outflaring, everted, and thickened 1.0–1.5 cm. below the lip producing a trianguloid cross-

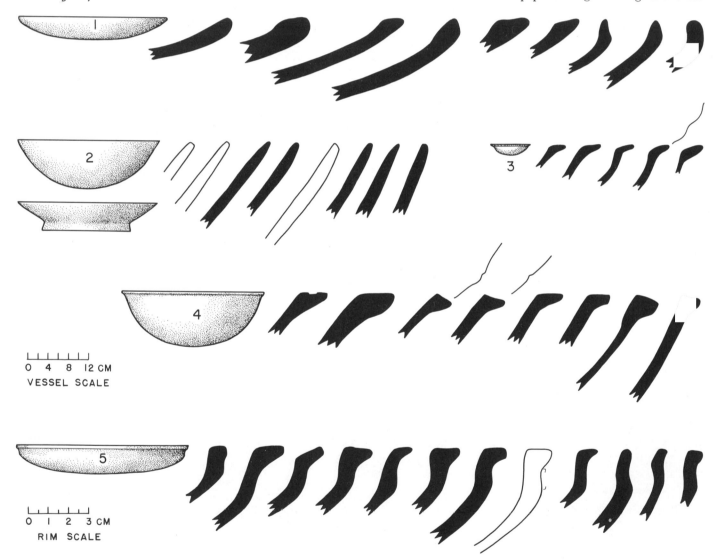

FIGURE 7.—Rim profiles and reconstructed vessel shapes of the Yasuní Phase, Common Forms 1–5. (Black=undecorated, white= decorated.)

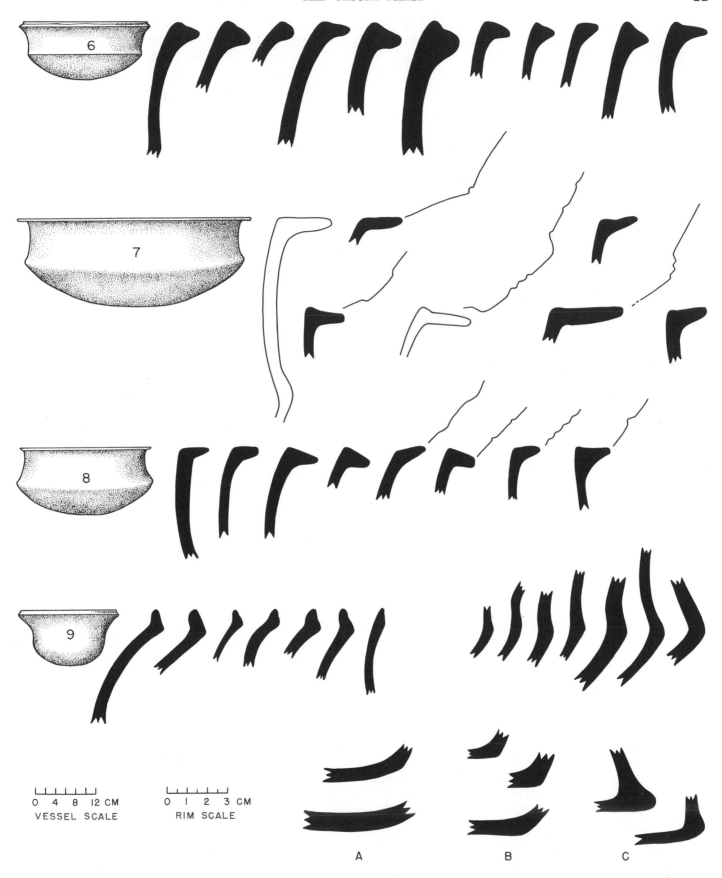

FIGURE 8.—Rim profiles and reconstructed vessel shapes of the Yasuní Phase, Common Forms 6–9 and Base Forms A–C. (Black= undecorated, white=decorated.)

section. The top is typically concave and sloping downward toward the exterior. Interior rim diameter 22–46 cm.; majority 30–40 cm.

Lip: Tapered or rounded.
Body wall thickness: 4.5–10.0 mm.
Base: Rounded or flattened.

7. Large carinated bowl with broad flange rim (fig. 8–7):
   Rim: Sharply everted to produce a broad horizontal or slightly upslanting or downslanting flange, 2.0–3.5 cm. wide; angle of eversion is more rounded on the exterior than the interior. Interior rim diameter 16–36 cm.
   Lip: Rounded or slightly flattened; typically embellished with lobes and notches.
   Body wall thickness: 4.5–6.5 mm.
   Base: Rounded or flattened.

8. Carinated bowl with everted rim (fig. 8–8):
   Rim: Sharply everted to produce a narrow flange (width about 1.5 cm.), with horizontal, upslanting or downslanting orientation. Angle of eversion is typically more rounded on the exterior. Interior rim diameter 22–42 cm.; majority 26–36 cm.
   Lip: Tapered, rounded, or slightly flattened; often embellished with notches or undulating.
   Body wall thickness: 4–7 mm.
   Base: Probably rounded or flattened.

9. Deep bowl with cambered rim (fig. 8–9):
   Rim: Outflaring to about 1 cm. below the lip, where it is inturned at an angle approximately 90 degrees to the previous direction, producing an inslanting camber with a slightly concave exterior. Rim diameter 16–26 cm.
   Lip: Rounded.
   Body wall thickness: 3–5 mm.
   Base: Probably rounded or slightly flattened.

Rare Forms

1. Deep bowl with a slightly incurving upper wall turning outward 2.5 cm. below the rounded lip. Rim diameter 28 cm. (fig. 9*a*).
2. Vessel with slightly outslanting upper wall with a flange attached on the exterior between 1 and 2 cm. below the rounded lip. The flange projects 1 cm. above the exterior surface, and is ornamented by vertical nicks 5–7 mm. apart. Rim diameter about 28 cm. (fig. 9*b*).
3. Deep bowl with nearly vertical wall slightly thickened on the exterior 2 cm. below the lip and tapering upward from that point. Rim diameter about 30 cm. (fig. 9*c*).
4. Vessel with slightly constricted mouth. Rim turns upward 1 cm. below the rounded lip. Mouth diameter 22 cm. (fig. 9*d*).
5. Jar with upper wall incurving and then upturned 2 cm. below the lip. Exteriorly thickened for 1 cm. below the rounded lip. Rim diameter 20 cm. (fig. 9*e*).
6. Jar with incurving upper wall, everted to produce a 1 cm. wide slightly outsloping collar. Tapered lip. Mouth diameter 16 cm. (fig. 9*f*).

7. Vessel with convex insloping upper wall joining lower wall at a 100 degree angle, exteriorly thickened rim, rounded lip. Mouth diameter about 12 cm. (fig. 9*g*).
8. Vessel with constricted mouth, direct rim, and rounded lip. Mouth diameter 14 cm. (fig. 9*h*).
9. Open bowl with a raised interior border produced by increasing the thickness of the wall by 2 mm., 3 cm. below the lip (fig. 9*i*). A slight change in curvature of the exterior wall occurs at the location of the increase in thickness on the interior. The lip is rounded and embellished by lobing and nicks. Two body sherds show a similar treatment on the interior.
10. Open bowl with outslanting wall, exteriorly thickened rim with triangular cross-section. Diameter at rim top, 18 cm. (fig. 9*j*).

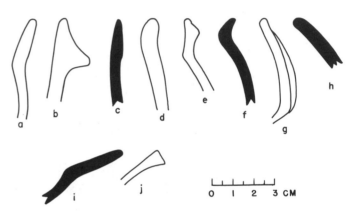

FIGURE 9.—Rim profiles of Yasuní Phase Rare Forms 1–10.

Base Forms

Four distinct base forms are represented in the sherds. Since there are no complete vessels, their association with the nine reconstructed vessel forms is hypothetical.

A. Rounded, unthickened, with a curved or slightly angular junction with the body wall. (fig. 8–A).
B. Flat, joining the body wall at an angle between 55 and 65 degrees. Junction more curved on interior than exterior as a result of slight thickening. (fig. 8–B).
C. Flat, joining the body wall at an angle of 90 to 110 degrees, and thickened on the exterior at the point of junction, forming a heel. Diameter 16–18 cm. (fig. 8–C).
D. Annular, tapering from point of attachment to lower edge and slightly outflaring. Identification is based on orientation and curvature of two small badly eroded fragments. Diameter 18 cm.

Pottery Type Descriptions

Miranda Modeled

PASTE AND SURFACE: All on Miranda Plain (p. 13); see that type description for details.

FORM:

Rim: Direct or slightly exteriorly thickened with tapered or flattened lip.

Body wall thickness: 3–5 mm., increasing to 9 mm. at carination.

Base: No direct evidence.

Reconstructed vessel shapes: The only rim represents Rare Form 7; other sherds are from the shoulder of carinated vessels.

DECORATION (fig. 10):

Technique: High relief nubbins (fig. 10 *b, c*) or low relief ribs (fig. 10*a*) applied to the exterior surface and smoothed over to obliterate the junction. One rib has sloughed off leaving a slight depression. Ribs are 3 cm. long, approximately 1 cm. wide at the surface, and 3

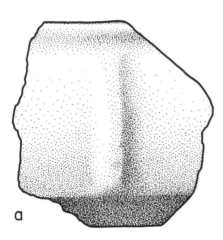

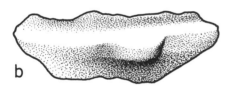

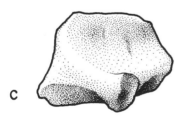

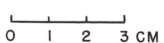

FIGURE 10.—Type sherds of Miranda Modeled.

mm. wide at the flattened top. Elevation is about 3 mm. Nubbins are prominent and the only complete example is smaller than average, measuring 1.5 cm. along the shoulder and projecting 5 mm.

Motif: Ribs run vertically about 4 cm. apart on the rim exterior; nubbins project from angle of carination (their frequency cannot be described because of the absence of sherds with more than one nubbin per sherd).

TEMPORAL DIFFERENCES WITHIN THE TYPE: None observable.

CHRONOLOGICAL POSITION OF THE TYPE: Yasuní Phase.

Miranda Plain

PASTE:

Temper: Waterworn sand, principally clear and white quartz. Grains rarely exceed 1 mm., and typically are smaller than 0.5 mm. Temper is well distributed and abundant enough to give eroded surfaces a sandpaper texture. A minority have very little sand temper.

Texture: Abrasive like fine-grained sandpaper; compact without air pockets. Breaks with a jagged edge, which is not friable.

Color: About 50 percent are completely oxidized, light orange to bright orange through the cross-section; the the remainder are dark gray throughout or oxidized on the surface leaving a medium to dark gray core.

Method of manufacture: Coiling; coil line breaks are rare.

SURFACE:

Color: Light tan to light brown most typical, with variations toward light orange and gray brown. Occasional small medium gray irregularly shaped fire clouds. Interior rarely a uniform black.

Treatment: Less than 5 percent have original surfaces intact. These were smoothed sufficiently to depress temper grains, producing a compact, fine-grained texture smooth and even to touch although with imperfections visible. One sherd has broad (1–2 mm.) horizontal smoothing tracks.

Hardness: 2.5.

FORM:

Rim: Exteriorly thickened, interiorly thickened, everted, cambered or direct, with rounded, flattened, or tapered lip.

Body wall thickness: Range 2–9 mm.; majority 4–6 mm.

Base: Flat (Form B, fig. 8–B); rounded, curving gradually to side walls (Form A, fig. 8–A).

Reconstructed common vessel shapes (figs. 7, 8):

Form 8: 18.2 percent.
Form 4: 13.2 percent.
Form 2: 12.1 percent.
Form 1: 12.1 percent.
Form 3: 7.7 percent.
Form 5: 7.7 percent.
Form 6: 6.6 percent.

Minor vessel shapes (frequency less than 5 percent; figs. 8, 9): Forms 7 and 9; Rare Forms 3, 8, and 9.

OCCASIONAL DECORATION: Vessels of Common Forms 3, 4, 7, and 8 often have nicked or lobed lips.

TEMPORAL DIFFERENCES WITHIN THE TYPE: None observable.

CHRONOLOGICAL POSITION OF THE TYPE: Yasuní Phase.

Yasuní Incised

PASTE AND SURFACE: Predominantly on Yasuní Plain (p. 15), rarely on Miranda Plain (p. 13); see those type descriptions for details.

FORM:

Rim: Direct or flange, with rounded lip; large lobes occur on open bowls of Form 2.

Body wall thickness: 5–8 mm.

Base: Annular (Form D) or flattened (Forms B and C).

Reconstructed common vessel shapes (figs. 7, 8):

  Form 2: 4 rims; decoration on interior.

  Form 6: 1 rim; decoration on exterior.

  Form 7: 3 rims; decoration on rim top and exterior above waist.

DECORATION (fig. 11):

Technique: Incised lines on a plain surface. Execution varies from thin sharp marks resembling knife cuts (width 0.1–0.2 mm.) to lines 0.5–1.0 mm. wide and about 0.5 mm. deep. Wider lines may have very irregular margins, but the extent of surface erosion makes it impossible to determine whether this reflects sloppy technique of incision or damage subsequent to burial. (Where arrangement of pits was sufficiently regular to appear intentional, the sherd was classified as Yasuní Incised and Punctate.) Well preserved incisions are straight and sharply defined, although sometimes interrupted where they cross small surface defects. Intersections often undershot. Straight lines tend to be parallel but not evenly spaced. Separation 0.6–1.2 cm.

Motif: Patterns are composed principally of arrangements of parallel straight lines. The most frequent are parallel horizontal lines spaced 5–12 mm. apart, creating bands broken by vertical incisions into rectangular

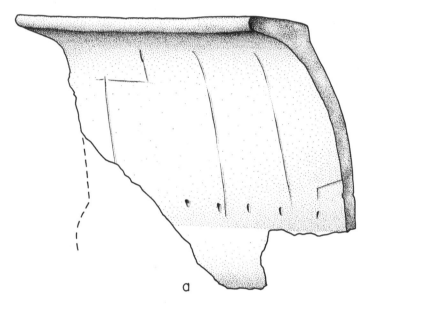

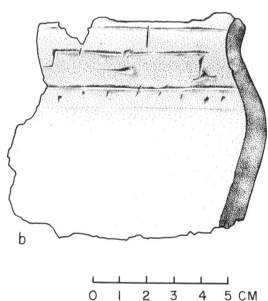

0 1 2 3 4 5 CM

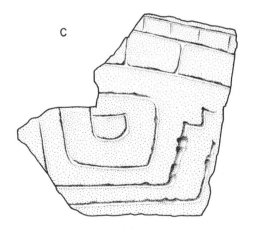

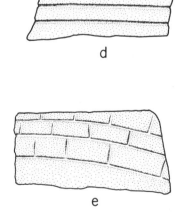

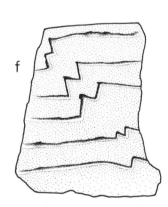

FIGURE 11.—Type sherds of Yasuní Incised.

zones (fig. 11*a–b*, *d–e*), and parallel horizontal lines displaced by several steps at intervals (fig. 11*f*). One design features a squared spiral (fig. 11*c*).

Associated techniques: A row of small vertical nicks may occur along the lower edge of the decorated zone (fig. 11*a–b*).

TEMPORAL DIFFERENCES WITHIN THE TYPE: None observable.

CHRONOLOGICAL POSITION OF THE TYPE: Yasuní Phase.

Yasuní Incised and Punctate

PASTE AND SURFACE: All on Yasuní Plain (p. 15); see that type description for details.

FORM:

Rim: Flange with flattened lip ornamented with small broad lobes and notches.

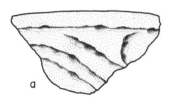
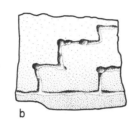
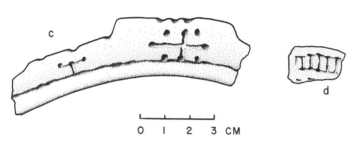

FIGURE 12.—Type sherds of Yasuní Incised and Punctate.

Body wall thickness: 3–5 mm.
Base: No direct evidence.
Reconstructed vessel shapes (figs. 8, 9):
Form 7: 1 rim; decoration on rim top.
Rare Form 10: 1 rim; decoration on interior.

DECORATION (fig. 12):

Technique: Relatively broad (about 1.5 mm.), deep (1 mm.), U-shaped incisions terminating in, or accompanied by, circular punctates about 2 mm. diameter at the surface. Punctates are considerably deeper than incisions and have a conical or rounded contour. Although erosion obscures details of execution, several sherds give the appearance of drag-and-jab or "dotted" lines creating parts of the design (fig. 12 *a–b*).

Motif: Parallel and intersecting lines on the rim top, symmetrically accented by single punctates or terminating in a punctate, or parallel incisions on the surface, some of which terminate in a punctation or have "dotted" segments.

TEMPORAL DIFFERENCES WITHIN THE TYPE: None observable.

CHRONOLOGICAL POSITION OF THE TYPE: Yasuní Phase.

Yasuní Nicked

PASTE AND SURFACE: Four on Yasuní Plain (p. 15), one on Miranda Plain (p. 13); see those type descriptions for details.

FORM:

Rim: Exteriorly thickened at or below the lip.
Body wall thickness: 3–9 mm.
Base: No direct evidence.
Resconstructed vessel shapes (figs. 7, 9):
Form 5: 1 rim; decoration on vertical exterior wall.
Rare Form 2: 1 rim; decoration on lip of flange.
Rare Form 5: 1 rim; decoration on upper surface of rim thickening.

DECORATION (fig. 13):

Technique: Parallel vertical cuts or nicks, in one case probably made with fingernail, in others by a pointed tool. Length 5–7 mm., width about 1 mm., separation 1–11 mm., with little variation on a single example. Depth less than 1 mm.

Motif: Single row adjacent to lip, on lip of flange rim or on exterior wall above carination. (Nicked lips, common on vessels of Form 8, have been considered occasional embellishments of plain types.)

Associated technique: Two sherds have small rim lobes.

TEMPORAL DIFFERENCES WITHIN THE TYPE: None observable.

CHRONOLOGICAL DISTRIBUTION OF THE TYPE: Yasuní Phase.

Yasuní Plain

PASTE:

Temper: Black ash, the larger particles elongated and showing the cellular structure characteristic of cariapé. Size ranges from minute specks to particles 4 mm. long; the majority are intermediate between these extremes. Glossy lumps of irregular form are characteristic; black color contrasts sharply with gray paste producing a speckled appearance. Light gray siliceous particles representing the typical appearance of cariapé (Meggers and Evans, 1957, p. 81) occur in about 5 percent of the sherds. Waterworn sand is characteristically also present, and often abundant.

Texture: Extremely friable, probably in part because of the badly deteriorated condition of the sherds. Sand temper gives a sandy texture, but the paste is less abrasive to the touch than that of Miranda Plain. Air pockets are absent, but holes left by leached organic temper occur.

Color: Typically medium to light gray throughout the cross-section; about 20 percent are light orange or light tan throughout the cross-section.

Method of manufacture: Coiling; rare fractures along coil junctions show overlapping union.

SURFACE:

Texture: Observation is limited to about 5 percent of the sherds with traces of the original surface. These

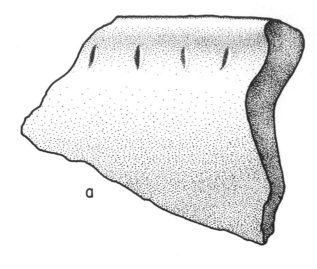

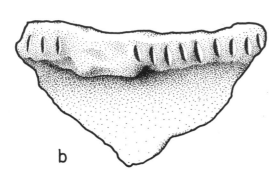

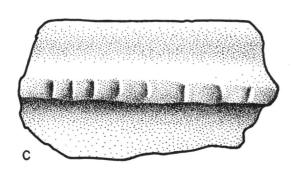

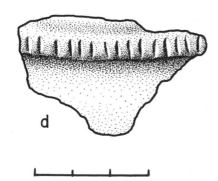

O   I   2   3 CM

FIGURE 13.—Type sherds of Yasuní Nicked.

are smooth to the touch and generally even although some temper grains remain visible. One sherd shows polishing striations on interior and exterior. Some have a low gloss.

Color: Typically light tan to grayish tan, shading to whitish or light orange. Small medium gray fire clouds probably are characteristic, since they are common on the few sherds with the surface preserved. Dark gray to black surfaces are excessively rare.

Hardness: 2 (in view of the extent of erosion, this softness may not accurately reflect the original condition).

FORM:

Rim: Exteriorly thickened, interiorly thickened, everted, cambered, flange or direct, with rounded, flattened, or tapered lip.

Body wall thickness: Range 2–8 mm.; majority 5–6 mm. Loss of surfaces suggests that these measurements may be about 1 mm. too small.

Base: Thickened (Form C, fig. 8–C); flat or slightly flattened (Form B, fig. 8–B). Two small fragments may represent annular bases, but their eroded condition makes broken surfaces impossible to distinguish conclusively from finished ones so that their present appearance may be deceptive.

Reconstructed common vessel shapes (figs. 7, 8):
Form 6: 36.2 percent.
Form 8: 14.7 percent.
Form 5: 13.7 percent.
Form 4: 10.8 percent.
Form 7: 8.8 percent.
Form 1: 5.9 percent.

Minor vessel shapes (frequency less than 5 percent; figs. 7–9): Form 2, 3, 9, Rare Form 6.

OCCASIONAL DECORATION: Vessels of Forms 4, 7, and 8 often have nicked or lobed lips.

TEMPORAL DIFFERENCES WITHIN THE TYPE: None observable.

CHRONOLOGICAL POSITION OF THE TYPE: Yasuní Phase.

Yasuní Red

PASTE AND SURFACE: All on Yasuní Plain (p. 15); see that type description for details.

FORM:

Rim: Flange (lip missing).
Body wall thickness: 4–7 mm.
Base: No direct evidence.
Reconstructed common vessel shapes (fig. 7):
Form 5 with flange rim; paint on interior and exterior.
Carinated body sherd; paint on exterior.

DECORATION:

Technique: Rich red slip, well preserved on one sherd, faint trace on the remainder. Fine grained, even, thin.

Motif: Completely covering the surface or applied to the rim and body wall above shoulder.

TEMPORAL DIFFERENCES WITHIN THE TYPE: None observable.

CHRONOLOGICAL POSITION OF THE TYPE: Yasuní Phase.

Yasuní Zoned Hachure

PASTE AND SURFACE: On Yasuní Plain (p. 15); see that type description for details.

FORM:

Rim: Direct or exteriorly thickened with rounded lip.

Body wall thickness: 4–6 mm.

Base: No direct evidence.

Reconstructed vessel shapes (figs. 7, 9):

Form 2: 1 rim; decoration on interior.

Form 4: 1 rim; decoration on interior.

Rare Form 4: 1 rim; decoration on exterior.

Rare Form 10: 1 rim; decoration on interior.

DECORATION (fig. 14):

Technique: Incised lines bounding bands and zones textured with fine hachure. Incisions 0.5–1.0 mm. wide, straight, generally parallel, and evenly spaced. Intersections may be overshot or fall short of junction. Hachure composed of very fine, shallow, closely spaced lines typically perpendicular to the longest axis of the zone, or of more haphazardly arranged and widely spaced fine lines, or crossed lines.

Motif: Parallel incisions 6–10 mm. apart appear to define bands or rectangular zones filled with fine parallel or cross hachure; alternatively, straight and stepped incisions form more irregularly shaped zones containing fine hachure. Severe erosion makes most patterns impossible to reconstruct.

TEMPORAL DIFFERENCES WITHIN THE TYPE: None observable.

CHRONOLOGICAL POSITION OF THE TYPE: Yasuní Phase.

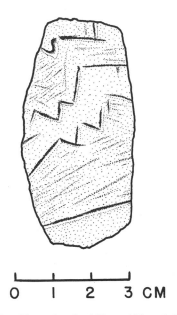

FIGURE 14.—Type sherd of Yasuní Zoned Hachure.

THE SERIATED SEQUENCE AND ITS IMPLICATIONS

The shallowness of the refuse deposit at both of the habitation sites assigned to the Yasuní Phase obviated the possibility of securing stratigraphic information on trends of ceramic change. Consequently, the phase characteristics must be viewed as representing a single point in time, However, pronounced differences in the relative frequency of vessel shapes at the two sites (Appendix table 1) suggest that they are not contemporary, and that further work in the area will bring to light additional sites that may permit establishment of a seriated sequence.

A single carbon-14 date was obtained by extracting the organic temper from 2 kilograms of Yasuní Plain sherds from N–P–10. The date of 2000±90 years ago, or 50 B.C. (SI–300) seems acceptable in view of the prehistoric sequence on the Rio Napo and the probable affiliations of the Yasuní Phase.

DIAGNOSTIC FEATURES OF THE YASUNÍ PHASE

The Yasuní Phase is defined from investigation of two sites on the right bank of the Rio Napo, neither with sufficient depth of refuse to permit stratigraphic excavation. One of the sites is situated on an elevated section of the river bank, the location favored by all of the other phases. The other is unique in occupying the summit of a high hill adjacent to the river. Both have suffered badly from erosion making the original dimensions difficult to reconstruct. However, the smaller site on the hilltop was estimated at 20–30 meters in diameter, while the other appeared to extend about 145 meters along the bank and 15 meters inland. No evidence was found of disposal of the dead.

There is no evidence bearing on subsistence pattern.

Hunting, fishing, and gathering resources must have been exploited, and slash-and-burn agriculture can also be assumed to have been practiced. However, the absence of griddle fragments implies that bitter manioc was absent or not processed for consumption in the manner typically employed in later times. Although rim forms and body contours of pottery vessels are distinct from those of other phases identified in the area, the differences do not seem to reflect significant differences in function.

The pottery of the Yasuní Phase has been classified into two plain and six decorated types. Miranda Plain is sand tempered, abrasive in texture, and incompletely to completely oxidized in firing. Yasuní Plain is tempered with particles of charcoal and cariapé, producing a very friable texture, and predominantly incompletely oxidized in firing. Both types occur with approximately equal frequency at the point in time represented by the unselected sherd sample from N–P–10.

With the exception of red slipping covering the entire surface (Yasuní Red), decoration is by incision or modeling. It must be kept in mind, however, that these techniques are most resistant to obliteration and the surfaces of all sherds are in extremely poor condition. The extreme rarity of all the decorated pottery types probably also reflects the condition of the sample rather than the original frequency of decoration. Incision may occur alone (Yasuní Incised), in conjunction with punctation (Yasuní Incised and Punctate) or be used to delimit rectilinear zones textured with fine parallel or cross hachure (Yasuní Zoned Hachure). Other forms of embellishment are a row of nicks along the lip or exterior surface (Yasuní Nicked), and simple applique (Miranda Modeled).

Vessel shapes emphasize open containers, wide in comparison to depth. Rims are typically everted to produce a narrow to broad horizontal to sloping flange, often thickened on the exterior at the angle of eversion and frequently ornamented with lobes or nicks. Direct and short cambered rims also occur. In addition to rounded or flat bases, an unusual "heeled" form occurs. Low annular bases may occur.

The only shaped stone tool is a fragment of a percussion chipped ax. A few natural stones showed wear from use in pounding or abrading. No pottery artifacts were found.

No pottery of trade origin was identified from either of the Yasuní Phase sites. This factor, added to the relatively greater degree of deterioration of the pottery surfaces, argues in favor of an early position in the regional sequence. This inference is supported by the single carbon-14 date, which places the occupation of N–P–10 at 2000 ± 90 years ago, or 50 B.C. (SI–300).

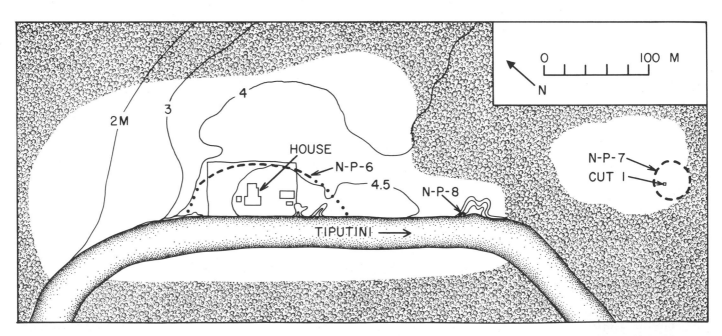

FIGURE 15.—Sketch map showing the locations of sites N–P–6 of the Napo Phase and N–P–7 and N–P–8 of the Tivacundo Phase on the left bank of the Rio Tiputini.

The Tivacundo Phase

DESCRIPTION OF SITES AND EXCAVATIONS

Two habitation sites of the Tivacundo Phase were found in close proximity on the left bank of the Rio Tiputini, a tributary entering the right bank of the Rio Napo (fig. 3, pl. 7).

N–P–7: Chacra Alfaro

At the time of our visit in November 1956, a small area about 100 meters inward from the left bank of the Rio Tiputini was cleared and planted in manioc, plantain, banana, and papaya. Although grass covered most of the surface, sherds and potrest fragments were abundant over an area 30–35 meters in diameter toward the southeast edge (fig. 15). Concentration was greatest near the center, becoming sparser toward the margins. The soil throughout the clearing was medium to dark brown with a high proportion of clay, causing it to bake hard with exposure to the sun. A surface collection was made, which was supplemented with material derived from scattered tests.

A 1 by 1 meter stratigraphic test pit was excavated northwest of the center of the site, where the refuse accumulation appeared to reach maximum depth. Levels were controlled in arbitrary depths of 8 cm. Level 0–8 cm. was largely occupied by grass roots. Soil was contaminated with ash of the recently burned clearing and contained relatively few sherds. In Level 8–16 cm. the soil was looser and slightly darker brownish tan; sherds were abundant. In Level 16–24 cm. sherds became sparser, disappearing as the brown loamy clay of the natural soil was reached.

N–P–8: Barranco Alfaro

A little upstream from N–P–7, the Rio Tiputini makes a 180 degree bend. The force of the current in the rainy season has eaten into the bank, causing slumping and exposing fragments of pottery for a distance of about 2.5 meters (fig. 15). Tests revealed nothing, however, suggesting that all but a remnant of the site has been washed away. As a result of displacement of the soil, sherds extended from 75 cm. below the surface down to the water's edge (a depth of 4 meters). While the original depth and thickness of the refuse deposit could not be clearly ascertained, it was probably relatively shallow.

Repeated exposure to percolating rainwater and to river action had produced an advanced degree of deterioration in the pottery, especially the surfaces, which often adhered to the sticky clay soil when the attempt was made to remove them. Moisture has also made sherds soft and easily fractured. In spite of the difficulties, a relatively large sample was obtained. Because of the impossibility of stratigraphic control, all materials were combined into a single collection.

Data from Other Investigations

No other sites or vessels, either complete or fragmentary, of Tivacundo Phase pottery types have been recorded from the Rio Napo or the Rio Tiputini.

ANALYSIS OF MATERIALS

Stone Artifacts

The only stone artifact from the Tivacundo Phase is a small irregularly shaped andesite pebble with several flat slick surfaces resulting from use as a polishing tool (fig. 16). Elongated with a trianguloid cross-section, it measures 3.5 cm. long, 1.5 cm. wide at the base, 0.5 cm. wide at the top, and 2.2 cm. in maximum height. Provenience is N–P–7, Cut 1, Level 16–24 cm.

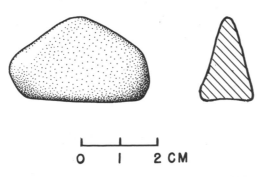

0   I   2 CM

FIGURE 16.—Tivacundo Phase polishing pebble.

Pottery Artifacts

In terms of their origin, Tivacundo Phase pottery artifacts fall into two categories: manufactured objects and reused sherds. Examples of the former are limited to potrests; the latter consist only of abraders.

Abraders

FIGURE 17

Three sherds of Chacra Plain containing a large amount of sand in addition to the charcoal particles diagnostic of this pottery type show two or more deep grooves on the exterior surface produced by abrasion. Width has a different range of variation on each sherd, probably reflecting differences in the diameter of the shaft being abraded, since depth on all three examples is 1–2 mm. The ranges of variation are 3–4 mm., 4–5 mm., and 5–6 mm. Grooves are generally parallel to the rim, but may be horizontal or diagonal in orientation. The sherds include a rim of Form 2, a base of Form B, and a body sherd. All are from N–P–7, Surface.

Potrests

PLATE 8*h–i*

Forty-three irregularly shaped hunks of fired clay represent an unknown number of potrests. The majority have very sandy paste and are fired dark to bright orange throughout. Rare variations in com-

position include almost pure clay, and fine sand and charcoal temper. This lack of consistency suggests that potrests were made from leftover material for pottery manufacture, or from whatever clay was at hand. They were constructed by shaping one large or several small lumps into a cylinder with flattened ends. Their poor state of preservation suggests that what firing they received resulted from use to support a cooking vessel.

Surfaces typically remain uneven, retaining pits, scars, and high spots. A few show vertical grooves, probably finger smoothing marks. Form is cylindrical, with slightly concave sides, flattened ends, and rounded corners. The absence of complete examples makes height unmeasurable, but fragments suggest that it was about 15 cm. Base diameters range from 8–12 cm.; one upper end has a diameter of 9 cm.

Ceramic Classification

The pottery types of the Tivacundo Phase are based on classification of 2241 sherds. If the selected sample from N–P–8 is eliminated from the calculation,

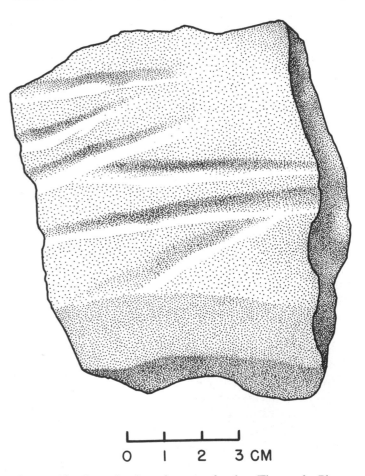

0   I   2   3 CM

FIGURE 17.—Base sherd used as an abrader, Tivacundo Phase.

decoration occurs on 5.6 percent of the sherds. The extensive erosion of the surfaces, which would remove painted designs, may have distorted the frequency to some extent, but there is no reason to assume that it was originally markedly higher.

Tivacundo Phase pottery in general is characterized by sandy texture and oxidized surfaces. Cross-sections sometimes show a laminated structure but paste is typically compact. All surfaces have been badly damaged by exposure to acid soil, making their original condition difficult to describe. In general, they appear to have been even, but neither floated sufficiently to eliminate defects nor polished. A thin red wash has been tentatively identified on a few sherds, but red or white slips were not observed.

Three plain pottery types have been recognized on the basis of temper and firing differences: Alfaro Plain, sand tempered and incompletely oxidized; Tivacundo Plain, sand tempered and completely oxidized; and Chacra Plain, tempered with charcoal particles. Two additional varieties of temper are represented in rare sherds: These are cariapé and fine muscovite sand. Decorative techniques are restricted to fine incision and red painting, which are typically combined in zoned patterns. Vessel shapes are few and simple; ovoid as well as circular outline occurs. Symmetry is good.

With the exception of Form 3, represented by a complete ovoid bowl of Tivacundo Incised and Zoned Red, all vessel shapes have been reconstructed from evidence provided by sherds. Association of the different base forms with body and rim profiles has been inferred from considerations of diameter and inclination, except in Forms 1–3 where large sherds extend from lip to bottom. Worthy of special note are several sherds representing flat bottoms riddled with perforations made when the clay was wet.

Pottery type descriptions have been arranged in alphabetical order, following description of vessel shape characteristics. Provenience and frequency of both pottery types and vessel shapes are given on Appendix tables 4 and 6.

Reconstructed Vessel Forms

Common Forms

1. Rounded bowl with direct rim (fig. 18–1):
   Rim: Outcurving to upcurving, unthickened. Diameter 14–36 cm.; majority 24–32 cm.
   Lip: Rounded, rarely slightly flattened.
   Body wall thickness: 4–8 mm.
   Base: Probably rounded or slightly flattened.
2. Rounded bowl with slightly thickened rim (fig. 18–2):
   Rim: Outcurving to nearly vertical, with small thick-ening or beading on the upper 5 mm. of the exterior not exceeding the body wall thickness by more than 1.5 mm. A similar effect is occasionally produced on unthickened rims by a narrow groove 2–6 mm. below the lip on the exterior. Diameter 16–30 cm.; some vessels may be ovoid rather than circular.
   Lip: Rounded or flattened at center.
   Body wall thickness: 5–7 mm.
   Base: Probably rounded or slightly flattened.
3. Depressed globular bowl with slightly thickened rim (fig. 18–3):
   Rim: Incurving, with slight thickening or beading on the upper 3–5 mm. of the exterior not exceeding the body wall thickness by more than 1 mm. The effect may be accomplished by slight eversion rather than thickening. Rim diameter 14–36 cm., majority 20–30 cm.; ovoid as well as circular examples occur.
   Lip: Rounded; rarely slightly flattened at center.
   Body wall thickness: 3.5–6.0 mm.
   Base: Probably rounded or slightly flattened.
4. Depressed globular bowl with everted, thickened rim (fig. 18–4):
   Rim: Sharply everted (angle between 50 and 90 degrees) 1.0–2.5 cm. below the lip, producing a flat insloping top, and thickened on the exterior producing a trianguloid cross-section. The lower edge of the thickening is unerased and demarcated in cross-section by 1–2 mm. increase in thickness. Interior rim diameter 12–36 cm.; majority 16–26 cm.
   Lip: Tapering or flattened.
   Body wall thickness: 4–9 mm.
   Base: Probably pedestal (Form A) or flat (Form B).
5. Collared jar (fig. 19–5):
   Rim: Upper 1.5–4.0 cm. of the incurving wall is bent upward producing a nearly vertical or insloping collar. Diameter 20–30 cm.; majority 22–26 cm.
   Lip: Rounded or slightly flattened at the center.
   Body: A number of body sherds showing an angular change in contour on the exterior may be associated with this form (fig. 20g).
   Body wall thickness: 4–7 mm.
   Base: Probably flat (Form B) or concave (Form C).
6. Large globular jar with slightly thickened rim (fig. 19–6):
   Rim: Upper 0.8–1.6 cm. of incurving wall is bent upward, producing a narrow beading or collar, which may be accentuated by slight thickening. The lower edge may be a step-like elevation or a narrow groove. Mouth diameter 18–46 cm.; majority 30–42 cm. On several sherds interior junctions are unobliterated on the last three coils adjacent to the lip.
   Lip: Rounded or flattened, resulting in a circular or rectanguloid cross-section.
   Body wall thickness: 0.8–1.9 cm.
   Base: Probably pedestal (Form A) or flat (Form B).

Rare Forms

1. Flat platter or griddle, 1.2–2.2 cm. thick, with direct rim and rounded or tapering lip. Three examples with

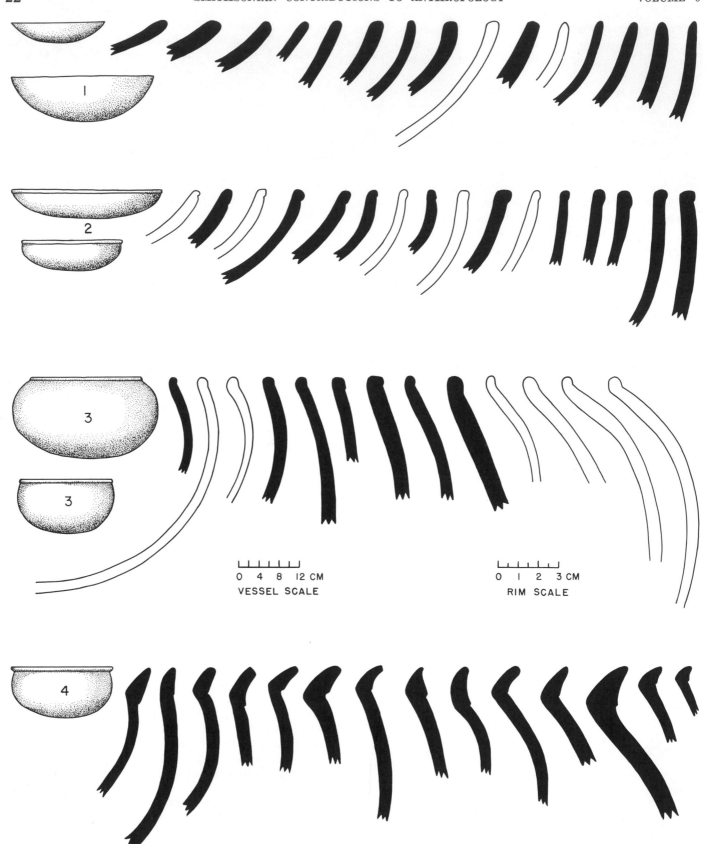

0 4 8 12 CM
VESSEL SCALE

0 1 2 3 CM
RIM SCALE

FIGURE 18.—Rim profiles and reconstructed vessel shapes of the Tivacundo Phase, Common Forms 1–4. (Black=undecorated, white=decorated.)

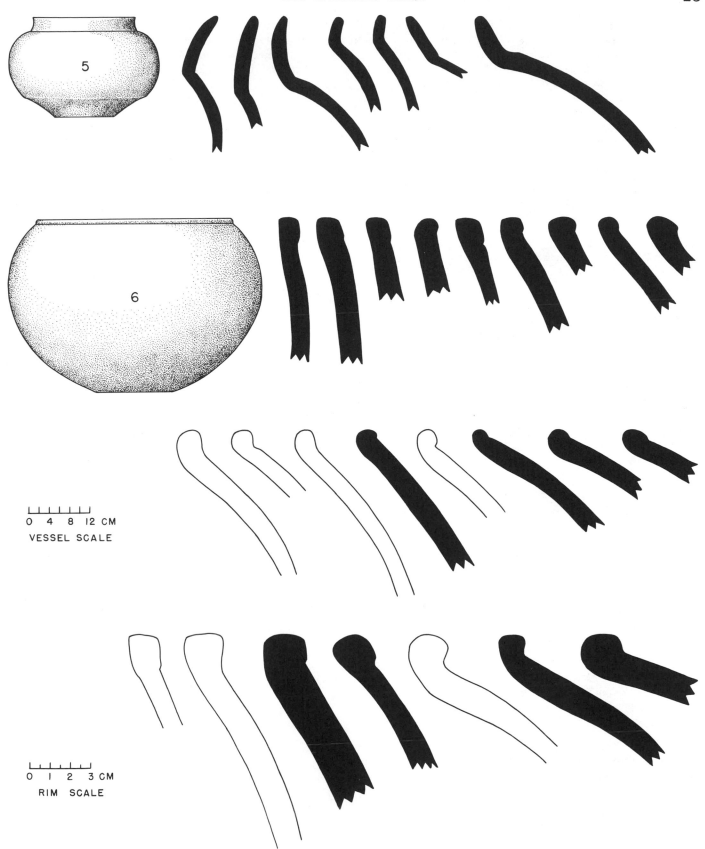

FIGURE 19.—Rim profiles and reconstructed vessel shapes of the Tivacundo Phase, Common Forms 5 and 6. (Black=undecorated, white=decorated.)

diameters of 24–26 cm. may represent griddles, but two with diameters of 14 and 18 cm. are smaller than the usual range of griddle size (fig. 20a).

2. Globular jar with constricted mouth and direct or expanding rim, rounded lip. Mouth diameter 14 cm. (fig. 20b–c).

3. Rounded bowl with expanding rim, rounded lip. Interior rim diameter 26 cm. (fig. 20d).

4. Ovoid bowl with rounded shoulder and slightly everted rim accompanied by slight thickening of the interior wall (fig. 20e).

5. Large shallow vessel with concave bottom, nearly vertical curved walls and broad horizontal flange rim (lip missing). Depth 7.5 cm.; base diameter 24 cm. (fig. 20f).

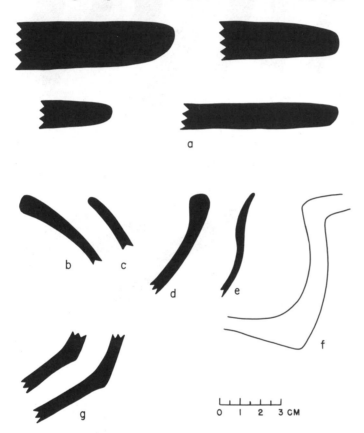

FIGURE 20.—Rim profiles of Tivacundo Phase Rare Forms. a, Rare Form 1. b–c, Rare Form 2. d, Rare Form 3. e, Rare Form 4. f, Rare Form 5. g, Typical shoulder treatment. (Black=undecorated, white=decorated.)

Base Forms

Five base forms can be distinguished in the sherd sample. The rarity of complete vessels makes association of base and rim forms dependent upon correlation of dimensions and general body contour. Only the occurrence of rounded or slightly flattened bases (Form E) with rims of Vessel Forms 1–3 is confirmed by complete vessels.

A. Flat and sharply demarcated from the body wall on the exterior by a nearly vertical to outsloping "pedestal" 5–10 mm. high, sometimes reflected by a convexity on the interior. Diameter 10–28 cm. (fig. 21–A).

B. Flat, typically joining the body wall at an angle of 40–50 degrees, but occasionally falling above or below this range. Junction is typically angular on the exterior and rounded on the interior, and 2–5 mm. thicker than the body wall. Several examples are riddled with unequally spaced (2–10 mm. apart) perforations 3–5 mm. in diameter, punched from the exterior when clay was very wet before firing and creating a ridge about 1 mm. elevation around the opening on the interior (pl. 8f–g). Diameter of perforated examples 8–12 cm.; diameter of unperforated examples 18–24 cm. (fig. 21–B).

C. Concave, with an angular or rounded junction to the body wall. A concavity of 2–5 mm. is produced by thinning of the wall and does not result in convexity on the interior. Diameter 12–18 cm. (fig. 21–C).

D. Incipient annular base, resulting from combining the pedestal of Form A with the concavity of Form C. Diameter 16 cm. (fig. 21–D).

E. Rounded, continuation of curvature and thickness of the body wall (pl. 9).

Pottery Type Descriptions

Alfaro Plain

PASTE:

Temper: Abundant angular grains of multicolored (pink, white, black) sand, estimated to comprise about 50 percent of the volume. Size rarely exceeds 1 mm. Occasional sherds have additional rare grains of black charcoal.

Texture: Very sandy and friable; eroded surfaces and broken edges crumble into sand when rubbed, probably in part because of deterioration of paste in the ground. Compact.

Color: Typically medium to dark gray throughout the cross-section; occasionally oxidized in a band adjacent to one or both surfaces leaving a gray core. Rarely, the the gray core is displaced to the inner half of the cross section, oxidation penetrating from the exterior surface to the center.

Method of manufacture: Coiling.

SURFACE:

Color: Brown, grayish brown, or brownish orange. Darker hues tend to occur on the interior. A minority of sherds show a whitish to light orange tint. Dark gray fire clouds occur.

Treatment: Few sherds retain their original surface; these are even but not smooth or polished, and retain minor defects and visible temper grains.

Hardness: 3.

FORM:

Rim: Exteriorly thickened, everted or expanded, with rounded or tapered lip.

Body wall thickness: Range 4–10 mm.; majority 4–7 mm.

Base: Rounded or slightly flattened (Form E); flat (Form B, fig. 21–B); pedestal (Form A, fig. 21–A); concave (Form C, fig. 21–C).

Reconstructed common vessel shapes (figs. 18, 19):
  Form 2: 27.0 percent.
  Form 5: 23.1 percent.
  Form 4: 21.2 percent.
  Form 3: 11.5 percent.
  Form 6: 9.7 percent.
Minor vessel shapes (frequency less than 5 percent, figs. 18, 20): Form 1; Rare forms 2 and 3.
TEMPORAL DIFFERENCES WITHIN THE TYPE: Whitish to light orange surfaces are most frequent at the earliest site (N–P–8). Vessel Form 5 is restricted to this same portion of the sequence (Appendix table 4).
CHRONOLOGICAL POSITION OF THE TYPE: A common plain type throughout the seriated sequence, with a trend of slightly declining frequency (fig. 26).

Chacra Plain

PASTE:
Temper: Small irregularly shaped lumps of charcoal

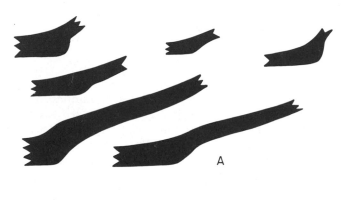

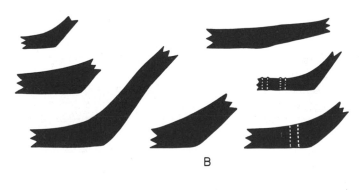

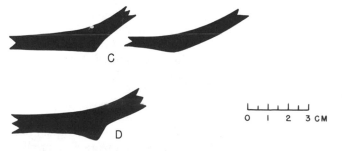

FIGURE 21.—Base forms of Tivacundo Phase plain pottery. A, Flat, "pedestal". B, Flat, angular junction with body wall. C, Concave. D, Incipient annular.

and angular grains of multicolored sand; either may predominate or they may be equally abundant (when charcoal is rare, i.e., only one or two particles could be detected, the sherd was classified as Alfaro Plain or Tivacundo Plain). Charcoal particles range from pinpoint size to about 1 mm. diameter, rarely reaching 3 mm. in length. Elongated hunks may resemble cariapé but the striated cellular structure of the latter is absent. Carbon may also take the form of irregular small black or medium gray splotches, sometimes visible only under 5✕ magnification. Sand grains are under 1 mm. diameter. Distribution of charcoal particles is often uneven, but the gaps are occupied by less prominent sand particles with the result that temper is well distributed.
Texture: Compact, sandy but not friable. Air pockets are not characteristic but small cavities may occur between coil junctions where kneading is not complete. Occasional examples have a laminated appearance.
Color: Dark gray or medium gray throughout cross-section; rarely, light brown. Carbonizing effect of charcoal temper causes blotchy appearance in some light brown pastes. Oxidation seldom penetrates beyond the surface, but occasional sherds have an oxidized layer of relatively even width extending to 1 mm. inward.
Method of manufacture: Coiling, exhibited in unobliterated junctions on some interior surfaces, and occasionally in cross-section.

SURFACE:
Color: Light orange to buff to light brown of relatively even hue except where marred by small (2–3 cm. dia.) dark gray fire clouds. Oxidation sometimes produces a whitish surface film. Interior surfaces are typically less completely oxidized than the exterior and occasionally have a grayish hue.
Treatment: Few sherds retain their original surfaces; these show smoothing sufficient to obliterate most sand and charcoal temper particles but leaving scattered irregular scars up to 1 by 3 mm. in size. Even but slightly abrasive to the touch.
Hardness: 2.5–3.

FORM:
Rim: Direct, exteriorly thickened or everted, with rounded, tapered or flattened lip (pl. 8*a–e*).
Body wall thickness: Range 0.4–1.5 cm.; majority 5–8 mm.
Base: Rounded or slightly flattened (Form E); flat (Form B, fig. 21–B, pl. 8*f–g*); pedestal (Form A, fig. 21–A); incipient annular (Form D, fig. 21–D).
Reconstructed common vessel shapes (figs. 18, 19):
  Form 4: 28.0 percent.
  Form 3: 21.5 percent.
  Form 6: 15.9 percent.
  Form 1: 14.0 percent.
  Form 2: 11.2 percent.
  Form 5: 5.6 percent.
Minor vessel shapes (frequency less than 5 percent; fig. 20): Rare form 1.
TEMPORAL DIFFERENCES WITHIN THE TYPE: Vessels of Form 5 are common only at the earliest site, while Form 2 is absent (Appendix table 4).

CHRONOLOGICAL POSITION OF THE TYPE: Present throughout the seriated sequence, increasing from 12.3 to 34.8 percent and then declining to 23.3 percent (fig. 26).

Tivacundo Incised and Zoned Red

PASTE: Decoration was applied to all of the plain types, with the following frequencies: Alfaro Plain (p. 24), 46.5 percent; Tivacundo Plain (p. 27), 39.1 percent; Chacra Plain (p. 25), 8.6 percent; Unclassified sand-tempered Plain (p. 29), 0.5 percent; see those type descriptions for details.

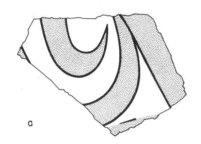

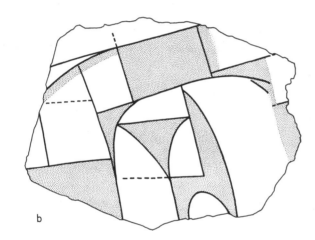

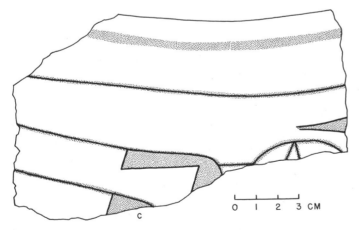

FIGURE 22.—Type sherds of Tivacundo Incised and Zoned Red. *a–b*, Technique 1. *c*, Technique 2.

SURFACE:

Color: Pale orange to buff.

Treatment: All suffer from some degree of erosion. Those in good condition are even and smooth to the touch, although some temper grains remain visible and fine horizontal scratches left by the smoothing tool can be seen under $5\times$ magnification.

FORM:

Rim: Exteriorly thickened or slightly everted with rounded flattened or tapered lip.

Body wall thickness: Range 0.4–1.4 cm.

Base: Rounded or slightly flattened (Form E); pedestal (Form A, fig. 21–A).

Reconstructed common vessel shapes (figs. 18, 19):

Form 3: 50.0 percent.
Form 6: 19.3 percent.
Form 2: 11.5 percent.
Form 4: 7.8 percent.

Minor vessel shapes (frequency less than 5 percent; figs. 18, 20): Form 1; Rare Form 5.

DECORATION (figs. 22, 23; pl. 9):

Technique: Fine incised lines superimposed with a red painted line, or demarcating zones filled with red. Incisions 0.2–0.5 mm. wide, straight, and even in appearance to the unaided eye. Magnification to $5\times$ shows irregularities in depth and discontinuities. Margins may be even or jagged. Long lines are straight although parallelism is imperfect especially when separation exceeds 1 cm. Overshot or undershot junctions are typical. Faint or broken lines occur in some areas unrelated to the final pattern, suggesting that guidelines were sketched onto the surface to orient the artist. Red coloring is applied in two ways:

1. In bands and zones bounded by incisions (the most common technique). Rich, dark, even color subject to flaking off especially when the underlying surface is well smoothed inhibiting penetration. Paint may fill the zone or fall short of reaching the boundary leaving an unpainted strip 0.5–1.0 mm. wide. None of the examples show overlap of paint to surface outside the boundary incision (figs. 22*a–b*, 23; pl. 9*b–d*).

2. Covering fine incisions (less common and used in conjunction with Technique 1). Rich red band, 1.5–2.5 mm. wide applied so as to evenly straddle an incised line, overlapping the surface on both sides (fig. 22*c*; pl. 9*e*).

Motif: Complicated all-over patterns on the exterior, composed of small symmetrical or asymmetrical zones and broad bands, are characteristic of Technique 1. Zones typically combine straight and curved lines. The most distinctive element is a small concave-sided equilateral triangle. Scale is correlated with vessel size: zones tend to be small on small vessels and large on large ones, the constituent elements remaining similar. Technique 2, also restricted to the exterior, is applied to parallel lines drawn independently or connecting red zones.

TEMPORAL DIFFERENCES WITHIN THE TYPE: None observable.

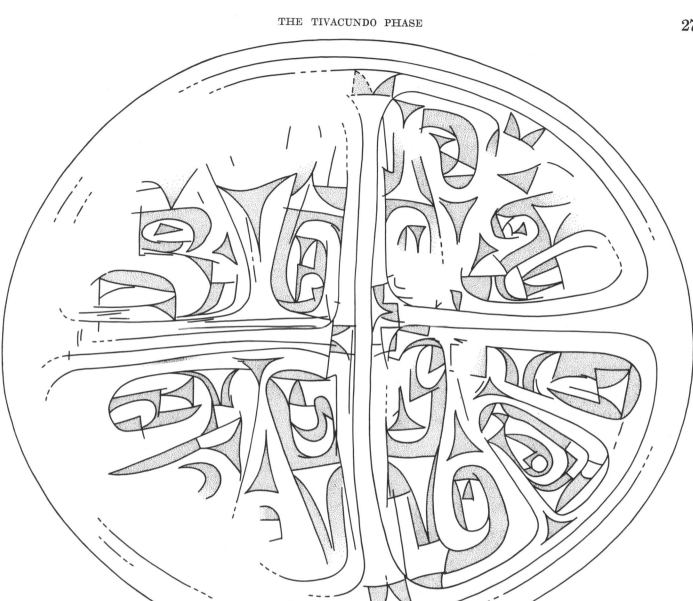

FIGURE 23.—Rolled out design on exterior of Tivacundo Incised and Zoned Red oval bowl (cf. pl. 9).

CHRONOLOGICAL POSITION OF THE TYPE: Limited to N–P–8, the earliest site in the seriated sequence (fig. 26).

Tivacundo Plain

PASTE:

Temper: Angular grains of multicolored sand, diameter typically less than 0.5 mm. but sometimes larger than 1 mm. Abundant with a tendancy toward clustering. Some sherds also have rare grains of charcoal.

Texture: Sandy and friable, crumbling into sand on eroded surfaces and broken edges. Tendency to lamination, with air pockets occurring between layers.

Color: Bright orange, reddish orange, or rarely brownish orange through cross-section. A few examples hav orange core and gray band adjacent to the surface.

Method of manufacture: Coiling, evident in occasional coil line fractures and incompletely obliterated junctions on some jar rim interiors.

SURFACE:

Color: Light orange, reddish orange, brownish orange, buff or tan, with the tone generally uniform on small sherds. Rarely medium to dark gray, probably localized fire clouding. Exterior and interior of a single sherd generally have a similar hue.

Treatment: Few sherds retain their original surface; these are even and smoothed sufficiently to create slight floating but leaving some temper grains exposed and small irregularities.

Hardness: 3 to 3.5.

FORM:

Rim: Direct, exteriorly thickened or everted, with tapered, rounded or flattened lip (pl. 10*a–h*).

Body wall thickness: Range 0.3–1.5 cm.; majority 5–9 mm.

Base: Rounded or slightly flattened (Form E); flat (Form B, fig. 21–B), sometimes perforated (Form B, pl. 10*i–j*); pedestal (Form A, fig. 21–A); concave (Form C, fig. 21–C).

Reconstructed common vessel shapes (figs. 18, 19):

Form 2: 25.0 percent.
Form 4: 19.8 percent.
Form 1: 16.7 percent.
Form 3: 16.7 percent.
Form 6: 14.6 percent.

Minor vessel shapes (frequency less than 5 percent, fig. 19): Form 5.

TEMPORAL DIFFERENCES WITHIN THE TYPE: Surface color of examples from N–P–8 is lighter orange than on examples from N–P–7. Vessels of Form 5 occur only at N–P–8.

CHRONOLOGICAL POSITION OF THE TYPE: Tivacundo Plain shows a pronounced increase in frequency and constitutes the most abundant type in the latest levels of the seriated sequence (fig. 26).

Tivacundo Red Painted

PASTE: Decoration occurs on the following plain types: Chacra Plain (p. 25), 41.8 percent; Alfaro Plain (p. 24), 32.7 percent; Tivacundo Plain (p. 27), 25.5 percent. When segregated by levels, frequencies generally duplicate the trends of popularity exhibited in the plain types, implying that selection was not practiced in vessels for decoration. See plain type descriptions for details of paste.

SURFACE: All surfaces are badly eroded, but evidence suggests their original condition was similar to that of Tivacundo Incised and Zoned Red.

FORM:

Rim: Direct or exteriorly thickened with rounded or flattened lip.

Body wall thickness: Range 4–10 mm.

Base: Rounded or slightly flattened (Form E); flat, sometimes perforated (Form B).

Reconstructed common vessel shapes (figs. 18, 19):

Form 2: 42.2 percent.
Form 6: 36.8 percent.
Form 1: 10.5 percent.
Form 3: 10.5 percent.

DECORATION: (fig. 24; pl. 11*a–e*):

Technique: Rich dark red paint applied in narrow (2–3 mm.) or wide (5–10 mm.) bands or irregularly shaped areas. Extensive damage by erosion makes details of

execution impossible to observe.

Motif: Patterns of straight and curved parallel lines on the exterior. Only two sherds (both from N–P–8) have complicated designs in the style associated with Tivacundo Incised and Zoned Red. Rim exterior is painted red on larger jars.

TEMPORAL DIFFERENCES WITHIN THE TYPE: Complicated patterns are restricted to N–P–8, the only site producing Tivacundo Incised and Zoned Red.

CHRONOLOGICAL POSITION OF THE TYPE: Present throughout the seriated sequence as the most common decorated type (fig. 26).

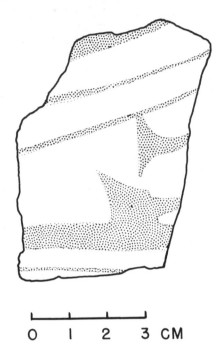

FIGURE 24.—Type sherds of Tivacundo Red Painted.

Unclassified Cariapé-tempered Plain

PASTE:

Temper: Cariapé; particles typically 1–2 mm. in length, occasionally 5 mm. Color predominantly white, but gray and black particles also occur, as well as some black charcoal lumps like the tempering of Chacra Plain. Orientation is random. Rare sherds contain sand in addition to cariapé.

Texture: Compact; no lamination or air pockets.

Color: Typically medium to dark gray core leaving oxidized band up to 2 mm. wide adjacent to one or both surfaces; rarely light orange through cross-section.

Method of manufacture: Coiling.

SURFACE:

Color: Light orange to whitish on exterior; light orange or medium gray on interior.

Treatment: All badly eroded; rare patches of original

surface show smoothing sufficient to obliterate most temper particles but not removing all pits and defects.
Hardness: 2.5.

FORM:

Rim: Direct or upturned and "beaded," with rounded lip (pl. 11*f*).

Body wall thickness: Range 0.5–2.0 cm.

Base: Flat (Form B, fig. 21–B).

Reconstructed common vessel shapes (fig. 19): The single rim sherd represents Form 6.

TEMPORAL DIFFERENCES WITHIN THE TYPE: None observable.

CHRONOLOGICAL POSITION OF THE TYPE: Limited to N–P–8, the earliest site in the seriated sequence (fig. 26).

Unclassified Sand-tempered Plain

PASTE:

Temper: Very fine sand grains up to 0.5 mm. diameter and smaller particles of muscovite that glitter as specks on eroded surfaces.

Texture: Very compact, fine grained.

Color: Cream or buff throughout the cross-section or adjacent to exterior surface leaving a pale gray band along the interior; rarely, light gray throughout the cross-section.

Method of manufacture: Coiling; coil junction fracture relatively common, and showing steep angle of overlap.

SURFACE:

Color: Pale cream or buff of even tone on both interior and exterior; rarely pinkish orange. Medium gray discoloration results from fire clouding.

Treatment: No sherds retain their original surfaces; present condition suggests only that it was relatively even.

Hardness: 3.5.

FORM:

Rim: Direct, exteriorly thickened or everted, with rounded or tapered lip.

Body wall thickness: 5–7 mm.

Base: Probably rounded or slightly flattened (Form E).

Reconstructed common vessel shapes (figs. 18, 20): Forms 2, 4, and Rare Form 2.

TEMPORAL DIFFERENCES WITHIN THE TYPE: None observable.

CHRONOLOGICAL POSITION OF THE TYPE: Limited to the early part of the seriated sequence (fig. 26).

Unclassified Decorated

INCISED (fig. 25*a*).—Two body sherds have broad (2–3 mm.) shallow (less than 1 mm.) incisions, curved in cross-section. Incisions are straight and parallel. Execution is poor so that width and depth are not consistently maintained. One on Chacra Plain, one on Tivacundo Plain; both from N–P–7, Cut 1, Level 0–8 cm.

One fragment, a constricted mouthed vessel with direct rim, has fine incision on the exterior, similar in technique to that of Tivacundo Incised and Zoned Red, although executed with less precision (fig. 25*a*). Paste is Tivacundo Plain. The last two coils adjacent to the lip are unobliterated on the interior. N–P–7, Cut 1, Level 8–16 cm.

NICKED SHOULDER (fig. 25*b*).—One sherd has a row of nicks or notches of variable length (4–7 mm.) and separation (4–6 mm.) along a slightly angular shoulder. A narrow horizontal red-painted line is faintly visible just above. Paste is Chacra Plain. N–P–7, Cut 1, Level 8–16 cm.

RED SLIP.—Several sherds have a reddish film on the exterior or both surfaces that may be the remnant of a wash or slip. Color is a dull reddish brown rather than the rich red of painted decoration. Five on Chacra Plain, three on Tivacundo Plain, one on Alfaro Plain; Vessel shapes 4, 5, and 6 are represented. All from N–P–8.

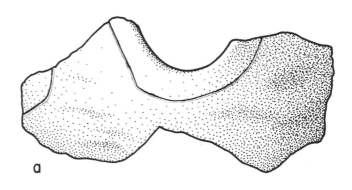

a

b

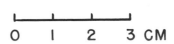

0   1   2   3 CM

FIGURE 25.—Unclassified decorated sherds from the Tivacundo Phase. *a*, Incised. *b*, Nicked shoulder.

THE SERIATED SEQUENCE AND ITS IMPLICATIONS

The seriated sequence of the Tivacundo Phase is based on tendencies exhibited by plain pottery types in successive levels of the stratigraphic excavation at N–P–7 (fig. 26). Two of the types show marked and regular changes in frequency, Chacra Plain declining from 31 percent to 22 percent, and Tivacundo Plain increasing from 32 percent to 45 percent during the period of time represented by the refuse accumulation. Alfaro Plain shows a smaller decline in frequency, from 27 to 25 percent. Tivacundo Red Painted, the only decorated type present throughout the sequence, shows no consistent pattern of change.

The relatively frequencies of pottery types in the sample from N–P–8 appear to fit the trends shown by the plain types best when seriated below the earliest level at N–P–7. If the distorting influence on plain type frequencies resulting from the abnormal amount of Tivacundo Incised and Zoned Red is overcome by classifying the decorated sherds in terms of the plain types on which the decoration was applied, the best agreement is still achieved by placing N–P–8 at the lower end of the sequence. A single carbon-14 date, obtained by extracting the organic material from 2 kilograms of sherds of Chacra Plain from N–P–7, Cut 1, Level 0–8 cm., places the latter portion of the seriated sequence at 1440 ± 70 years ago, or A.D. 510 (SI–330).

The relative chronological position of the two sites is of importance because of several marked differences in the occurrence of minor plain and decorated types, which are of potential utility in tracing the affiliations of the Tivacundo Phase. A small number of undecorated sherds with cariapé temper were identified in the sample from N–P–8, while none were found in the larger sample from N–P–7. The other unclassified plain type, tempered with fine muscovite sand, is more frequent at N–P–8 than at N–P–7, where it occurs only in the earliest level of the stratigraphic excavation. Of the decorated types, Tivacundo Incised and Zoned Red is limited to N–P–8 (fig. 26).

Differences between the relative frequencies of most of the pottery types suggest that there is a gap between the occupation of N–P–8 and N–P–7. This inference is strengthened by examination of differences in vessel shape popularity. Since the upper and lower levels of the excavation at N–P–7 produced too few rim sherds to constitute a reliable sample (Appendix table 4), the rims from all three levels have been combined. This procedure results in rim samples of nearly equal size from the two sites, minimizing errors that might be attributed to differences in size of the samples compared.

When the relative popularity of the six common

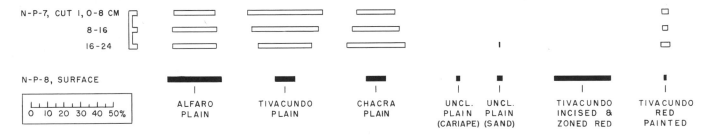

FIGURE 26.—Seriated sequence of Tivacundo Phase sites based on changes in pottery type frequency (see appendix table 6).

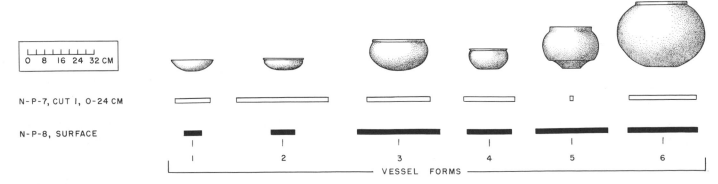

FIGURE 27.—Changes in relative frequency of Tivacundo Phase Common Forms 1–6. Sites are arranged in seriated order.

vessel shapes at N–P–8 and N–P–7 is compared, marked differences are evident in two: Forms 2 and 5 (fig. 27). The pronounced increase in popularity of Form 2 can be accounted for to a limited extent by the corresponding decrease in the frequency of Form 3, from which it differs only in inclination of the rim (fig. 18). Since Form 3 is the one most often chosen for incised and red zoned decoration, its greater frequency at N–P–8 may reflect selection of the sample for decorated sherds. However, an even sharper contrast in the popularity of Form 5 at the two sites cannot be dismissed on such grounds, since this form is always undecorated, as far as can be determined from the present condition of sherd surfaces. The only example of an incipient annular base (fig. 21–D) comes from N–P–8, but the general infrequency of base sherds makes it possible to attribute this restriction to the inadequacy of the available sample.

DIAGNOSTIC FEATURES OF THE TIVACUNDO PHASE

The archeological description of the Tivacundo Phase is based on evidence from two habitation sites occupying adjacent locations on the left bank of the Rio Tiputini where the elevation is above flood level. Only one is intact, the other having been nearly destroyed by erosion of the river bank. The former has a diameter of 30–35 meters, and the refuse accumulation does not exceed 24 cm. This is the only phase not encountered on the Rio Napo, suggesting that smaller streams may have been the preferred location. No evidence was found of burial practices.

Although no direct evidence of subsistence pattern was encountered, it can be assumed that fishing, hunting, and slash-and-burn agriculture were practiced. A few sherds of flat, circular pottery griddles were identified, but their rarity as well as the relatively small reconstructed diameter make it appear improbable that they were utilized for preparation of bitter manioc. Also of problematic significance are vessels with flat bottoms riddled with small perforations, which would have permitted draining or steaming of the contents.

The pottery of the Tivacundo Phase has been classified into three plain and two decorated types. Alfaro Plain, an incompletely oxidized sand-tempered ware, declines slightly in frequency, while Tivacundo Plain, sand tempered and completely oxidized, shows a considerable increase from early to late. Chacra Plain, tempered with ash, attains maximum popularity in the middle of the seriated sequence. Two minor plain types, one tempered with cariapé and the other with fine sand, are restricted to the early levels. The most striking decorated type, Tivacundo Incised and Zoned Red, is also an early diagnostic, while red painted designs not bounded by incision (Tivacundo Red Painted) occur with similar frequency throughout the sequence. Vessel shapes are rounded, open or globular, and typically have a slightly modified "beaded" rim. Some are ovoid rather than circular. A conical-based vertical-necked jar is an early form.

Pottery artifacts are limited to sherds used as abraders and large solid, cylindrical potrests. No shaped stone tools have been reported, and the only stone artifact found was a small polishing stone.

The only carbon-14 date available (see p. 93) indicates that the Tivacundo Phase occupied the region subsequent to the end of the Yasuní Phase and prior to the arrival of the Napo Phase, or around the middle of the first millenium A.D.

The Napo Phase

DESCRIPTION OF SITES AND EXCAVATIONS

The best represented of the archeological phases along the Rio Napo and its tributaries is the Napo Phase. Seven habitation sites were investigated, but although the majority were extensive in area the refuse deposit was too shallow or too disturbed by modern occupation for stratigraphic excavation except in the case of N–P–2. Information on disposal of the dead comes from numerous accidental finds of burial urns in the region.

N–P–1: Tiputini

The main headquarters of the Shell Petroleum Company during exploration in the eastern Ecuadorian lowlands was on the left bank of the Rio Napo a few kilometers above the mouth of the Rio Tiputini (fig. 3). The buildings subsequently were taken over by the Ecuadorian Army and have remained in use. This location was probably selected for modern occupation because the land from the river bank inward for a considerable distance maintains an elevation above flood level, providing not only a large area for habitation but also conditions suitable for an airstrip. The elevation also made it attractive as a village site to earlier immigrants, and the segment paralleling the river bank is occupied by one of the principal sites of the Napo Phase.

The area of Napo Phase habitation coincides almost

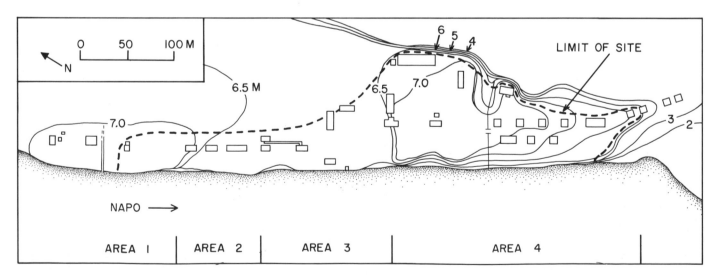

FIGURE 28.—Sketch map of the Napo Phase site of N–P–1, showing the relationship of the archeological remains to modern buildings and the arbitrary divisions made for surface collection.

exactly with that on which modern buildings have been erected (fig. 28), extending some 650 meters along the river bank and increasing from about 40 meters wide at the northwest end to about 120 meters in maximum width in the southeastern half. The southeastern portion occupies the summit of a peninsula-like elevation, the edges of which drop off rapidly on the east and more gradually on the southeast. Here, and at the northwest end of the site, elevation reaches about 7 meters above low water level, while the center is depressed slightly to 6 meters above water level. The vertical river bank becomes more sloping as the summit narrows, and with descending elevation becomes low and subject to flooding immediately below the southeastern edge of the site. The Napo is very wide here and a low island lying opposite Tiputini (pl. 1a) is inundated during the rainy season.

Modern occupation of the site has done extensive damage to the archeological deposit. The surface around most of the buildings is kept clean of vegetation, with the result that up to a meter of the soil has been removed, along with sherds and other kinds of cultural evidence (pl. 12a). It was consequently impossible to find a spot with sufficient depth for stratigraphic testing, and only surface collections could be made. Since it was important to determine whether the site area represented a large population for a short period of time or a small population successively occupying various portions of the area over a longer period of time, the surface material was collected in four spatial units (fig. 28). Comparison of the percent-

age frequency of the various pottery types in the four collections permits evaluation of the nature of the occupation at the site (see pp. 78–80).

With the exception that sherds were less abundant in Area 1, no significant differences were observed in occurrence or distribution of the archeological remains. Most of the sample was collected from eroding banks, drainage ditches, and less disturbed portions of the surface. Where all vegetation had been eliminated, the soil was hard packed and baked and sherds were badly eroded and easily broken. The circular bodies of several badly fractured vessels were exposed in the path in front of the mess hall and two vessels attributed to Tiputini have been preserved in the Colegio Militar in Quito (pls. 54a, 64). Fragments of stone tools were collected from Area 4.

Two other polychrome anthropomorphic jars are said to have come from N–P–1 (pls. 58a, 63).

N–P–2: Nueva Armenia

A group of low rolling hills occupies the right bank of the Rio Napo about halfway between the Rio Tiputini and the Rio Yasuní (fig. 3). Much of the area has been cleared of forest and converted into grassland for cattle raising, making the contour of the terrain clearly visible (pl. 13). A cluster of houses and other modern buildings occupies a section along the river bank where the hills retreat inland leaving a relatively level area about 4 meters above the low

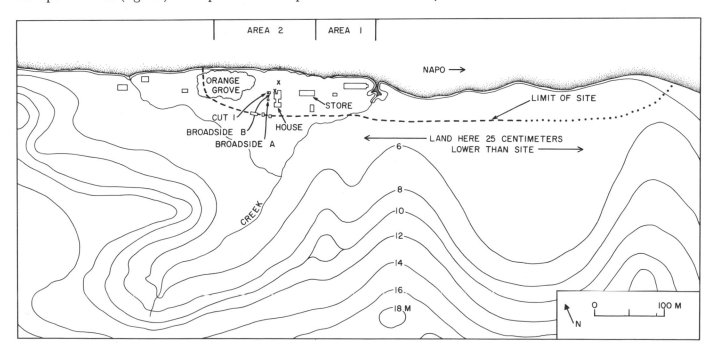

FIGURE 29.—Sketch map of the Napo Phase site of N–P–2, showing modern occupation, arbitrary divisions used for surface collection, and the location of excavations.

water level (pls. 13a–b, 14a). The surface, including much of the present occupation but continuing farther to the southeast, shows evidence of habitation by people of the Napo Phase (fig. 29).

The habitation area, recognized by the presence of sherds, is bisected by the eastern arm of a small creek flowing down from the hills to the west. The greatest concentration of pottery occurred adjacent to the river, extending along the bank of the Rio Napo for approximately 250 meters. Inland extension varied from 30 to 65 meters. Absence of surface vegetation around the buildings and the sandy nature of the soil has facilitated erosion, but damage to the archeological deposit is much less than what has taken place at N–P–1. The sandy condition of the soil, permitting drainage, has also maintained the sherds in far better condition than at any other site. Sherd refuse continues on the downriver side of the creek for at least 250 meters. It may extend farther but the thick grass and hard soil made verification impossible.

Depth of accumulation was sufficient on the highest part of the site, on the west side of the house (fig. 29), to permit stratigraphic excavation. The 3 by 3 meter cut was divided into two artificial 15 cm. levels. The soil was dark brown sandy loam, becoming darker gray toward the southwest, where sherds were most abundant. The soft loose composition of the soil made digging with a trowel possible, and sherds and other inclusions easy to detect (pl. 14b). At 22–25 cm. in depth, the soil color changed sharply from grayish brown of the occupation layer to light yellowish brown sterile sand. The surface of the sterile deposit was uneven, especially in the south corner, where sherds occurred in a pocket 50 cm. in depth. Testing to a depth of 2 meters showed the deposit to continue sterile, sandy loam giving way to light gray clay intermixed with red streaks.

The abundance, large size, and excellent surface condition of the sherds in the vicinity of Cut 1 made it desirable to increase the size of the sample. This was done by extending the excavation 3 meters to the southeast. Conditions were similar to those in Cut 1, and only extremely small plain body sherds were discarded. Most of the pottery came from the upper 15 cm. of the deposit. A pocket 25 cm. in diameter and 50 cm. in depth was filled with fragments of many different vessels. Material from this extension of the Cut 1 was designated as Broadside A and cataloged as a separate unit. A second large sample, including two small complete vessels, was obtained from an irregular area about 3 meters in diameter south of Cut 1 by the women of the household. For identification, it was labelled Broadside B.

For general surface collection, the site was divided into two areas. Area 1, from the store eastward to the creek (fig. 29), presented characteristics similar to those encountered in the excavation, except that sherds were sparser. The surface distribution tended toward a clustering pattern, with areas of relatively great concentration separated by nearly sterile regions. Testing showed the depth of the refuse to repeat that found east of the house. A smaller sample was obtained from the surface of Area 2, west of the store. Sherds collected by local children from a subarea within Area 2 adjacent to the north side of the house, were kept as a separate classificatory unit (Area 2a).

A complete anthropomorphic vessel with polychrome decoration (pl. 52) was excavated prior to our visit from immediately in front of the house. A second of similar construction (pl. 53) and a restorable bowl with Rocafuerte Incised decoration on one side of the rim (pl. 42) have since been collected and deposited in the Museo Arqueológico del Banco Central, Quito. Several stone axes (fig. 31 a–c) were also attributed by local residents to the site.

N–P–3: Nuevo Rocafuerte

The modern village of Nuevo Rocafuerte occupies the right bank of the Rio Napo about 2 kilometers above the mouth of the Rio Yasuní and the Ecuadorian-Peruvian border (fig. 3). Most of the houses are lined in a row paralleling the shore (pl. 12b) and separated from the bank by a double avenue broken down the center by a series of rectangular grass plots (fig. 30). The surface of the avenue and around most of the buildings is kept free of vegetation, and consequent erosion by annual rains has increased surface indications of aboriginal occupation. Sherds are scattered along the bank for more than half a kilometer, extending both to the east and west of the modern village. Maximum elevation is at the central portion of the site, where the vertical bank rises to about 4 meters above low water level. The western portion is about a meter lower. Because of irregularities in the contour of the river bank, inland extension varies from 50 to 100 meters.

Random testing of the deposit produced sherds to a depth of 12 cm. or less, but showed no concentration except along the bank opposite the easternmost of the modern buildings. Test A, 2 by 1 meters, revealed medium gray clay with only a few sherds, which were added to the general surface collection for study. Test B, a few meters to the west (fig. 30), was more rewarding. In this 1.5 meter square area, sherds were closely packed in black sandy loam to a depth of 15–30 cm. Extension of Test B to the southeast showed the dense accumulation to occupy an ovoid area about 75 by 100 cm. in diameter and 1

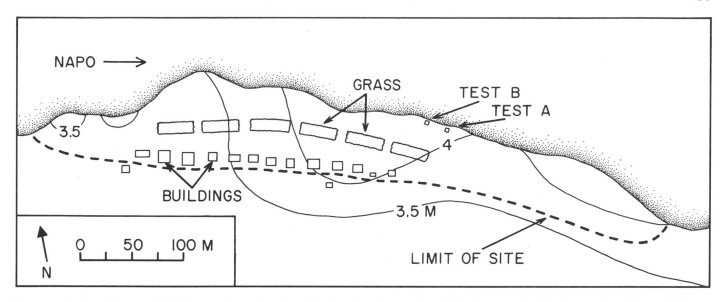

FIGURE 30.—Sketch map of the Napo Phase site of N–P–3, showing the portion of the site occupied by the modern village of Nuevo Rocafuerte and the location of test excavations.

meter in depth. The presence of numerous fragments from a single large painted vessel suggests that the latter may have been interred with the mouth at ground level and after its original function had ceased, it may have been used as a refuse depository. The cavity was surrounded by the sterile light tan clay, which cccurred elsewhere in the site at a depth typically less than 10 cm. below the existing surface.

Although no anthropomorphic urns were encountered during our visit, residents stated that several had been found in the past and were taken to the Jijón y Caamaño Museum in Quito.

N–P–4: Bello Horizonte

For about 3 kilometers upriver from N–P–3, the bank is a rolling succession of hills and depressions. Surface sherds are scattered throughout this area but no concentration was observed until N–P–4, where the highest elevation is attained by the bank (fig. 3; pl. 15a). Sherds were most abundant adjacent to the nearly vertical river bank, where three small summits reach an elevation of about 6 meters above low water level. A modern house had been built behind this slight ridge, and the surface of the western two-thirds of the site had been kept clear of vegetation since the construction of the house some 30 years prior to our visit. The owner contended that the river bank was then much farther to the north.

Sherds were most abundant in the area of highest elevation, extending about 100 meters along the bank and 20 meters inland. Testing of spots with greatest concentration of surface sherds produced little or nothing. Soil was sandy, slightly grayer in the refuse deposit than below. Sherds were typically restricted to the upper 5 cm., occasionally occurring to a depth of 10 cm. The sample was collected mainly from the 90 by 40 meter area east and north of the house, where the surface was free from debris and vegetation.

The owner reported that an anthropomorphic urn with modeled legs was found at the site some years before and sold to a passing American.

N–P–5: Florencia

A cluster of high hills about half way between N–P–2 and N–P–4 embraces a small level area (fig. 3; pl. 15b). A creek flowing northward near the western edge serves as the source of fresh water to the modern residents during the dry season, when the Rio Napo channel retreats northward behind a 500–800 meter wide sandbar. The entire area has been cleared of forest and is covered with pasture, resembling the situation at N–P–2. Remains of Napo Phase habitation were traced over an area about 75 meters along the bank by 30 meters inland, where the elevation was 2 to 4 meters above low water level. The refuse deposit was very thin, rarely exceeding 5 cm. The soil over most of the site consisted of red-orange sandy clay with occasional spots of grayish hue, representing remnants of the habitation layer.

N–P–6: Puerto Alfaro

A relatively small Napo Phase habitation site is located on the high left bank of the Rio Tiputini about 100 meters upstream from the Tivacundo Phase site of

N–P–8 (fig. 15). Sherds occur over an area about 150 meters long by 50 meters inland. Most of the surface lies within the dooryard of a modern house, which is kept free of vegetation (pl. 16a). The opposite bank is low (pl. 16b). The light tan soil bakes hard in dry weather and is reduced to mud during the rainy season, with detrimental effects on the pottery. Testing showed sherds to be restricted to the surface. Several stone tools were also collected (fig. 31f).

N–P–9: Cotacocha

About 8 kilometers above N–P–1 (fig. 3), the left bank of the Rio Napo attains an elevation of 7 meters above low water. A modern house occupies the eastern quarter of a cleared area extending about 25 meters along the bank and a slightly greater distance inland. Beyond its limits, the ground was obscured by grass and banana trees. Within the cleared area, the soil was light tan to brown, hard-baked clay. Sherds were scattered on the surface and extended to a depth of 5 cm. The majority were classified as belonging to the Cotacocha Phase, but 26 were of Napo Phase origin, only one of which was decorated.

N–P–13: Pañacocha

A fragmentary Rocafuerte Painted (red-on-white) vessel of Form 6 was collected by one of the soldiers from Pañacocha, said to be near the mouth of the Rio Cuyabeno, a tributary on the left bank of the Rio Aguarico (fig. 3). The paste is sand tempered.

Data From Other Investigations

The exotic and often beautifully painted anthropomorphic burial urns of the Napo Phase have found their way into a remarkably large number of museums, considering the remoteness of the area of their origin. Unfortunately, few have exact provenience identification. Where a location is specified it is sometimes unidentifiable because the name is no longer used or distances cannot be computed with confidence on a modern map. In spite of these drawbacks, the data enlarge the geographical distribution of Napo Phase pottery.

Rio Aguarico

Three complete vessels with characteristic Napo Phase form and decoration have been found on the Rio Aguarico. An Armenia White-on-red jar of Form 17 (pl. 20c), in the Peabody Museum, Harvard University, was collected by John Gillin (1936, p. 469) who gives the following description of its provenience:

The specimen was presented to me by two Aguarico Indians who happened to share our camping place . . . . I went next morning to the spot where the specimen was alleged to have been found. A hole was found in the side of a mud bank with evidences of considerable digging by sticks and cutlasses. The writer is convinced that the urn was found by the Indians in situ, four feet six inches deep in alluvial, gray clay. The surface of the ground was covered to a depth of about nine inches with vegetable mould and a matting of roots from the forest growing there . . . . We had no tools for digging, but a day spent in working with cutlasses revealed several sherds of gray, undecorated pottery and a hearth of charcoal at a depth of five feet nine inches from the surface. The creek in question, which is nameless, is a right tributary of the Aguarico which joins the latter an estimated forty-five miles above its mouth. The site is located on the left bank of the creek about one and a half miles above its mouth.

An unnamed tributary of the Rio Aguarico in the approximate location specified by Gillin lies almost due north of N–P–9. Overland distance from the Rio Napo here is only about 20 kilometers (fig. 3).

The second vessel, a Rocafuerte Painted (red and black-on-white) jar of Form 6 with an anthropomorphic face on a rim lobe (pl. 46), was acquired during our survey from a local resident who said it had been found on the right bank of the Rio Aguarico a short distance above the mouth of the Rio Cuyabeno (fig. 3). The paste is sand tempered. No associated material was observed.

An anthropomorphic urn of type B, with the orifice in the base, is said by Alan C. Lapiner to have come from the Rio Aguarico at the mouth of the Rio Eno, located approximately at 76 degrees 25 minutes west longitude (fig. 3), which places it farther up river than other documented finds of Napo Phase ceramics. The vessel has both polychrome and grooved decoration, and painted designs surround both eyes (pl. 62b). Details are given on Table A.

Eden

A Napo Plain Incised bowl (USNM Archeology No. 385647), a side-notched stone ax (USNM Archeology No. 385649; fig. 31d) and a T-shaped stone ax (USNM Archeology No. 385648; fig. 31e) are attributed to the vicinity of Eden. Recent maps show Eden on the right bank of the Rio Napo, above the mouth of the Rio Dumbique, or about 80 kilometers upstream from N–P–1 (fig. 3).

Rio Indillama

A Rocafuerte Painted (black-on-white) jar of Form 17 (pl. 54b) is said to have come from the right bank of the Rio Napo a little below the mouth of the Rio Indillama (fig. 3).

Oasis

A collection of 40 sherds, 37 of them decorated, in the Museum of the American Indian, Heye Foundation, New York, are from Oasis on the right bank of the Rio Napo, a few kilometers upstream from Eden (fig. 3). The range of decorated techniques and vessel shapes is comparable to that at other Napo Phase habitation sites. Although selected for decorated sherds, the attempt has been made to seriate this collection in the Napo Phase sequence (figs. 61–63) after correcting it by allowing for a 61.8 percent frequency of plain sherds, which is the average figure for unselected Napo Phase samples. (Appendix table 8.)

Providencia

An excised bowl (pl. 32b) was found by Howard S. Strouth near Providencia on the left bank of the Rio Napo (fig. 3). Diameter is 28 cm.

Rumi-tuni

Two pottery vessels of Napo Phase types in the American Museum of Natural History, New York (AMNH, 41.1/3985 and 41.0/9141), are attributed to "Rumi-tuni", located on the right bank, 315 kilometers above the mouth of the Rio Napo. Measurement of this distance on the most accurate map available places it in the vicinity of the mouth of the Rio Curaray, in what is now Peruvian territory (fig. 3). The specimens consist of a Napo Red Incised bowl of Form 5 and a Rocafuerte Painted (red and black-on-white) semi-cylindrical anthropomorphic jar lacking the head (pl. 65).

Rio Yasuní

A Napo Phase site has been reported by Pedro I. Porras (personal communication) near Puerto Vargas, on the left bank of the Rio Yasuní about 4 kilometers from the mouth (fig. 3). The bank here rises 3 meters above low water level. A 2 by 2 meter stratigraphic excavation showed the Napo Phase refuse to be overlain by 20 cm. of humus, which contained fragments of a modern painted vessel. Below 20 cm., Napo Phase sherds were sparse and neither of the two 10 cm. levels produced a sample of 100 sherds. Sterile clay appeared at about 37 cm.

Classification of the sherd sample by temper resulted in 93.6 percent sand, 3.8 percent cariapé, and 2.6 percent charcoal, a combination that seriates between N–P–1, Area 4, and Oasis, in the upper third of the sequence (fig. 60). Tabulation of single-line and double-line incision shows 45 percent frequency of single-line and 55 percent frequency of double-line technique, equivalent to that of N–P–3, Surface and Test A, which seriates early (fig. 61). The inconsistency of these results may stem from insufficient sample size. The presence of all decorated types except Napo Negative and Tiputini White Excised favors the earlier position, since many are absent from the late portion of the sequence (fig. 63).

A large anthropomorphic figure is reported to have been found about 80 meters upstream from the location of the excavation. The figure is seated, with abbreviated legs, a cylindrical body expanding slightly at rounded shoulders, a constructed neck and globular head. Ears, eyes, nose and mouth are in relief; the mouth is shown open. Treatment is not like that of any of the other anthropomorphic urns, but wide variation in rendition of anthropomorphic features is characteristic of Napo Phase art.

Unspecified Location on Rio Napo

An anthropomorphic urn in the possession of a Rio Napo resident in 1956 (now owned by Thomas Flannery) is of interest because of the circumstances reported by the finder concerning its discovery. The vessel is of type B with the orifice at the bottom, and has arms and legs in full round (see Table A for details). It was encountered during excavation for a house post, buried upside down. The opening was covered with a lid of unspecified type. The arms and legs had been broken off and placed inside. No remnants of bones or teeth were reported.

Other vessels are illustrated in various publications or preserved in museum collections. They are either attributed because of their style to the Rio Napo or have only this generalized provenience identification. Anthropomorphic examples are described on Table A. Rocafuerte Painted vessels illustrated by Jijón y Caamaño (1951) include jars of Forms 16 and 17, the latter with a bowl-shaped lid (op. cit., figs. 497–8, 502) and a basin of Rare Form 5 (op. cit., fig. 503).

ANALYSIS OF MATERIALS

Stone Artifacts

The soil along the Rio Napo is devoid of large stones at the longitude of the Napo Phase sites. However, above the mouth of the Rio Suno (fig. 1), bars of rounded cobbles and pebbles provide a ready source of this raw material. Both shaped and polished tools and unshaped rock fragments showing use were collected from most of the Napo Phase sites. Proveniences are indicated on Appendix table 7.

Abraders

Five small stones from various sites (Appendix table 7) have facets worn on parts of the surface from use as abraders. Rock materials are fine sandstone or pumice. One quartz pebble appears to be polished from use.

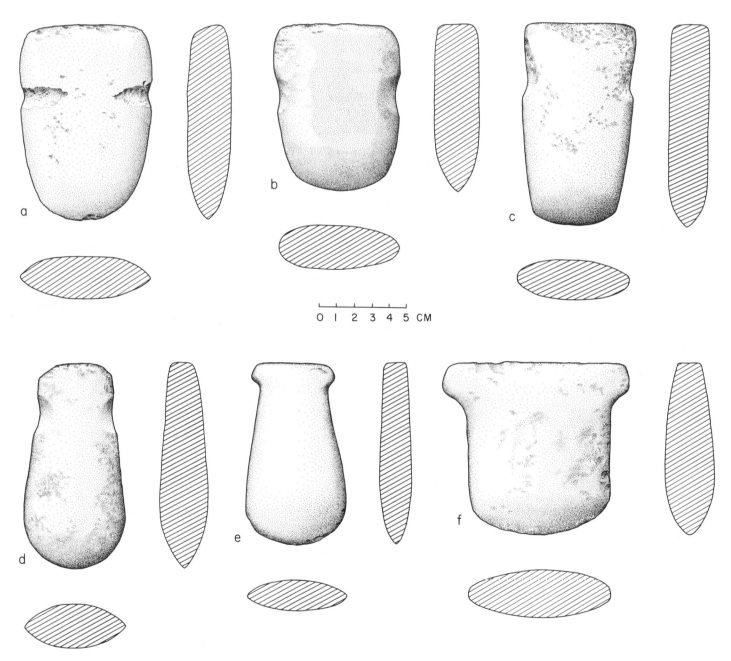

0 1 2 3 4 5 CM

FIGURE 31.—Napo Phase stone axes. *a–d*, Side notched. *e–f*, T-shaped.

Form is irregular and size varies from 5.0 by 3.5 by 3.0 cm. to 3.5 by 2.5 by 1.0 cm.

Axes

FIGURE 31

The majority of the stone axes, represented by four complete and two broken examples with the blades missing, are side-notched, fashioned from granite, andesite, greenstone, and slightly metamorphosed tuffaceous sandstone. The butt is nearly flat, and sides tend to be generally parallel, tapering gradually toward the convex blade. One example (fig. 31d) is atypical in form, the sides diverging below the notch to an expanded blade. Notches are shallow, with a maximum depth of 3–4 mm. except for one unusually large sample where depth reaches 7 mm. The notched area is even but not polished, and pecking may extend inward along the surface to produce a slight depression (fig. 31a). Surface polish may be nearly complete, leaving a few pits and flaws especially near the butt. More typically, however, polishing is best adjacent to the blade and may also occur at both edges or on the face. The butt edge is battered principally from use, but to some extent from shaping by pecking without subsequent polishing.

Vertical sections show the two faces to be parallel except on one example, flattened at the butt, and curving to a sharp edge at the blade. The horizontal section varies from the butt, which tends to be rectanguloid, to the region immediately below the notches, where the edges become rounded. About half the distance between the notches and the blade, the cross-section becomes ovoid with blunt to sharp ends.

Length of complete examples varies from 9.5 to 11.5 cm., with one fragment of considerably larger size. Width at the butt is 6.4 to 7.4 cm., at the blade about 5 cm., except for one example in which the butt is 4.5 cm. wide and the blade 5.7 cm. Maximum thickness is 2.3 to 2.7 cm., except for the above mentioned unusually large fragment with a thickness of 3.7 cm.

Two axes have a T-shaped or "eared" form, but one has parallel sides (fig. 31f) while the other expands toward the blade (fig. 31e). The former is tuffaceous sandstone, polished adjacent to the blade and on the end of the butt, with the remainder of the surface evenly pecked and unpolished. Thickness increases from 1.3 cm. at the flat butt to 2.8 cm. toward the blade. The sides are slightly flattened. Maximum width at the butt is 10.8 cm., width below the ears is 8 cm. Length is 9.5 cm. The second example, fashioned from silicified volcanic rock, has a completely polished surface leaving two small flaws adjacent to the butt.

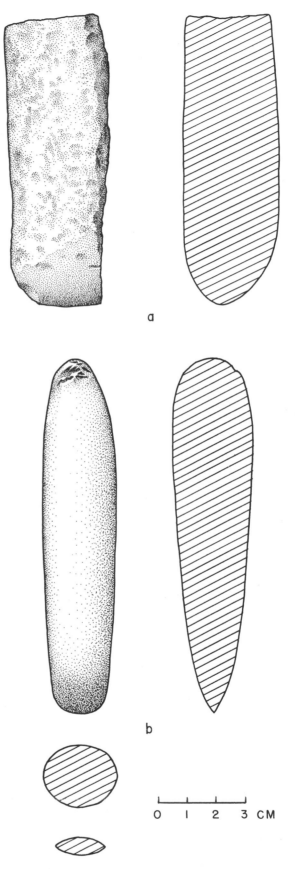

a

b

0 1 2 3 CM

FIGURE 32.—Napo Phase stone tools. a, Grinding stone. b, Chisel.

The blade shows slight battering from use. Width at the ears is 4.6 cm., maximum width 5.6 cm.; total length is 10.3 cm. Thickness increases slightly from 1.3 cm. at the flat butt to 1.8 cm. toward the blade.

Chisel

FIGURE 32b

The only tool in this category comes from the surface at N–P–6. It is fine-grained slate, incompletely shaped from an elongated waterworn pebble, leaving the original contour unmodified at the naturally rounded butt end. The sides are slightly convex, and the faces taper toward a well sharpened convex blade. As a result, the cross-section is nearly circular at the middle, becoming almond-shaped at the blade. The surface is even and polished to a slick finish except adjacent to the butt. Total length is 12.2 cm., maximum diameter 2.5 cm. at the center, blade width 1.7 cm.

Cores

The only two examples are from N–P–1. Both are chert. Dimensions are 3.5 by 2.5 by 1.8 cm. and 2 by 2 by 1 cm.

Grinding Stones

FIGURE 32a

Two fragments, both from N–P–1, Area 4, show use polish on one or more surfaces. One is a thick fragment of dark grayish green andesite that has been altered to reddish tan on the worn surfaces. The fragment is at present a rectanguloid block (fig. 32a). One surface is slightly convex and the other slightly concave when viewed in the long axis. In cross-section, the former is slightly convex and the latter markedly so. Projection of the contours of the most strongly curved faces suggests that the original form may have resembled that of a large mano. Thickness ranges from 4.2 to 5.5 cm., existing length is about 11 cm.

The other fragment is also grayish green andesite. Asymmetrical use polish occurs on the end, extending about 3 cm. backward on one face and 2 cm. on the other. The remaining surface is roughly shaped by pecking. Cross-section is ovoid. Existing length is 10 cm., thickness 3.5 cm., and reconstructed width about 6 cm.

Hammerstones

FIGURE 33

Hammerstones may be divided into two categories: those that were intentionally shaped and natural rocks that show traces of use. The first category includes two specimens, one disk-shaped and the other rectanguloid.

The disk-shaped hammerstone (fig. 33b), from the surface of N–P–2, is grayish tan andesite with black pyroxene crystals. It has an even, but not polished surface, with numerous shallow to deep pits. Shape is not perfectly circular, so that diameter varies from 7.3 to 7.5 cm., with a maximum thickness of 2 cm. The faces are parallel and slightly convex, tapering to rounded edges.

The rectanguloid example (fig. 33a) is grayish white granite. It comes from N–P–1, Area 3. Both ends and one side are severely battered. The outline resembles that of the notched axes, with flat butt, parallel sides, and a convex lower end, suggesting that it may be an unfinished ax. Cross-section is ovoid with rounded edges. Most of one face and half of the other are even but not smooth to the touch, with deep pits and irregularities unobliterated. Length is 11.5 cm., width 5.6 cm. and thickness 2.1 cm. The upper portion of a similar object has an even surface and a considerably battered butt. The rock is dark gray porphyry. Provenience is N–P–1, Area 4. Width is 7.1 cm., maximum thickness 2.9 cm., existing length 6.3 cm.

Eleven natural stones show traces of battering on one or more edges. Rock materials represented are andesite, quartz, quartzite, porphyry, and sandstone. The majority are fragments of waterworn pebbles with existing dimensions between 7.5 by 7.5 by 2.5 cm. and 4.5 by 3.0 by 1.5 cm. Their condition suggests temporary use and there is no evidence of intentional shaping.

Two pebbles, both from N–P–1, Area 4, show evidence of more extended use (fig. 33 c, d). One is quartz, cylindroid with rounded ends, one of which is severely worn. A smaller area of similar wear occurs on the other end. Length is 5.8 cm., width 4.8 cm., and thickness 4.2 cm. The other is a naturally trianguloid andesite pebble with one flat and one convex face. The effects of battering are visible in two areas along the edge and at the center of the flat face. Diameter is 6.5 by 7.0 cm., maximum thickness 4.3 cm.

Natural Pebbles

Complete or fragmentary pebbles of chert, quartz, sandstone, quartzite, and granite were collected from most sites. Since these types of stone were all represented in objects showing use, the presence of unworked stones may be of cultural origin. Size varies between 6.5 by 4.0 by 1.8 cm. and 4.0 by 2.8 by 2.2 cm.

Paint Stone

An irregularly shaped hunk of limonite from N–P–3, Test B Extension shows striations from rubbing. Dimensions are 6.5 by 5.5 by 3.0 cm.

Spalls

Andesite, quartzite, and sandstone spalls from waterworn pebbles or tools with worked surfaces (axes?) appear to be by-products of manufacture or use of stones for pounding. None show evidence of use in their present condition.

Pottery Artifacts

All Napo Phase pottery artifacts are objects of primary manufacture. No sherds were observed to show signs of use or reworking.

Disk

One fragment of a small pottery disk may represent a spindle whorl. The paste is fine sand tempered and fired tannish orange. Surfaces are even and smooth but not polished or floated sufficiently to obliterate temper particles. Outline is not perfectly circular, and one surface is flat while the other is slightly convex. Diameter is about 3 cm., thickness at the center 3.5 mm. Perforation diameter 3 mm. Provenience is N–P–2, Broadside B.

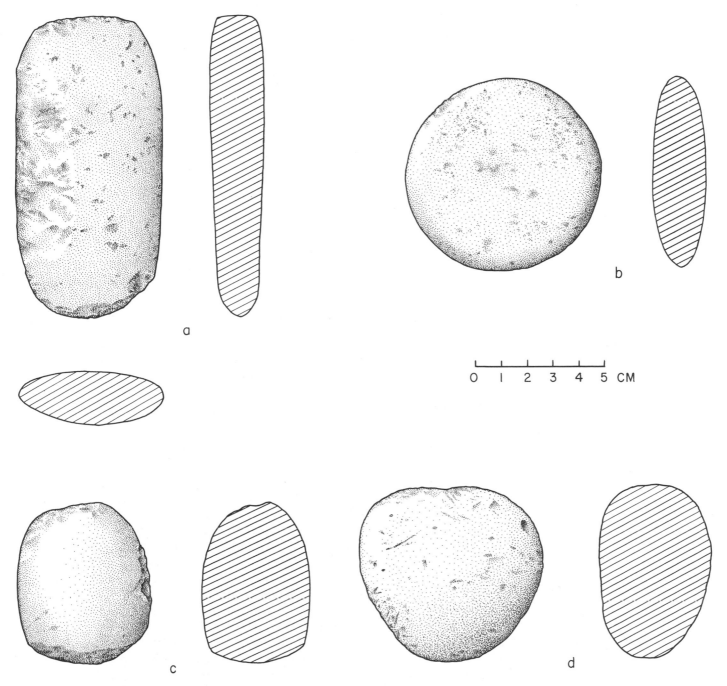

FIGURE 33.—Napo Phase hammerstones. *a–b*, Shaped stones, *c–d*, Natural pebbles.

Potrests

FIGURE 34; PLATE 17

More than 200 fragments of potrests were collected, representing all of the Napo Phase sites. A number of upper or lower ends are included, but the majority are irregularly shaped body fragments, 2–6 cm. in diameter. Form is not symmetrical, making diameter measurement of fragments unreliable. The majority of diameter measurements ranged from 8–12 cm. at the upper end and 10–18 cm. at the base. The only example complete enough to provide both height and diameter was 9 cm. in diameter and 13 cm. tall. Another measured 15 cm. with part of the height missing.

Most of the fragments are made of untempered clay. A minority have sandy paste, perhaps being made of clay left over from vessel manufacture. Color is light orange to pinkish orange, or occasionally pale tan or grayish. A layer 2 to 10 mm. wide adjacent to the surface may be paler buff or orange than the core. Texture is laminated with abundant air pockets. Characteristic fracture into irregular hunks (pl. 17 *c, e*) suggests construction by aggregation of lumps of clay until the desired volume was achieved. A number of surface fragments have irregular inner walls suggesting that the interior either was hollow or was never sufficiently well fired to be preserved under the destructive action of weathering. Others were clearly of solid construction.

Surface is brown, tan or rarely pale orange, often with small irregularly shaped fire clouds. Treatment varies from smoothed to produce an even surface to irregular and uneven, especially on the ends. Horizontal or vertical smoothing marks may occur, made by the finger or possibly a pebble tool.

Only one example is decorated on the upper end with incision and excision (fig. 34). It came from N–P–2, Broadside A.

Roller Stamps

FIGURE 35

Although no roller stamps or fragments were collected at any of the Napo Phase sites included in the survey, one example in the Museo Víctor Emilio Estrada, Guayaquil, is attributed to the Rio Napo. The roller surface bears a deeply excised pattern resembling that on pottery vessels, suggesting that the artifact is of Napo Phase origin. The design area consumes less than half the total length, the remainder being divided between two tapering handles that give the object a rolling pin form. Total length is 15 cm., length of the design portion 6 cm., and maximum diameter about 6.6 cm.

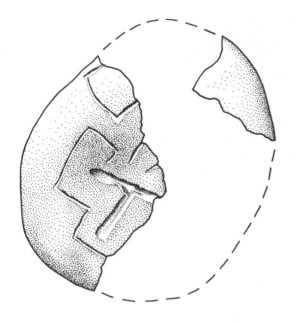

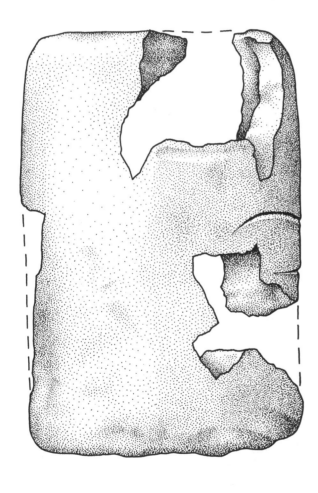

0   1   2   3 CM

FIGURE 34.—Decorated potrest from the Napo Phase.

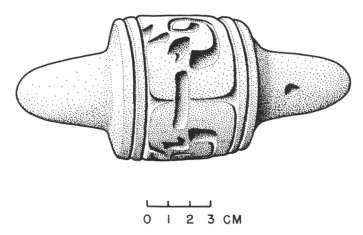

└─┴─┴─┴─┘
0 1 2 3 CM

FIGURE 35.—Roller stamp probably of Napo Phase origin.

Ceramic Classification

The pottery types of the Napo Phase are based on classification of 13,896 sherds from 8 habitation sites, supplemented by a number of complete vessels in private collections and museums. Decoration is more frequent than in the other archeological phases on the Rio Napo, varying between 34 to 47 percent of the sherds where the sample seemed adequate.

Although Napo Phase pottery frequently exhibits surface erosion, preservation is much better than in the Tivacundo and Yasuní Phases. Surfaces are often intact, showing traces of smoothing and in some cases polishing, but rarely achieving a slick or lustrous finish. Both red and white slips occur in association with painting, incision and excision, and more complicated treatments involve the application of red or white pigment to incised lines. In a few cases, more than one technique was applied to a single vessel, usually a combination of incised or excised exteriors with painted interiors.

The undecorated pottery was classified on the basis of temper differences into three plain types: cariapé-tempered Armenia Plain, sand-tempered Napo Plain, and charcoal-tempered Tiputini Plain. An unusually large number of decorated types—19 in all—has been established after much deliberation. Incised and excised designs occur in two varieties, one done with a single pointed tool and the other with a double- or multiple-pointed tool. Each technique occurs with plain, red and white slipped surfaces, so that subdivision of the incised types by technique doubles the number of types. Differences in vessel shape and temporal position presented by the single-line and double-line techniques in the Napo Phase ceramic complex are sufficient to warrant their separation into distinct types, and this procedure is further justified by the differences in geographical distribution

of the two techniques in the Amazon Basin. Other characteristic Napo Phase decorated techniques are red-on-white, black-on-white, and red and black-on-white painting, white-on-red painting, negative painting, and red slipping without further embellishment.

Twenty-one common shapes have been recognized for Napo Phase pottery, nearly all represented by one or more complete vessels. The outstanding characteristic is avoidance of circular form. The majority of all vessels are squarish when viewed from above, and many have concave sides and projecting corners. Even the most nearly circular examples often have slightly flattened sides, although truly circular outline also occurs. Annular bases, channeled and cambered rims, and several kinds of anthropomorphic treatment are additional features setting Napo Phase pottery apart from that of other complexes in the area.

Since most rim sherds did not provide measurable diameters, vessel shapes have been drawn to the size and proportions of a complete specimen, in contrast to the procedure followed for illustrations of pottery types in other phases. In several cases, the same rim profile is associated with two distinct body shapes; where this is known to occur, both forms have been shown. Rim profiles have been selected to illustrate both the range of variation exhibited by a form and the association of the form with plain and decorated pottery types. Plain rims are drawn in all figures in solid black, while red slipped ones are hachured; decorated (incised, excised, painted) rims are shown in outline. Decorated portions of the surface are usually identified by arrows or brackets.

Pottery type descriptions have been arranged in alphabetical order following the description of vessel and base forms. Provenience and frequency of both pottery types and vessel shapes can be found in Appendix tables 8 and 10.

Reconstructed Vessel Forms

Common Forms

1. Open bowl with exteriorly thickened rim (fig. 36–1):
   Rim: Upcurving or incurving and thickened on the exterior to produce an elevated band 2–4 (rarely, 5) cm. wide adjacent to the lip. Thickness is 2–3 mm. greater at the center than the body wall, and typically decreases slightly both above and below. Noncircular.
   Lip: Flattened; very rarely, rounded.
   Body wall thickness: Range 3–7 mm.; majority 3–5 mm.
   Base: Rounded or slightly flattened (Form C).

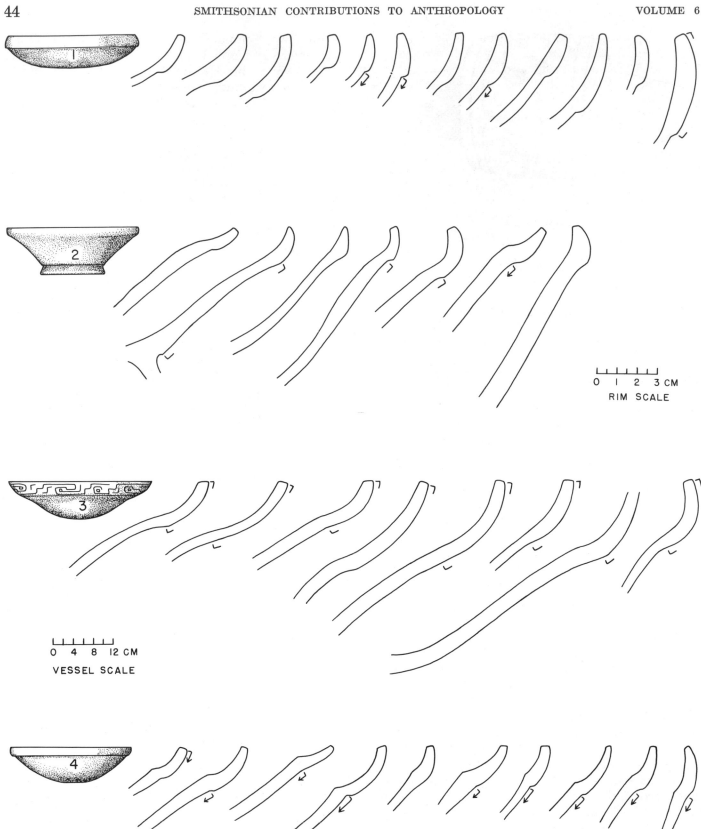

FIGURE 36.—Rim profiles and reconstructed vessel shapes of the Napo Phase, Common Forms 1–4. Arrows and brackets designate decorated zone.

2. Deep bowl with outslanting wall (fig. 36–2):
   Rim: Outslanting or slightly everted, turning upward 1.5–2.5 cm. below lip often assuming a nearly vertical orientation. Upturned section is convex on the exterior, either because of thickening or corresponding concavity on the interior. Lower edge of upturned section may blend into the wall or change direction abruptly. Noncircular.
   Lip: Tapered and flattened.
   Body wall thickness: Range 4.0–9.5 mm.; variable on a single vessel.

Base: Annular (Form D), or flattened (Form A).

3. Bowl with curved cambered rim (fig. 36–3):
   Rim: Outcurving wall, concave on exterior, turns upward producing a convex exterior contour 3.0–5.5 cm. below the lip. This curved camber typically results from gradual change in direction and is rarely accompanied by thickening of the wall. Noncircular.
   Lip: Flattened.
   Body wall thickness: Range 4.5–7.0 mm.
   Base: Flattened (Form A).

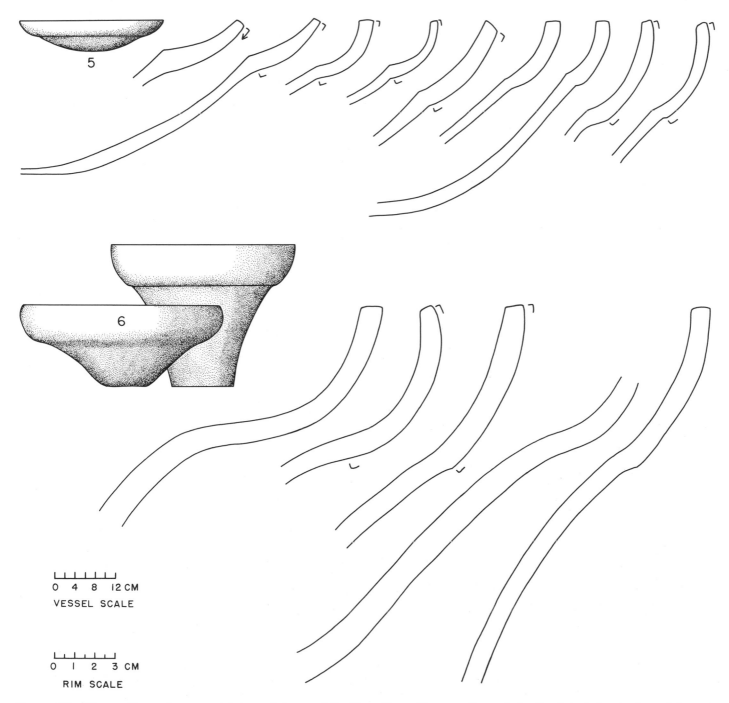

0 4 8 12 CM
VESSEL SCALE

0 1 2 3 CM
RIM SCALE

FIGURE 37.—Rim profiles and reconstructed vessel shapes of the Napo Phase, Common Forms 5–6. Brackets designate decorated zone.

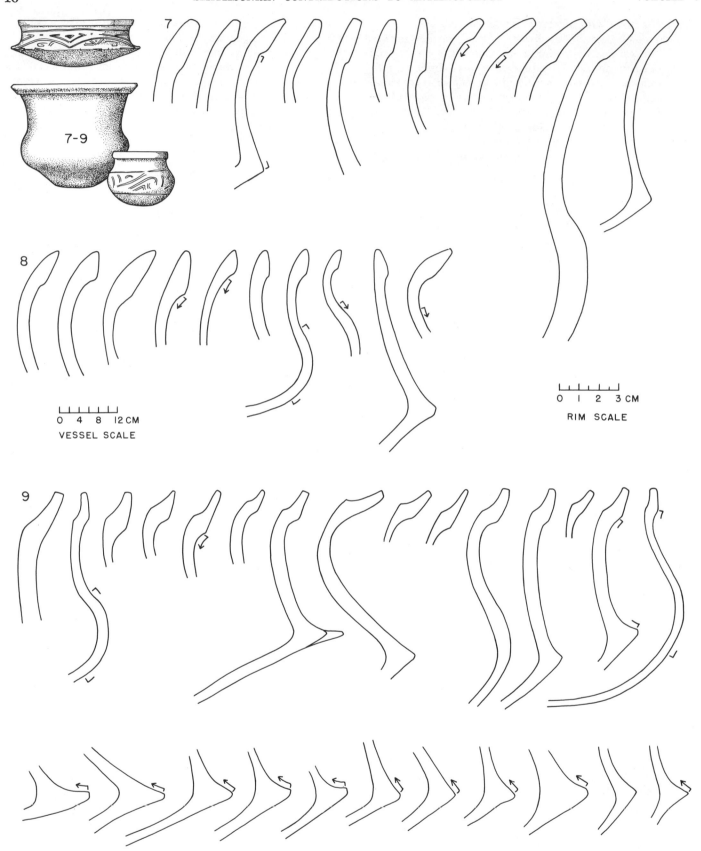

FIGURE 38.—Rim profiles and reconstructed vessel shapes of the Napo Phase, Common Forms 7–9. Arrows and brackets designate decorated zones.

4. Open bowl with "channel" rim (fig. 36–4):

Rim: Curvature of the body wall is markedly increased 2–3 mm. below the lip, producing an effect on the exterior similar to that of Form 1 both in contour and orientation. This is accomplished without thickening, with the result that a channel or marked concavity is produced on the corresponding portion of the interior. Slight thickening of the wall increases the abruptness of the change of direction on the interior, and it typically appears as a sharp ridge. Change of direction on the exterior may be gradual or abrupt and step-like. Noncircular.

Lip: Flattened.

Body wall thickness: Range 4–6 mm.; thickened to 6–9 mm. at lower border of channel.

Base: Flattened (Form A), or rounded (Form C).

5. Open bowl with broad "channel" rim (fig. 37–5):

Rim: Construction similar to Form 4, but with with channel width 3–5 cm. Noncircular.

Lip: Flattened.

Body wall thickness: Range 4–6 mm.; thickened to 6–10 mm. at lower border of channel.

Base: Flattened (Form A), or rounded (Form C).

6. Large deep bowl or jar with curved cambered rim (fig. 37–6):

Rim: Construction similar to Form 3, but with change in curvature beginning 9–11 cm. below the lip. Change in direction on the exterior may be continuous and gradual or abrupt, the latter condition produced by slight thickening. Diameter may reach 50 cm.

Lip: Flattened.

Body wall thickness: Range 9–13 mm.

Base: Flat (Form A, B, or E).

7. Bowl or jar with everted, exteriorly thickened rim (fig. 38–7):

Rim: Slightly to strongly everted and thickened abruptly 1–3 cm. below the lip, tapering from a maximum thickness at this point toward the lip. Lower edge of thickening is smoothed over typically producing a concave zone of junction on the exterior. The interior surface continues the curvature of the wall eversion. Thickened band is generally convex on the exterior surface; rarely, it is concave. Eversion is frequently greater at corners than at sides.

Lip: Flattened.

Body wall thickness: Range 4–9 mm.; lower edge of exterior rim thickening, 6.5–12.0 mm.; thickness at carination 1.0–2.7 cm.

Body form: Two distinct shoulder forms occur with this rim construction (also with Forms 8, 9, and 10).

A. Carinated and typically thickened to increase the prominence of the angle (fig. 38, bottom). Thickening is often greater at the corners than at the sides; when this occurs, the sides are concave when the vessel is seen from above. Corners vary from rounded to projecting (fig. 39).

B. Rounded and unthickened or slightly thickened.

Noncircular form when viewed from above is much less pronounced, but flattening of the sides is always perceptible.

Base: Rounded (Form C).

8. Bowl or jar with everted, exteriorly thickened tapered rim (fig. 38–8):

Rim: Everted and exteriorly thickened 1–3 cm. below the lip, tapering from that point to the lip. Curvature of inner wall and of convex surface of tapering outer wall often meet at the midline to form a symmetrical cross-section. Noncircular.

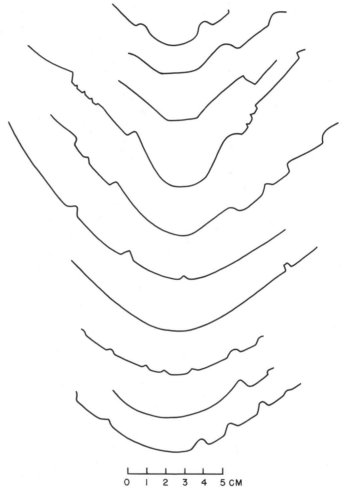

FIGURE 39.—Shoulder corner contour of carinated vessels of Napo Phase Common Forms 7–10, showing decorative notching.

Lip: Tapering and slightly rounded.

Body wall thickness: Range 4–6 mm.

Body form: See Form 7.

Base: Rounded (Form C).

9. Bowl or jar with everted "channel" rim (fig. 38–9):

Rim: Everted and bent abruptly 1.2–2.5 cm. below the lip creating an external appearance similar to that of Form 7 but with a clearly defined channel on the interior produced either by a combination of thickening at the lower edge and thinning toward the lip, or by allowing the inner wall contour to parallel that of the outer wall. Noncircular.

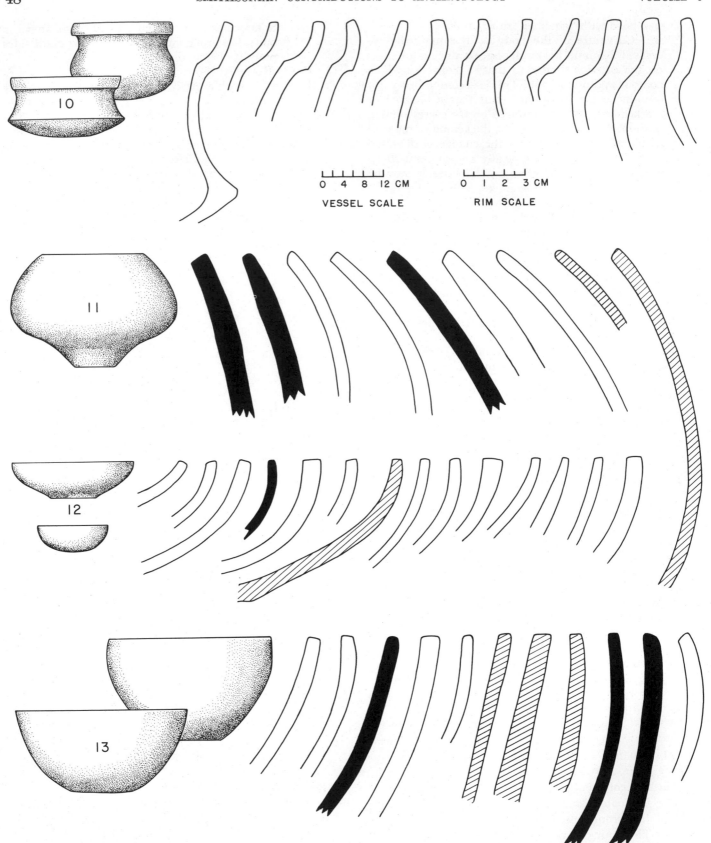

FIGURE 40.—Rim profiles and reconstructed vessel shapes of the Napo Phase, Common Forms 10–13. Arrows designate decorated zones. (Black=undecorated, white=decorated, hachure=red slipped.)

Lip: Flat.
Body wall thickness: Range 4–9 mm.; majority 4–7 mm.
Body form: See Form 7.
Base: Rounded (Form C).

10. Bowl or jar with cambered rim (fig. 40–10):
    Rim: Cambered, curved, or angular on the exterior but typically angular on the interior, frequently changing direction at an angle approaching 90 degrees. This form is distinguished from the "channel" rim of Form 9 both by its greater length (height) and by greater uniformity of thickness of the cross-section, although there is a continuum from one to the other. Noncircular.
    Lip: Flat.
    Body wall thickness: Range 2–9 mm.; majority 4–6 mm.
    Body form: See Form 7.
    Base: Rounded (Form C).

11. Constricted mouth jar (fig. 40–11, pls. 52, 53).
    Rim: Direct and incurving.
    Lip: Flat or rounded.
    Body wall thickness: Range 6–13 mm.
    Body form: Some complete vessels have a strongly curved shoulder, others may be more globular.
    Base: Flat (Form B).

12. Shallow bowl with direct rim (fig. 40–12):
    Rim: The outslanting wall curves upward about 3–5 cm. below the lip, depending on the diameter of the bowl. Change of direction is gradual but sufficient so that the rim orientation approaches vertical and the lip is typically horizontal. Rim form is usually direct but rarely expanded or tapered. Diameter 14–42 cm.
    Lip: Flat; rarely rounded.
    Body wall thickness: Range 4–9 mm.
    Base: Flat (Form B) or rounded (Form C).

13. Large deep bowl with direct rim (fig. 40–13):
    Rim: Direct, continuing the outward slope of the body wall or curving upward about 5–9 cm. below the lip to assume a vertical or slightly incurving orientation. Change of direction is typically gradual but occasionally perceptible on the exterior as a rounded angle. Diameter 28–46 cm.
    Lip: Flat or rarely rounded.
    Body wall thickness: Range 6–12 mm.
    Base: Flat (Form A) or rounded (Form C).

14. Large shallow basin (fig. 41–14; frontispiece; pls. 42, 51*a*).
    Rim: Strongly outsloping and slightly everted to produce a convex interior contour, sometimes enhanced by slight thickening of the wall. Noncircular.
    Lip: Flat and usually lobed or ornamented with an elaborate pattern of steps and notches.
    Body wall thickness: Range 5–13 mm.
    Base: Rounded (Form C).

15. Flange rim jar (fig. 41–15):
    Rim: Everted at an angle of approximately 90 degrees and thickened to produce an angular contour on the interior and a curved one on the exterior. The flattened or slightly convex top 1.3–1.5 cm. wide, is usually level, but occasionally insloping or outsloping. Interior diameter of two specimens measures 20–24 cm., but others are probably noncircular.
    Lip: Tapering or flattened.
    Body wall thickness: Range 3–6 mm.
    Base: Probably rounded (Form C).

16. Large collared jar (fig. 41–16):
    Rim: The effect of a broad collar is produced either by thickening of the wall or by alteration of curvature or both. Collar height ranges from 4.5–14.5 cm., with the majority about 9–12 cm. high. Thickening is usually 2–4 mm. greater than the lower body wall. The collar surface is convex on the exterior, and the upper portion is slightly incurved. Diameters of 36–42 cm. were measured, but the majority are probably noncircular.
    Lip: Flat, rarely curved.
    Body wall thickness: Range 4–10 mm.; majority 4–6 mm.
    Base: Probably flat (Form A).

17. Semicylindrical jar (fig. 42–17; pl. 54):
    Rim: Slightly everted, vertical or insloping; wall thickness may remain uniform, increase or decrease in the upper 3 cm. Diameter 17–48 cm.
    Lip: Flat and generally horizontal.
    Body wall thickness: Range 7–13 mm.
    Body form: Range of variation from a tall jar to a broader, more open vessel results from different combinations of diameter and height. A pronounced to gently rounded shoulder occurs at the junction between the outflaring lower wall and the more vertical upper one, and diameter is equal or greater than that of the rim.
    Base: Flat (Form A) or rounded (Form C).

18. Globular jar with constricted neck (fig. 42–18):
    Rim: Everted to produce an outsloping neck. Junction with incurving body wall may be curved or slightly angular. One example is thickened on the exterior 5 cm. below the lip, producing a collar-like band.
    Lip: Flat.
    Body wall thickness: Range 4–6 mm.
    Base: Probably rounded (Form C).

19. Constricted mouth jar with exteriorly thickened rim (fig. 42–19):
    Rim: Incurving wall is upturned and thickened 1.0–1.5 cm. below the lip producing a narrow "beaded" edge. Interior diameter 28–46 cm.
    Lip: Rounded.
    Body wall thickness: Range 6–12 mm.
    Base: Probably flattened (Form A).

20. Large shallow basin (fig. 43–20):
    Rim: Upslanting and direct or narrowing slightly beginning 2 cm. below the lip. Diameter of one example, 42 cm.

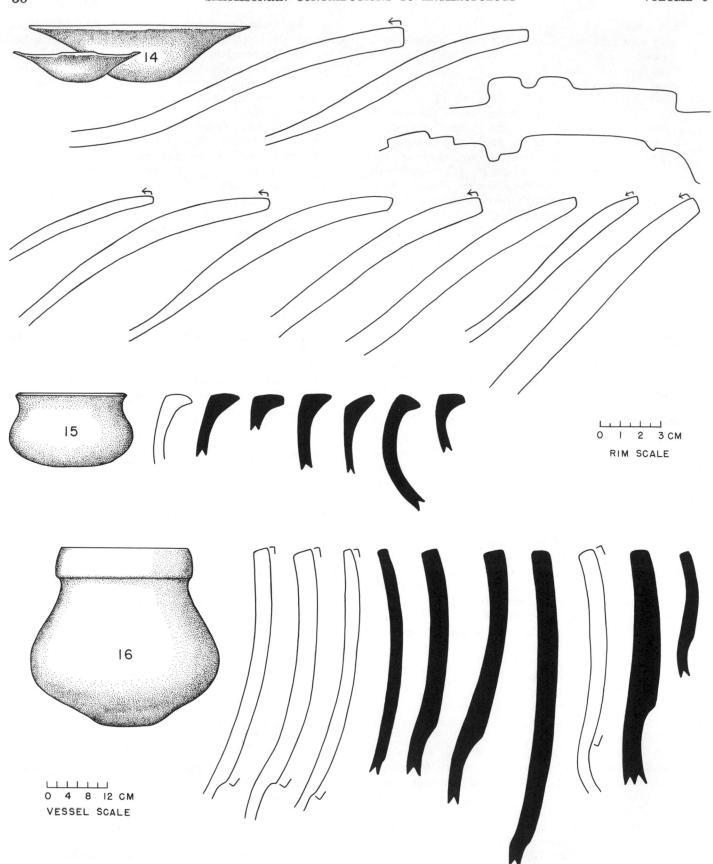

FIGURE 41.—Rim profiles and reconstructed vessel shapes of the Napo Phase, Common Forms 14–16. Arrows designate decorated zones. (Black=undecorated, white=decorated.)

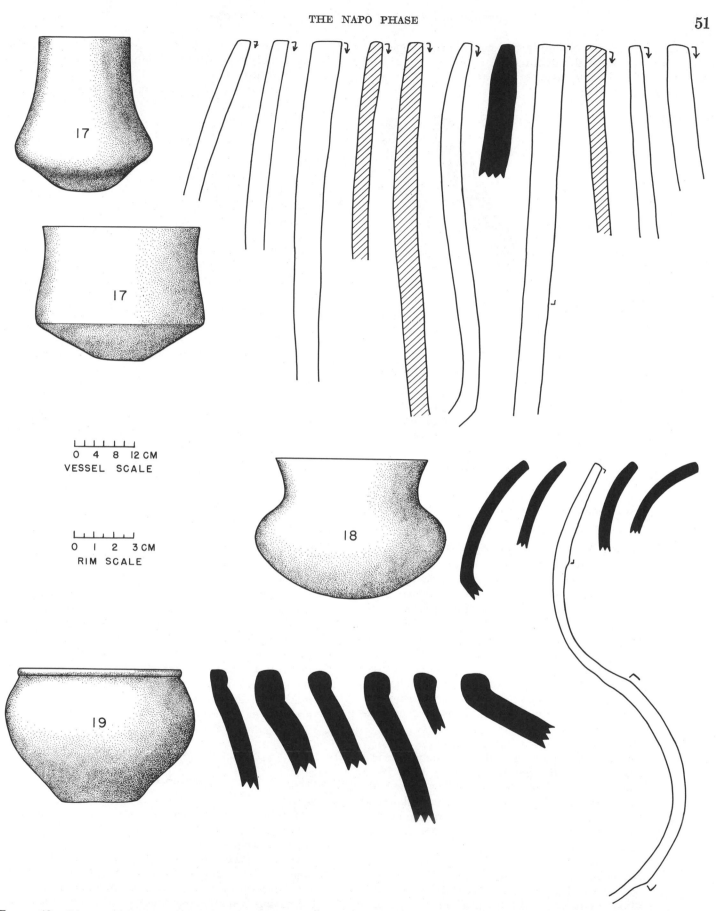

FIGURE 42.—Rim profiles and reconstructed vessel shapes of the Napo Phase, Common Forms 17–19. Arrows and brackets designate decorated zone. (Black=undecorated, white=decorated, hachure=red slipped.)

Lip: Rounded or slightly flattened; one example is ornamented with nubbins.
Body wall thickness: Range 1.2–2.0 mm.
Base: Flat (Form A).

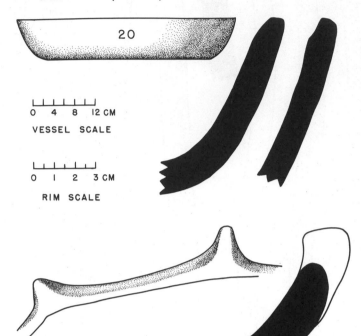

VESSEL SCALE

RIM SCALE

FIGURE 43.—Rim profiles and reconstructed vessel shapes of the Napo Phase, Common Form 20. (Black=undecorated.)

21. Anthropomorphic vessels (table A; pls. 55–65):

Three general types of anthropomorphic vessels (not including common forms occasionally receiving minor anthropomorphic treatment) can be distinguished on the basis of location of the orifice. Elevation of relief, style of facial features, and degree of realism or stylization seem to be independent variables.

A. Orifice at top of head (pls. 55–56).

The face occupies one side of a collared rim (cf. Form 16); body is cylindroid or rounded, bottom flat or slightly concave. Limbs project free of the body or are partly in relief. Height of one example is 38 cm.

B. Orifice at the bottom (pls. 57–61, 62*b*).

The face occupies one side of a hemispherical head, separated from the rounded body by a narrow constriction. The lower edges of the body wall curve inward to a direct rim with flattened lip leaving the central bottom open. Limbs may be absent, shown as relief, or project free. Height of two examples is 23.5 and 48.0 cm.

C. Orifice at neck, removable head (pls. 62*a*, 63–65). No heads are represented. The rounded body wall curves inward at the neck and is cut back about 2 cm. below the lip producing a channel into which the lid forming the head would fit. Limbs are shown as discontinuous relief or project free; legs may be vestigial. Seated and kneeling positions are shown. Heights of three examples are 15.0, 34.5, and 43.0 cm. from base to rim at neck.

Rare Forms

1. Rounded jar with constricted mouth and everted rim, thickened at the angle of eversion and tapering to a rounded lip. Mouth diameter 14–28 cm. (fig. 44–*a*).
2. Griddle with slightly raised and expanded rim, rounded lip. Diameter 40 cm. (fig. 44–*b*).
3. Open bowl with flaring rim thickened on the exterior about 11 cm. below the lip, from 2–4 mm. greater than the thickness of the body wall, forming a raised band. Flat lip. Rim diameter 28 cm. (fig. 44–*c*).
4. Shallow rounded bowl with sharply everted rim broken into large flat insloping lobes. Noncircular (fig. 44–*d*).
5. Bowl with outflaring walls and sharply everted rim with an outsloping to nearly vertical flat top, flat or tapered, and notched or lobed lip. Noncircular (fig. 44–*e*).

Base Forms

Five base forms are represented in Napo Phase pottery (see also Appendix table 10). The existence of complete vessels and large fragments makes it possible to associate most of them with one or more of the rim variations.

A. Flat, curving junction with the wall; unthickened to slightly thickened either at bottom or at curve. Diameter 6–20 cm. (fig. 45–A).
B. Flat, angular junction with the wall. Junction thickened to produce a gradual curve on the interior. Bottom sometimes thickened. Exterior may have leaf impression (pls. 18 *i–l*, 21*h*). Diameter 10–18 cm. (fig. 45–B).
C. Rounded and unthickened or slightly thickened at center (fig. 45–C).
D. Annular, vertical or flaring ring, varying greatly in height and profile. Height 0.5–3.0 cm.; diameter 8–16 cm. (fig. 45–D).
E. Flat, joining the wall at an angle approximating 90 degrees; typically thickened at angle to produce a slightly less abrupt transition on the interior. Bottom may be of greater or less thickness than wall. Noncircular (fig. 45–E).

Pottery Types

Armenia Plain

PASTE:

Method of manufacture: Coiling; fracture along coil junctions common; widths of 1.8, 2.0, and 2.2 cm. observed.
Temper: Cariapé, varying from small scattered white siliceous particles to large and easily observed cellular "bundles." More finely ground cariapé typically associated with moderate to large amounts of fine sand containing hematite particles up to 3 mm. diameter.

TABLE A.—*Characteristics of Napo Phase anthropomorphic urns*

Characteristics	Type A				Type B
Sex Temper	Female	Male Sand	Male ? Sand	Male ?	Male ?

Form:
  Arms
 	
  Legs
	Full round (missing)
	
	Relief
	Full round
		Full round
		Bulging lower arm
		Relief
		Bulging calf
			Full round
			Bulging lower arm
			Full round
			Bulging calf
				Full round
				
				Relief except feet
				Bulging calf
					Full round
					
					Full round
					Bulging calf

Decoration:
  Head
  Face
  Body
	Hair black
	Unpainted
	R & B/W
	Techs. 2 & 3
		Hair black
		Red
		R & B/W
		Technique 2
			R/W
			(eroded)
			R/W
				Painted	Hair black
					Painted
					R & B/W
					Technique 2

Dimensions:
  Total height
  Body height
  Max. diameter
  Head diameter
 	
  Base diameter
  Body wall th.
	38 cm.
	
	18.5 cm.
	(orifice)
		42.5 cm.
		
		21.9 cm.
		(orifice)
		25.5 cm.
		1.5 cm.
			38 cm.
			26 cm.
			38 cm.
			23 cm.
			
			20 cm.
			7–8 mm.
					34 cm.
					25 cm.
					21.5 cm.
					
					16.5 cm.

Special features	Ear lobes perforated
	Hair comes to point
	  at middle of back.
		Shield held with both
		  hands
			Shield in left hand
			Conical depression in
			  right hand
			Legs bent so soles
			  abut at center front
				Ear lobes perforated
				Elongated object held
				  by both hands
					Ear lobes perforated
					Long pigtail down
					  back
					"Rings" around
					  upper arm and calf

Provenience	Rio Napo 20 leagues above Rio Aguarico	Rio Napo	Rio Napo	N–P–3?	Rio Napo

Collection	Uhle, 1921, Lam. 3–4	Jay C. Leff, on loan
		  to Brooklyn
		  Museum
			AMNH 41.0/9183	Jijón y Caanaño,
				  1951, fig. 499
					Thomas Flannery

Plate	55	56	61b		57

TABLE A.—*Characteristics of Napo Phase anthropomorphic urns.*—Continued

Characteristics	Type B				
Sex Temper	Male	Male	Male Sand	Male	None Sand

Form:
  Arms
 	
  Legs
	Full round
	Bulging lower arm
	Full round
	Bulging calf
		None
		
		None
			Relief, bulging
			  lower arm
			Relief
			Bulging calf
				Full round
				
				Full round
				Bulging calf
					None
					
					None

Decoration:
  Head
  Face
  Body
	R & B/W
	(eroded)
	R & B/W
	Technique 2
		B/W
		Painted
		B/W
		Technique 4
			R & Brown/W
			Painted
			R & Brown/W
			  and grooving
				Hair black
				R & B/W
				R & B/W
				Technique 2
					R/W
					Painted
					R & B/W
					Technique 3

Dimensions:
  Total height
  Body height
  Max. diameter
  Head diameter
  Base diameter
 	
  Body wall th.
	34 cm.	36.8 cm.
		
		19 cm.
		20.3 cm.
			23.5 cm.
			13 cm.
			
			15.5 cm.
			
			7 mm.
				54 cm.
				
				16 cm.
				(orifice)
					48 cm.
					
					30 cm.

Special features	Hands joined
	Possibly once held
	  shield
			Shield or disk with
			  panpipe held in
			  both hands
				Shield held in both
				  hands
				Triangular relief on
				  chest
				Long pigtail down
				  back	

Provenience	N–P–1	Oriente region	Napo Area	Rio Napo 20 leagues above Rio Aguarico	Rio Napo
Collection	Museum of Primitive Art, 56.38	MAI–HF 6/1723	Casa de la Cultura, Quito	Uhle, 1921, Lam. 1–2	Musée de l'Homme 08.22.79
Plate	58a	58b	59	60	61a

TABLE A.—*Characteristics of Napo Phase anthropomorphic urns.*—Continued

Characteristics	Type B	Type C			
Sex	Male	Female	None	Male	None
Temper		Sand	Sand	Sand	Sand
Form:					
Arms	Relief	Relief	Full round	Relief and full round	Relief
Legs	Relief	Relief	Full round	Relief and full round	Relief
	Bulging calf	Bulging calf	Bulging calf		Bulging calf
Decoration:					
Head	R & B/W	(missing)	(missing)	(missing)	(missing)
Face	Painted				
Body	R & B/W	R & B/W	R & B/W	R & B/W	R & B/W
	Technique 3?	Techniques 2 & 3	Technique 2	Techs. 2 & 3	Techs. 2 & 3
Dimensions:					
Total height	29 cm.				
Body height		15 cm.	19.3 cm.	34.5 cm.	43 cm.
Max. diameter		20 cm.	20.6 cm.	27 cm.	26 cm.
Head diameter					
Base diameter		14 cm.		23 cm.	21–23 cm.
Body wall th.				10 mm.	7–9 mm.
Special features	Triangular relief on chest	Kneeling Center of bottom broken out Upper edge broken off Hands and feet have 4 digits	Upper edge recessed to receive lid	Arms bent backward	Upper edge recessed to receive lid Center of bottom broken out
Provenience	Rio Aguarico	Rio Napo	N–P–1	N–P–1	Rumi-tumi; right bank of Rio Napo 315 km. above mouth
Collection	Alan C. Lapiner	AMNH 41.0/9184	Museo Victor Emilio Estrada	Colegio Militar, Quito	AMNH 41.1/3985
Plate	62b	62a	63	64	65

Black ash also common, differing from charcoal temper in having elongated form resembling that of the siliceous cariapé. Evenly distributed; large particles tend to be aligned parallel to the surface, but there are many exceptions.

Texture: Majority sandy. Large airpockets (1.5 by 3.0 mm.) typical, some resulting from organic matter in the clay destroyed during firing, others from poor kneading of coil junctions.

Color: Cross-section ranges from solid orange to solid gray, with the majority incompletely oxidized leaving a gray core.

SURFACE:

Color: Tan, dull brownish orange to grayish brown; color variable over small areas due to poorly controlled firing. Medium gray fire clouds frequent on interior and exterior. Exterior may be blackened, possibly from use in cooking.

Treatment (pl. 18 *c–h*): Few surfaces are smoothed sufficiently to eliminate flaws. Majority relatively even but marred especially on the exterior by scratches caused by scraping with a rough-edged tool parallel to the rim. Where scratches are absent, pits and flaws common. A minority are better smoothed, floating

finer particles of clay to produce a fine textured finish. Broad (2–3 mm.) concave smoothing tracks visible on some, but not typical.

Hardness: 3.

FORM:

Rim: Direct with flat lip (pl. 18 *a–b*). Size of sample: 33.

Body wall thickness: Range 0.6–1.9 cm.; majority 8–10 mm.

Base: Flat (Forms A, B, and E); two of Form B have leaf impressions on the exterior (pl. 18 *i–l*). One annular (Form D) fragment with perforations.

Reconstructed common vessel shapes (figs. 40–43):

Form 12: 36.1 percent.
Form 17: 18.0 percent.
Form 20: 12.0 percent.
Form 16: 9.0 percent.
Form 13: 6.0 percent.

Minor vessel shapes (frequency less than 5 percent; figs. 40, 44): Form 11, Rare Form 4.

TEMPORAL DIFFERENCES WITHIN THE TYPE: None observed.

CHRONOLOGICAL POSITION OF THE TYPE: Present at maximum frequency (12.3 percent) in the early part of the seriated sequence and declining thereafter; absent from the latest site (fig. 63).

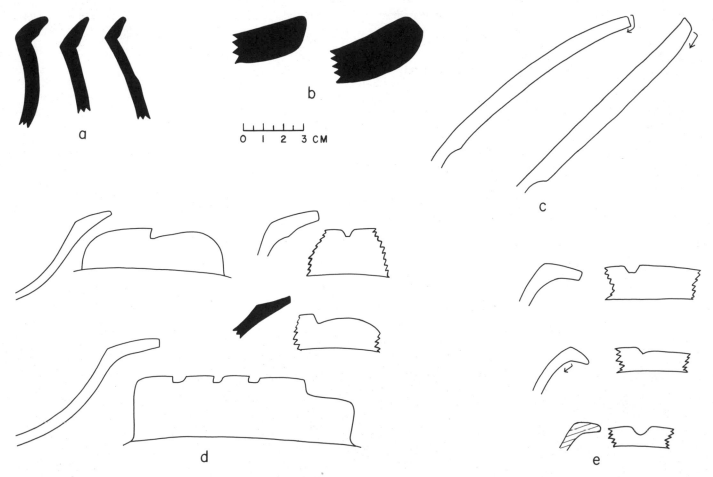

FIGURE 44.—Rim profiles of Napo Phase Rare Vessel Forms 1–5. Arrows designate decorated zone. (Black=undecorated, white=decorated, hachure=red slipped.)

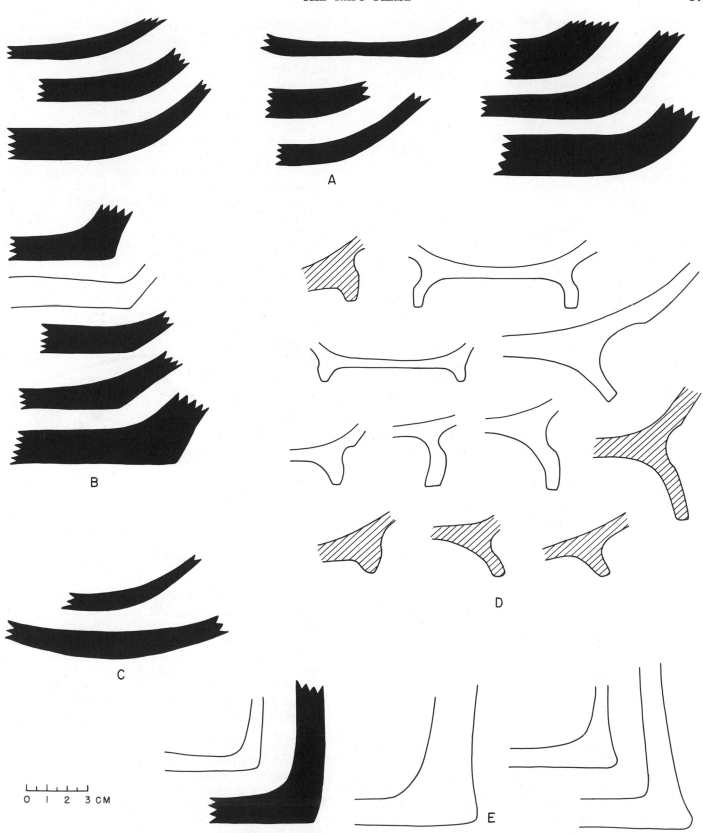

FIGURE 45.—Base forms of Napo Phase pottery. A, Flat, curving junction with body wall. B, Flat, angular junction with body wall. C, Rounded. D, Annular. E, Flat, joining body wall at angle of 90 degrees or more. (Black=undecorated, white=decorated, hachure=red slipped.)

Armenia White-on-red

PASTE: On Napo Plain (p. 58) or Armenia Plain (p. 52); see those type discriptions for details.

SURFACE:

Color: The undecorated interior is tan, brown, grayish brown, with light to dark gray fire clouds. A few examples are white slipped.

Treatment: Even but with pits, striations, exposed temper grains and occasionally scratches or larger flaws. Slightly to markedly less well finished than the decorated exterior.

Hardness: 2.5.

FORM:

Rim: Direct, everted, cambered or channel (rare), with flat lip. Size of sample: 14.

Body wall thickness: Range 4–10 mm.

Base: Probably rounded (Form C).

Reconstructed common vessel shapes (figs. 36–37, 40–42, 44): Forms 3, 4, 6, 11, 12, 14, 17, Rare Form 3.

DECORATION (pls. 19–20; Appendix table 11):

Technique: White painted designs on a red slipped exterior surface (continuing over the lip). Red slip varies from a coat thick enough to be of even color to a thin wash with a tendency to fire orange. Incomplete polishing may produce a striated effect because polishing tracks tend to fire deeper red than intervening unpolished streaks. White paint varies in thickness, thicker coatings providing more color contrast, but also tending to crackle and chip off. Thinner coatings have a streaky appearance resulting from nonuniform coverage of the underlying red slip. Execution is extremely variable, ranging from a few carefully done to a few crude and sloppy; the majority are intermediate. Bands often are of irregular width, but tend to be straight and parallel.

A rare variant (pl. 20 *a–b*) has the design laid out in narrow black lines, 1–2 mm. wide and 1–3 cm. apart. White paint applied between the outline, sometimes overlapping the black lines but rarely obliterating them.

Motif: Few sherds are large enough to show more than one or two parallel lines; however, coils, undulating bands and stepped elements occur.

TEMPORAL DIFFERENCES WITHIN THE TYPE: None observed.

CHRONOLOGICAL POSITION OF THE TYPE: Present throughout the seriated sequence with no consistent trend of changing frequency (fig. 63).

Napo Negative

PASTE: All on Napo Plain (p. 58); see that type description for details.

SURFACE:

Color: Buff to pale tan or light orange.

Treatment: Floated sufficiently to produce even, compact finish; slick to touch but not glossy.

Hardness: 3.

FORM:

Rim: Direct, exteriorly thickened or everted with flat or tapered (rare) lip. Size of sample: 3.

Body wall thickness: Range 4–8 mm.

Base: Probably rounded (Form C).

Reconstructed vessel shapes (figs. 36, 40, 44): Forms 1, 12, Rare Form 4.

DECORATION (fig. 46; pl. 25 *d, f*):

Technique: Resist painting forming gray to black bands and zones of irregular form on the interior of open bowls. One well preserved example (pl. 25*f*) has black bands 5–10 mm. wide, separated by narrow unpainted bands of more uniform width. Margins are sharply defined.

Motif: Parallel bands, interlocking coils, and asymmetrical zones.

ASSOCIATED TECHNIQUES: The exterior may be Napo Plain Excised, Napo Red Excised, or Napo Red Excised, White Retouched.

TEMPORAL DIFFERENCES WITHIN THE TYPE: None observed.

CHRONOLOGICAL POSITION OF THE TYPE: Very rare, but probably present throughout the seriated sequence (fig. 63).

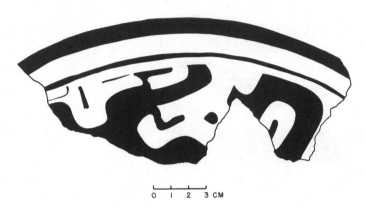

0 1 2 3 CM

FIGURE 46.—Napo Negative bowl interior.

Napo Plain

PASTE:

Method of manufacture: Coiling. Coil line fractures relatively common, showing coil widths of 1.3, 2.0, and 2.5 cm. (pl. 21 *i–k*). Junctions do not overlap strongly; edges tend to be slightly concavo-convex. Coil junctions occasionally incompletely obliterated on surface.

Temper: Sand grains usually less than 0.5 mm. in diameter, occasionally 0.5–1.0 mm. or, in thicker sherds 1.0–1.5 mm. diameter. White particles contrast sharply with gray paste, glossy black ones with orange paste (both colors generally present). Well distributed and sufficiently abundant to give fine sandpaper feel to eroded surfaces. Occasional large (up to 8 mm. diameter) red hematite inclusions, probably natural components of the clay.

Texture: Typically compact; breaks evenly, edges not friable. Occasional long thin airpockets.

Color: Complete variation from orange throughout the cross-section to gray throughout the cross-section. About half are completely oxidized. Orange usually uniform in shade throughout; light orange, light tan, or buff most typical; reddish orange or rusty brown less common. Gray varies from dark (black) to pale, with little variation on a single sherd. Dark gray core is rare. Incompletely oxidized examples may show a gray band along one surface instead of at the center of the core.

SURFACE:

Color: Typically light tan or light orange, including buff or cream; occasionally bright orange, reddish orange, gray-brown, or dark gray. Gray hues often result from fire clouding, making abrupt transition from orange color. Dark or light colored surfaces may occur with either gray or orange cross-section.

Treatment: Smoothed sufficiently to submerge larger temper grains and produce a fine-grained "floated" layer, but leaving smoothing tracks, defects, and irregularities. Both broad and fine smoothing tracks occur, but not on the same sherd; orientation is principally parallel to rim. Smoothing or scraping may drag temper particles leaving a scratch about 1 cm. long. Unevenness is common especially on thicker sherds, and reflected in unequal thickness of body wall. Some bowl interiors have polishing striations, but finish is never slick or lustrous. Smoothing less complete on jar interiors, leaving rough zones.

Hardness: 3–3.5.

FORM:

Rim: Direct with flat lip (pl. 21 *a, c–d*); rarely, exteriorly thickened or channel with flat or rounded lip (pl. 21 *b, e–f*); occasionally thickened lobes along a rounded lip (pl. 21*g*). Size of sample: 352.

Body wall thickness: Range 4–16 mm.; majority 8–10 mm.; variable on a single sherd.

Base: Flat (Forms A and B), rounded (Form C), or annular (Form D). Flat bases may show leaf impressions on exterior (pl. 21*h*).

Reconstructed common vessel shapes (figs. 36, 40–42; pl. 22*a*):
Form 16: 18. 2 percent.
Form 13: 13.4 percent.
Form 17: 11.7 percent.
Form 12: 10.2 percent.
Form 11: 8. 8 percent.
Form 15: 7. 4 percent.
Form 18: 5. 7 percent.
Form 1: 5. 4 percent.

Minor vessel shapes (frequency less than 5 percent; figs. 36, 42–44; pl. 22 *b–c*): Forms 4, 19, 20; Rare Forms 1, 2.

TEMPORAL DIFFERENCES WITHIN THE TYPE: None observed.

CHRONOLOGICAL POSITION OF THE TYPE: The principal plain type throughout the duration of the Napo Phase (fig. 63).

Napo Plain Excised

PASTE: Predominantly on Napo Plain (p. 58), occasionally on Armenia Plain (p. 52), rarely on Tiputini Plain (p. 72); see those type descriptions for details.

SURFACE:

Color: Pale buff, light orange, light tan, brown to grayish brown, with frequent large fire clouds on both interior and exterior.

Treatment: Variation from even and smooth with fine-grained texture and flaws obliterated, to sandy leaving broad smoothing tracks and pits visible. Interior of bowls typically better smoothed than exterior.

Hardness: 2.5–3.

FORM:

Rim: Collared, direct, channel, exteriorly thickened or cambered with flat or rounded lip. Size of sample: 34.

Body wall thickness: Range 5–12 mm. (not including carination).

Base: Probably rounded (Form C).

Reconstructed common vessel shapes (figs. 36, 38, 40, 41):
Form 16: 29. 4 percent.
Form 12: 26. 4 percent.
Form 4: 8. 8 percent.
Form 2: 5. 9 percent.
Form 7: 5. 9 percent.
Form 13: 5. 9 percent

Minor vessel shapes (frequency less than 5 percent; figs. 36–38, 41, 43): Forms 1, 3, 5, 9, 14, 20.

DECORATION (pls. 23–24, 25 *a–c, e*):

Technique: Double- or multiple-pointed tool used to produce lines and textured zones on an unslipped surface. Lines 2–5 mm. wide, and shallow (depth less than 1 mm.); typically poorly defined because of dragged edges and execution with successive strokes the ends of which do not coincide. Terminations often pushed up. Lines crooked and unevenly parallel.

Excised zones produced by multiple, often overlapping strokes of the incising tool, creating grooves and ridges parallel to the long axis of the zone. Depth is similar to that of incised lines on the same vessel. Excision is typically restricted to small zones such as widened intersections and corners. A rare treatment is addition of white pigment to the incisions and excised zones.

Motif: Complicated overall patterns sometimes divided into panels or bands by straight vertical or horizontal lines. Squared coils occur singly or interlocking, often with a short dash at the center. Patterns are rectilinear, softened by rounding of junctions and corners.

TEMPORAL DIFFERENCES WITHIN THE TYPE: None observed.

CHRONOLOGICAL POSITION OF THE TYPE: Present throughout the duration of the seriated sequence (fig. 63).

Napo Plain Incised

PASTE: Predominantly on Napo Plain (p. 58), rarely on Armenia Plain (p. 52) or Tiputini Plain (p. 72); see those type descriptions for details.

SURFACE:

Color: All shades from buff to black resulting from poorly controlled firing, fireclouding, and possibly refiring during domestic use.

Treatment: Incompletely smoothed, often showing pits, flaws, roughness, horizontal smoothing tracks and fine brush-like striations. Coil junction may remain incompletely obliterated on interior of carination.

Slight floating eliminates abrasive texture from most surfaces, but temper grains may remain visible. Best smoothing occurs on interior of open bowls. Decorated areas do not receive better treatment than undecorated ones.

Hardness: 2.5–3.

FORM:

Rim: Direct, exteriorly thickened, channel, everted or collared, with flattened or rarely rounded or tapered lip. Size of sample: 165.

Body wall thickness: Range 4–14 mm., reaching 2.4 cm. at carination.

Base: All forms.

Reconstructed common vessel shapes (figs. 36, 38–41; pl. 26):

    Form 16: 21.2 percent.
    Form 7: 15.3 percent.
    Form 9: 11.5 percent.
    Form 1: 11.5 percent.
    Form 8: 9.7 percent.
    Form 10: 8.5 percent.
    Form 12: 7.9 percent.

Minor vessel shapes (frequency less than 5 percent; figs. 36–37, 40–42, 44): Forms 2, 3, 4, 5, 13, 14, 15, 17, 18, Rare Form 5.

DECORATION (pls. 26–31):

Technique: Incision with a double- or triple-pointed tool on an unslipped surface, producing a mark with parallel striations in the bed. Rare examples show a multi-pointed tool. Incisions wide (2–6 mm.; majority 3–5 mm.) and typically about 1 mm. deep, but may vary from superficial to 2 mm. in depth. Width is often uniform on a single sherd, but may be erratic because of inconsistent orientation and pressure of the tool. Incisions with a double-pointed tool typically show parallel smooth tracks with a central ridge of lower elevation than the surface of the sherd. A rough texture and sporadic ridging is more characteristic of marks made with tri- or multi-pointed tools. Straight lines may be executed in successive strokes, the ends of which may not be perfectly superimposed. Lines are not evenly spaced or perfectly parallel. Corners are not overshot, but overlap is frequently visible. Ends are frequently pushed up, leaving a lump of clay 1 mm. in elevation. Dragged margins are typical of incisions with a rough trough. Short strokes (length 5 mm.) may occur, but punctates are absent.

Two rare variants occur: (1) the use of double lines in combination with lines executed with a single-pointed tool (pl. 31), and (2) addition of white pigment to the incisions. In the first variant, single and double lines may be interdigitated or may be used on different parts of the vessel, in which case they may reflect accidental or careless picking up of the wrong tool. The second variant, white fill, is difficult to distinguish from white slipping subsequent to incision, which often erodes the more exposed portions of the surface while remaining in the more protected beds of the incisions.

Motif: Complicated filling of space with interlocking vertical strokes attached to longer hroizontal ones, interlocking angular coils, and concentric rectanguloid elements. Predominantly straight lines are softened by rounding of corners and junctions. Even filling of space gives the impression of symmetry, but few patterns are completely symmetrical.

ASSOCIATED TECHNIQUES: Negative painting may occur on the interior.

TEMPORAL DIFFERENCES WITHIN THE TYPE: Examples combining double- and single-line techniques are restricted to the early half of the seriated sequence.

CHRONOLOGICAL POSITION OF THE TYPE: The second most common decorated type, present throughout the seriated sequence without consistent change in frequency (fig. 63).

Napo Red

PASTE: Red slip is applied to all varieties of paste; see type descriptions of Armenia Plain (p. 52), Napo Plain (p. 58) and Tiputini Plain (p. 72) for details.

SURFACE:

Color:

  Unslipped surfaces: Same range as Armenia Plain, Napo Plain, and Tiputini Plain.

  Slipped surfaces: Variation from deep rich red through red-orange to tile orange depending on thickness and firing; readily visible when paste is buff but difficult to detect when both slip and paste are orange. Dark gray fire clouds typical.

Treatment:

  Unslipped surfaces: Irregular to even but rarely smooth; texture remains granular on sand-tempered sherds; pits and flaws characteristic on interior of narrow mouthed vessels. Minor fluctuation in wall thickness evident in slight undulation of surface. Polishing striations sometimes appear adjacent to the rim on the interior.

  Slipped surfaces: Thicker slip forms an even coating, smooth to touch and with low luster. Horizontal polishing striations may occur. Applied to the exterior, usually above the region of maximum diameter.

Hardness: 2.5.

FORM:

Rim: Direct with flattened lip; rarely rounded or tapered lip. Size of sample: 86.

Body wall thickness: Range 5–14 mm.; majority 6–9 mm.

Base: No examples since slip does not extend to base; probably flat (Forms A and B) or rounded (Form C).

Reconstructed common vessel shapes (figs. 40, 42):

    Form 13: 33.8 percent.
    Form 11: 32.6 percent.
    Form 17: 17.4 percent.
    Form 12: 10.5 percent.

Minor vessel shapes (frequency less than 5 percent; figs. 41, 44): Form 15, Rare Form 5.

TEMPORAL DIFFERENCES WITHIN THE TYPE: None observed.

CHRONOLOGICAL POSITION OF THE TYPE: Napo Red occurs throughout the seriated sequence in a frequency not exceeding 12 percent (fig. 63).

Napo Red Excised

PASTE: Predominately on Napo Plain (p. 58), occasionally on Armenia Plain (p. 52), rarely on Tiputini Plain (p. 72); see those pottery type descriptions for details.

SURFACE: Like Napo Red Incised (p. 62); see that type description for details.

FORM:

Rim: Direct, exteriorly thickened, channel or cambered, with flat or rounded lip. Size of sample: 35.

Body wall thickness: Range 4–8 mm.

Base: Probably rounded (Form C).

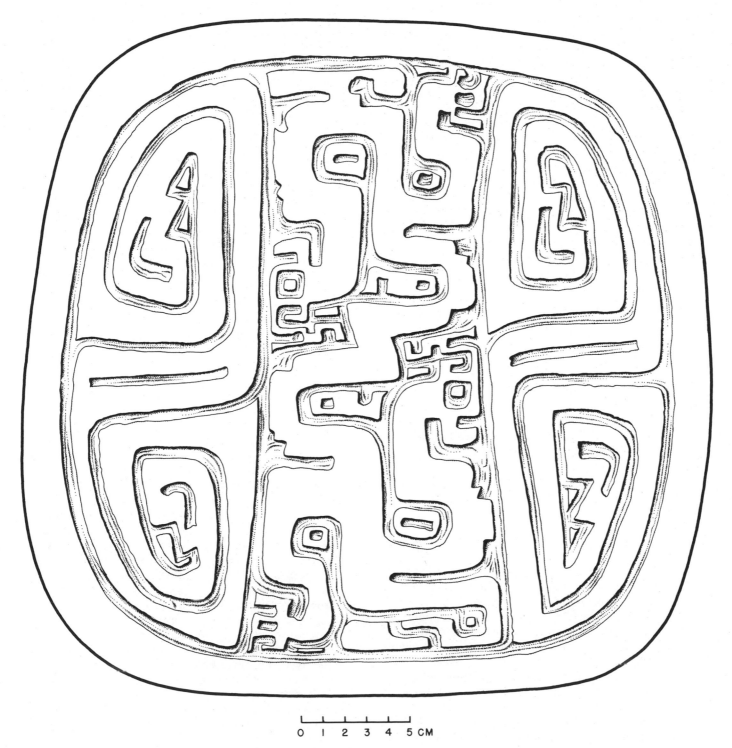

0 1 2 3 4 5 CM

FIGURE 47.—Reconstructed design of Napo Red Excised bowl exterior.

Reconstructed common vessel shapes (figs. 36, 38, 40; pl. 32*b*):
Form 12: 28.6 percent.
Form 4: 25.7 percent.
Form 2: 20.0 percent.
Form 1: 5.7 percent.
Form 3: 5.7 percent.
Form 7: 5.7 percent.

Minor vessel shapes (frequency less than 5 percent; figs. 37, 40): Forms 6, 10, 13.

DECORATION (fig. 47; pls. 32–33):

Technique: Incision and excision with a double- or multi-pointed tool prior to application of red coating to the surface. Incisions broad (2–5 mm.), shallow (generally less than 1 mm. deep; rarely 2 mm. deep), with square or tapered ends. Margins vary from sharply defined to ragged, and terminations may be pushed up. Trough texture is granular from exposed temper particles, which are typically suppressed by slight floating of the surface. Workmanship tends to be sloppy. Excised zones small, often restricted to widening of intersections and corners; unobtrusive.

Red slip was typically applied after incision, filling the cuts. The surface was not subsequently polished, so that finish depends upon treatment prior to decoration. Discoloration by firing may make slip invisible on part of a vessel, while other areas remain a rich dark red.

Motif: Similar to Napo Red Incised (p. 62); see that type description for details.

TEMPORAL DIFFERENCES WITHIN THE TYPE: None observed.

CHRONOLOGICAL POSITION OF THE TYPE: Present throughout the seriated sequence, with the possible exception of the latest levels (fig. 63).

Napo Red Excised, White Retouched

PASTE: Exclusively on Napo Plain (p. 58); see that type description for details.

SURFACE: Similar to Tiputini Red Excised, White Retouched (p. 76); see that type description for details.

FORM:

Rim: Channel, direct or exteriorly thickened, with flat or rounded lip. Size of sample: 9.

Body wall thickness: Range 4–12 mm.

Base: Rounded (Form C) or annular (Form D).

Reconstructed common vessel shapes (figs. 36 40): Forms 1, 2, 12.

DECORATION (pl. 34):

Technique: Incision and excision on a red slipped surface with a double- or multi-pointed tool. Incisions wide (3–6 mm.), shallow (less than 1 mm.), uniform in width and depth on a single sherd. Margins may be dragged or irregular; terminations square and sometimes pushed up.

Excision produced by repeated application of incising tool to widen area. Depth is similar to that of incised lines; floor is often uneven.

Red coating typically a thin wash contrasting poorly with the reddish orange natural surface, always applied prior to decoration.

White coating applied to cuts varies from a thick coating showing fine crackle to a thin wash slopping over onto the adjacent surface.

Motif: Complicated patterns of short straight lines often interdigitated so as to create a negative effect in which the motifs are formed by the intervening surfaces rather than the incisions.

ASSOCIATED TECHNIQUES: Negative painting may occur on the interior.

TEMPORAL DIFFERENCES WITHIN THE TYPE: None observed.

CHRONOLOGICAL POSITION OF THE TYPE: Sporadically represented but present throughout the seriated sequence except at the latest site (fig. 63).

Napo Red Incised

PASTE: Predominantly on Napo Plain (p. 58), rarely on Armenia Plain (p. 52) or Tiputini Plain (p. 72); see those type descriptions for details.

SURFACE:

Color: Light buff, tan, orange, brown to gray; widely variable over a small area from fire clouding and poorly controlled firing.

Treatment: Smoothed sufficiently to produce an even surface and sometimes floated but more commonly remaining slightly granular in texture. Fine smoothing striations may occur parallel to the rim. Interior generally slightly better smoothed than exterior, which bears the decoration.

Hardness: 2.5.

FORM:

Rim: Channel, exteriorly thickened, cambered or direct with flat or rarely rounded lip. Size of sample: 43.

Body wall thickness: Range 3–9 mm.; majority 5–6 mm.

Base: Rounded (Form C); possibly annular (Form D).

Reconstructed common vessel shapes (figs. 36, 40):
Form 12: 23.3 percent.
Form 4: 18.5 percent.
Form 1: 16.3 percent.
Form 13: 11.6 percent.
Form 2: 7.0 percent.

Minor vessel shapes (frequency less than 5 percent; figs. 36–38, 41, 44): Forms 3, 5, 8, 9, 15, Rare Form 4.

DECORATION (pl. 35):

Technique: Incision with a double- or multi-pointed tool before or after red slipping of the surface. Incisions wide (3–5 mm.) and relatively shallow (less than 1 mm.). The trough typically has a granular appearance from exposed temper grains, providing strong textural contrast with the surface especially when done subsequent to slipping. A double-pointed tool is most typical, leaving two parallel grooves with a slight but clearly visible ridge between; occasionally the ridge is off center. Terminations are square or tapered; square ends may have a thrown up margin. When incised prior to slipping, the slip fills and rounds over some roughness. Incisions may have a ragged or even margin; the former is more common. Margins are rarely thrown up. Spacing is a little more equal than on

Tiputini Red Incised, lines are less crooked and more evenly parallel.

Red slip varies from a good coating like that typical of Tiputini Red Incised to a thin wash that fires brownish or blends into the unslipped surface. Thin wash is more typical of Napo Red Incised.

On some examples, a white coating was added to the trough subsequent to red slipping. Thickness varies from a solid coating with fine crackle to a faint wash that may become blended into the surface by firing discoloration. White is often slopped over edges or ends of incisions onto the adjacent red surface.

Motif: Complicated arrangements of concentric and interlocking vertical and horizontal parallel lines.

ASSOCIATED TECHNIQUES: One bowl with Napo Red Incised, white retouched decoration on the exterior is polychrome painted on the interior.

TEMPORAL DIFFERENCES WITHIN THE TYPE: None observed.

CHRONOLOGICAL POSITION OF THE TYPE: Present throughout the seriated sequence in slightly increasing frequency (fig. 63).

Napo White Excised

PASTE AND SURFACE: On Napo Plain (p. 58); see that type description for details.

FORM: Only body sherds are represented; they appear to correspond to carinated and rounded bodies of vessel Forms 7–10 (figs. 38–40).

DECORATION (pl. 36):

Technique: Incision and excision with a multi-pointed tool prior to the application of a white coating to the surface. Technique and slight use of excision resemble Napo Plain Excised (see p. 59).

Motif: Straight vertical and horizontal lines in complicated arrangements (cf. Napo Plain Excised).

TEMPORAL DIFFERENCES WITHIN THE TYPE: None observed.

CHRONOLOGICAL POSITION OF THE TYPE: Very rare (fig. 63) but given status as a pottery type to facilitate comparison of the ceramic complex with that of other areas.

Napo White Incised

PASTE: Predominantly on Napo Plain (p. 58), rarely on Armenia Plain (p. 52) or Tiputini Plain (p. 72); see those type descriptions for details.

SURFACE:

Color: Orange, tan, reddish orange, buff; dark gray where fire clouded.

Treatment: Even but not smooth, retaining a granular texture and leaving pits and flaws unobliterated. Smoothing striations parallel to the rim vary from fine brush-like marks to deep cuts.

Hardness: 2.5.

FORM:

Rim: Channel, exteriorly thickened or collared (rare) with flattened, tapered or rounded (rare) lip. Size of sample: 29.

Body wall thickness: Range 3.5–8.5 mm., increasing to 3.3 cm. at carination (corner).

Base: Probably rounded (Form C).

Reconstructed common vessel shapes (figs. 38–40):
Form 9: 51.8 percent.
Form 7: 20.7 percent.
Form 8: 17.3 percent.
Form 10: 6.9 percent.

Minor vessel shapes (frequency less than 5 percent; fig. 41): Form 16.

DECORATION (pls. 37–40):

Technique: Incision with a double- or multiple- (rare) pointed tool on a plain surface subsequently coated with a thin white slip or wash. Incisions broad (2.5–6.0 mm.; majority 3–5 mm.), usually 0.5–1.0 mm. deep, with ragged, irregular margins. Pushed up terminations are common but thrown up margins are rare. Incisions typically are bifurcated by a fine ridge, whose straightness contrasts with the irregularity of the walls. Rarely, this ridge is at or near surface elevation. Execution is not careful; lines are unequally spaced, unevenly parallel and crooked.

Small circular applique nubbins may occur on lobes. Diameter is 0.5–1.0 mm., elevation 1–3 mm. A central punctate is typical.

A thin wash was applied to the decorated zone subsequent to incision. Color is typically cream rather than white. Present condition shows no sheen or evidence of polish, suggesting application by dipping or brushing without subsequent smoothing. Paper thin but tends to minimize the visibility of incision when lines are shallow. Eroded examples of this type are difficult to distinguish from Napo Plain Incised sherds with white fill in the incisions.

The carination may be expanded to broad horizontal lobes, which continue the incised decoration on their upper surfaces.

Motif: Complicated interlocking arrangements of horizontal and vertical parallel lines, sometimes forming symmetrical or asymmetrical panels.

TEMPORAL DIFFERENCES WITHIN THE TYPE: None observed.

CHRONOLOGICAL POSITION OF THE TYPE: Possibly absent from the latest levels of the seriated sequence (fig. 63).

Rocafuerte Incised

PASTE: Predominantly on Napo Plain (p. 58), rarely on Armenia Plain (p. 52); see those type descriptions for details.

SURFACE:

Color: Buff to light tan.

Treatment: Smoothed insufficiently to remove all flaws and eliminate granular texture of sandy paste.

Hardness: 3.

FORM:

Rim: Everted or direct with flat or rounded (rare) lip. Size of sample: 26.

Body wall thickness: Range 5–10 mm.

Base: Rounded (Form C) or flat (Form A).

Reconstructed vessel shapes (figs. 40–41, 44; frontispiece; pls. 41–42):
Form 14: 88.5 percent.
Form 11: 7.8 percent.
Rare Form 3: 3.7 percent.

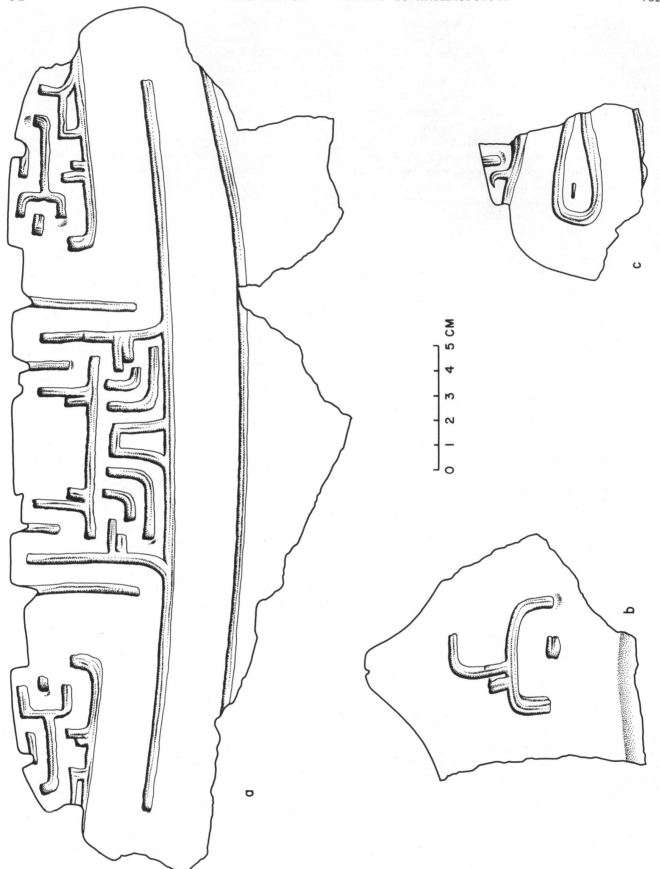

FIGURE 48.—Type sherds of Rocafuerte Incised, combined with red and black-on-white painting, showing relationships between incised and painted (overlay) portions of the design. (Stippling = red, black = black.)

DECORATION (figs. 48–49; frontispiece; pls. 41–43):

Technique: Incision with a double-pointed tool prior to white slipping; incisions painted red subsequent to slipping of the surface. Incised lines broad (4–6 mm.), shallow to deep (less than 1 mm. to 2 mm.), crudely executed, with very irregular margin, and marked variation in width and depth. Trough very uneven and showing parallel ridges left between tool points. Small areas excised by adjacent tool strokes in a zone previously outlined by incision.

Cream to off-white slip applied after incision covering surface and incised decoration. Some vessels have a smooth, even coating; others are uneven partly because of poor leveling of underlying surface. Fine crackle may occur.

A red coating was applied after slipping to incisions and excisions, following the irregular margins and rarely sloping slightly over onto the adjacent surface (pl. 43 *a–b, e*). Rich red to reddish orange color provides strong contrast with white slip. About 50 percent have decoration limited to red-retouched incisions.

Polychrome painting of the surface surrounding the incision (pl. 43 *c–d, f*) occurs on about 50 percent of the vessels. In such cases, the red retouch may extend beyond the incision to produce a red zone bordered by a narrow black line. This variant may not have all incisions retouched with red.

Motif: Rocafuerte Incised occurs almost exclusively on the upper interior surface of open basins, generally associated with complicated lobing of the lip. Typical elements are straight and hooked lines, many of which terminate in a notch in the lip.

TEMPORAL DIFFERENCES WITHIN THE TYPE: None observed; examples with and without associated polychrome painting occur with equal frequency throughout the seriated sequence (Appendix table 11).

CHRONOLOGICAL POSITION OF THE TYPE: Present in minor frequency except at the latest sites (fig. 63).

Rocafuerte Painted

PASTE: Predominantly on Napo Plain (p. 58), occasionally on Armenia Plain (p. 52) or Tiputini Plain (p. 72); see those type descriptions for details.

SURFACE:

Unslipped: Like Napo Plain, Armenia Plain, and Tiputini Plain; see those type descriptions for details.

White slipped:

Color: Off-white to cream, dirty white, or buff. Some correlation with thickness since thinner coatings are more transparent and incompletely obliterate the underlying buff to orange surface.

Treatment: Even, frequently smooth, and never slick or glossy. Paper thin coating often clearly visible in cross-section because of sharp contrast with paste color; this type provides the whitest and most even surface. A thinner application does not overcome the granular texture of the underlying surface. Fine crackle may occur, but is not typical.

Hardness: 3.

FORM:

Rim: Direct, everted, cambered, or exteriorly thickened; rarely, channel or collared; flat or rounded (rare) lip. Size of sample: 186.

Body wall thickness: Range 5–18 mm.; majority 6–10 mm.

Base: Flat (Forms A, B, E), rounded (Form C), or annular (Form D).

Reconstructed common vessel shapes (figs. 36–42): Although the principal vessel shapes are almost the same in the three varieties of painting, there is some difference in emphasis (table B).

TABLE B.—*Frequency of vessel shapes in decorated variants of Rocafuerte Painted*

Vessel shapes	Red and black-on-white		Black-on-white		Red-on-white	
	Form	Percent	Form	Percent	Form	Percent
Common	17	32.7	14	30.4	17	55.5
	14	23.1	17	23.9	11	11.2
	6	8.7	6	13.1	6	8.4
	13	6.7	7	10.9	14	8.4
	11	5.8	11	10.9	15	5.6
Minor	12	4.8	5	4.4	13	2.8
	7	3.8	12	4.4	16	2.8
	3	3.8	13	4.4		
	16	3.8				
	5	2.9				
	9	1.9				
	1	0.9				
	21	0.0				

DECORATION (figs. 50–58; pls. 44–65): Although painted decoration can be separated on the basis of paint color into three distinct varieties (red-on-white, black-on-white, and red plus black-on-white), the eroded condition and small size of most sherds makes recognition of these categories possible in less than 25 percent of the sherds classified as Rocafuerte Painted. The majority were placed in this type because they had a white slipped surface, sometimes with a trace of red or black paint. Even where preservation is good, subdivision is not always accurate. Reliability is greatest for red-on-white, since this typically occurs alone. Differentiation between black-on-white and polychrome may be difficult, however, since many polychrome designs make limited use of red so that small sherds may represent only black-on-white portions of the design. Examination of larger sherds and complete vessels shows several distinctive types of decoration within each of the three varieties.

Technique:

A. Red paint on a white slipped surface (fig. 50; pls. 44, 61*b*). Paint rich red to light orange, depending on thickness and firing. Line width not uniform because of uneven flow and use of multiple strokes to produce longer lines. Application may be in the form of thin lines (width 1.5–4.0 mm.), wider bands (width

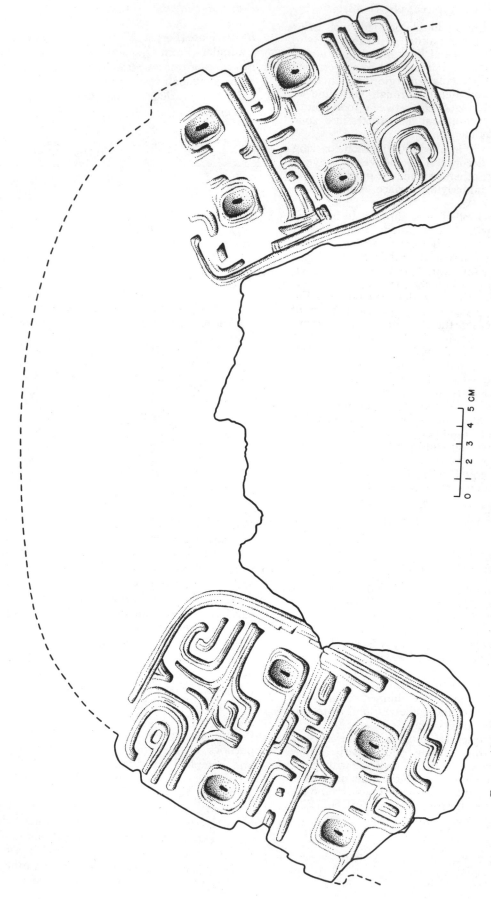

0 1 2 3 4 5 CM

FIGURE 49.—Fragment of Rocafuerte Incised bowl, combined with red and black-on-white painting, showing relationships between incised and painted (overlay) portions of the design. (Stippling=red, black=black.)

0.7–1.7 cm.), or solid zones. Solid zones may intervene between lines or occur independently; in both cases they are outlined with narrow lines and then filled in. Dots occur rarely either singly or in a row. Lines and bands are not straight or evenly parallel; intersections are often overshot. Designs generally incorporate broad and narrow lines and solid areas, although relative frequency varies considerably.

often remain visible. Corners are widened, suggesting splaying out of brush on curve; corners may be angular on the inner side and curved on the outer one.

Solid black zones and very wide bands are outlined with narrow lines and then filled in. If well done, fill blends with and renders invisible the outline; if sloppy, filling is a lighter gray and streaky from unequal thickness of the paint.

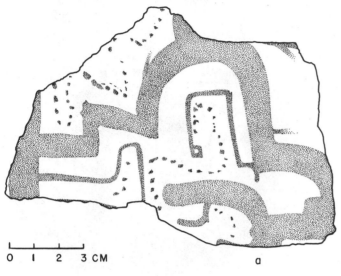

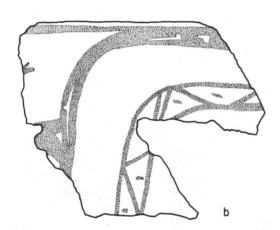

FIGURE 50.—Type sherds of Rocafuerte Painted, red-on-white.

FIGURE 51.—Decorative techniques of Rocafuerte Painted, black-on-white. *a*, Technique 1. *b–c*, Technique 2. *d*, Technique 3.

B. Black paint on a white slipped surface (fig. 51; pls. 45, 46-rim, 50, 54*b*, 58*b*). Line width varies but generally falls into two classes: (1) narrow (0.5–2.0 mm.) lines, and (2) wide (majority 1.0–1.5 cm., some 2.0 cm.) bands. Narrow lines may be consistent in width or vary throughout the range over a short distance because of unequal pressure or difference in the amount of paint on the applicator. Consecutive strokes often overlap or produce abrupt changes in line width. Intersections may be overshot (fig. 51 *b–c*). Wider bands may be done with a wide applicator or by repeated parallel strokes with a narrow one. Striations parallel to the length of the band

Dotted lines are carelessly executed, a single line being composed of "dots" of varying shape (circular, triangular, elongated, or shapeless "blobs"), size, and orientation. Spacing is unequal, varying from adjacent or even overlapping to 3 mm. apart. Failure to lift the applicator may produce a "drag-and-jab" effect.

Lines, bands, dots, and solid areas are employed in three principle ways, rarely combined on a single vessel:

1. Bands delimiting fields containing patterns of dotted lines (fig. 51*a*; pls. 45 *g–h*, 50*a*).

2. Narrow solid lines and dotted lines interspersed, or narrow solid lines defining fields occupied by dotted lines (fig. 51 *b–c*; pls. 45 *i–j*, 54*b*).

3. Pseudo-negative patterns produced by drawing the design in narrow lines and filling in the background, leaving the unpainted surface to carry the predominating motifs (figs. 51*d*, 54*a*, 55–body, 57*d*; pls. 45 *a–f*, 46–rim, 50 *b–d*, 58*b*).

C. Black and red paint combined on a white slipped surface (pls. 46–49, 51–65). Solid and dotted lines, bands and zones are of the same varieties and con-

struction as in red-on-white and black-on-white designs. Red and black painting is combined in five principal ways, several of which may occur on a single vessel:

1. Broad (1.0–1.5 cm.) red bands bordered by narrow (1 mm.) black lines, which may also occur independently. Black border may overlap the edge of the red band partly or completely, or may be adjacent (fig. 52*a*; pl. 46–body, 47 *a–b*).

FIGURE 52.—Decorative techniques of Rocafuerte Painted, red and black-on-white. (Stippling=red; black=black.)   *a*, Technique 1.   *b*, Technique 2.   *c*, Technique 3.   *d*, Technique 4.   *e*, Technique 5.

2. Broad black bands and narrow black solid or dotted lines used to create the design, portions of which are accented with narrow red lines or filled with red (figs. 52*b*, 53, 54*b*, 56–body, 57 *a–c*; pls. 48, 55*a*, 56–57, 58*a*, 60, 62*a*–side and rear, 63, 64–body, 65–body).

3. Narrow black solid or dotted lines used to form the design, portions of which are filled with red (figs. 52*c*, 55–rim, 56–rim, 58; pls. 47 *c–d*, 54*a*, 55*b*, 62*a*-front, 62*b*, 64–arms and legs, 65–arms and legs).

4. Thin paired red and black lines, each about 1 mm. wide, the inner edges abutting (fig. 52*d*; pl. 47*e*).

5. Pseudo-negative patterns produced by drawing the design in narrow black lines and filling in the background (cf. black-on-white Technique 3). Red is used for accent, filling small areas or bordering larger ones (fig. 52*e*; pls. 49, 51*a*).

Motif: Painted designs are difficult to describe because of their frequently complicated arrangement of asymmetrical elements drawn with straight and curved lines. Coils, hooks, S-shaped figures, stepped elements, and parallel lines are repeatedly employed.

TEMPORAL DIFFERENCES WITHIN THE TYPE: All techniques occur throughout the seriated sequence, with the possible exception of polychrome Technique 1, which is absent from the upper third (Appendix table 11).

0 1 2 3 4 5 CM

FIGURE 53.—Type sherd of Rocafuerte Painted, red and black-on-white, Technique 2. (Stippling=red, black=black.)

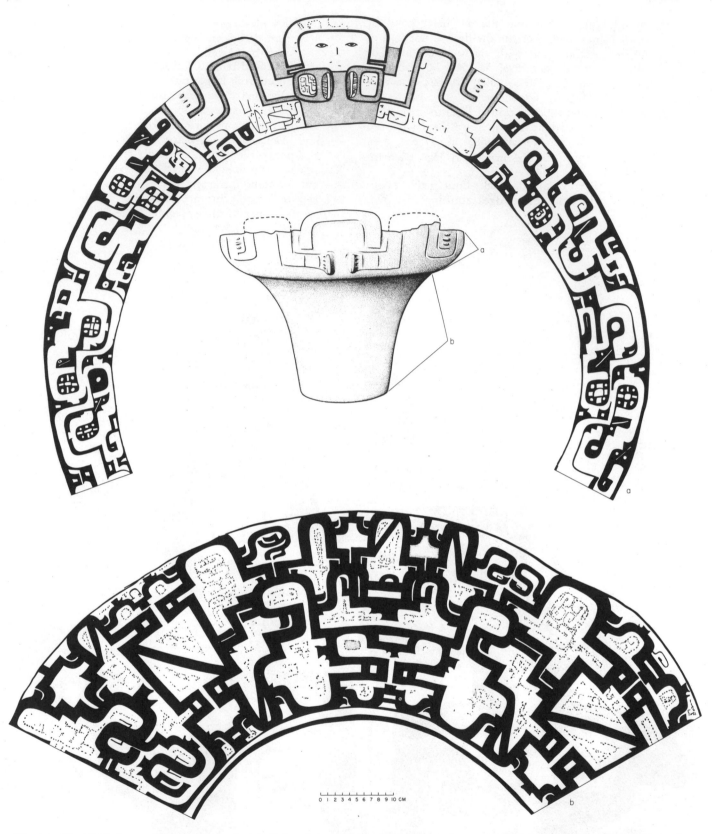

FIGURE 54.—Rolled-out design of Rocafuerte Painted jar of Form 6 with anthropomorphic face on rim. (Stippling=red, black=black.) *a*, Black-on-white Technique 3 on rim. *b*, Red and black-on-white Technique 2 on body. (cf. pl. 46).

FIGURE 55.—Rolled-out design of Rocafuerte Painted, red and black-on-white, Technique 3 on rim and black-on-white, Technique 3 on body. (Stippling=red, black=black.)

FIGURE 56.—Rolled-out design of Rocafuerte Painted, red and black-on-white. (Stippling=red, black=black.) Technique 3 on rim and Technique 2 on body.

CHRONOLOGICAL DISTRIBUTION OF THE TYPE: The principal decorated type, constituting between 10 and 15 percent of the pottery in most levels, throughout the duration of the seriated sequence (fig. 63).

Tiputini Plain

PASTE:

Method of manufacture: Coiling; occasional fractures expose coils 1.5–2.0 cm. wide.

Temper: Charcoal, varying in size from minute up to 2 mm., with rare particles up to 7 mm. Relatively abundant and easily visible in oxidized paste. Also fine sand containing mica flecks. Charcoal is typically rounded and does not have cellular structure of cariapé. A few sherds also have sparse amounts of cariapé.

Texture: Sandy, friable. Removal of charcoal by erosion leaves pits, weakening the sherds.

Color: Grayish tan to dark gray core, fired tan to light orange in a band 0.5–1.0 mm. wide along both surfaces; firing variable on a single sherd.

SURFACE:

Color: Buff, light tan, light orange, reddish tan, grayish tan to gray; considerable variation on a single sherd. Gray patches result from fire clouding.

Treatment: Smoothed with hand and possibly a scraping tool but leaving unevenness and irregularities. Smoothing may drag large temper particles, producing a short scratch. Never slick to touch.

Hardness: 3.5–4.

FORM:

Rim: Direct with flat lip. Size of sample: 26.

Body wall thickness: Range 0.7–1.7 cm.; majority 10–12 mm.

Base: Flat (Forms A and B), rounded (Form C); one annular (Form D).

Reconstructed common vessel shapes (figs. 40–42):
  Form 16: 54.0 percent.
  Form 12: 19.3 percent.
  Form 11: 7.7 percent.
  Form 17: 7.7 percent.

Minor vessel shapes (frequency less than 5 percent; figs. 40, 42, 44): Forms 13, 18, and Rare Form 2.

TEMPORAL DIFFERENCES WITHIN THE TYPE: None observed.

CHRONOLOGICAL POSITION OF THE TYPE: Occurs throughout the Napo Phase sequence in decreasing frequency (fig. 63).

Tiputini Plain Excised

PASTE: Predominantly on Napo Plain (p. 58), occasionally on Armenia Plain (p. 52), rarely on Tiputini Plain (p. 72); see those type descriptions for details.

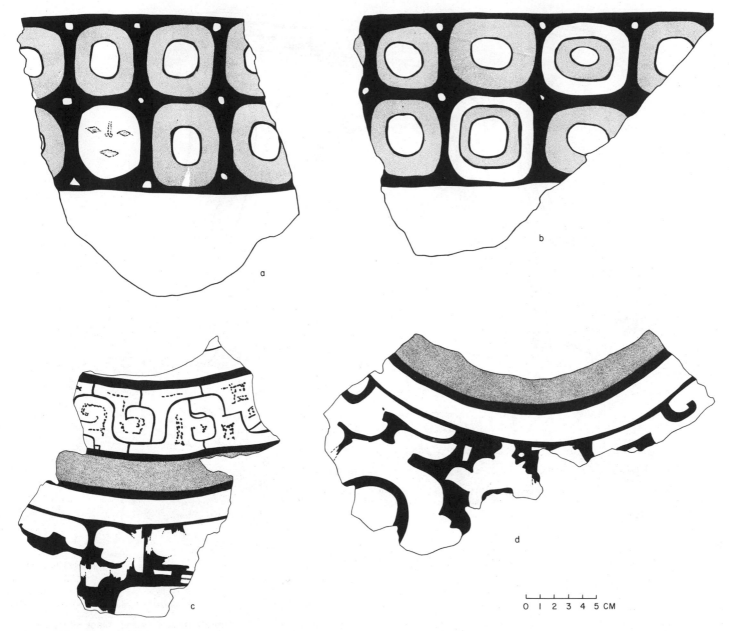

FIGURE 57.—Type sherds of Rocafuerte Painted, red and black-on-white. (Stippling=red, black=black.) *a–c*, Red and black-on- white Technique 2. *d*, Black-on-white, Technique 3 with red on upper border.

SURFACE: Like Napo Plain Excised (p. 59); see that type description for details.

FORM:

Rim: Direct, cambered, channel, or exteriorly thickened with flattened or rounded (rare) lip.

Body wall thickness: Range 4–9 mm.

Base: Probably rounded (Form C).

Reconstructed common vessel shapes (figs. 36–37, 40; pl. 66):

Form 12: 49.2 percent.

Form 33: 16.9 percent.

Form 5: 15.4 percent.

Form 4: 6.1 percent.

Minor vessel shapes (frequency less than 5 percent; figs. 37–38, 40–41): Forms 6, 7, 9, 13, 15.

DECORATION (pls. 66–69):

Technique: Incisions and excised areas executed with a single-pointed tool on an unslipped surface. More carefully done but with greater variation in width and depth than on Napo Plain Excised. Incisions 1–5 mm. wide, up to 2 mm. deep, with width and depth relatively uniform on a single vessel; rectanguloid cross-section. Edges and terminations sometimes thrown up. Intersections not overshot. Strokes straighter than in Napo Plain Excised, but not evenly parallel.

Excised zones outlined by incision and cut back to a depth equal or greater than incisions on the same vessel. When excision goes deeper than the outline, margins tend to be ragged. Bed of excision varies from

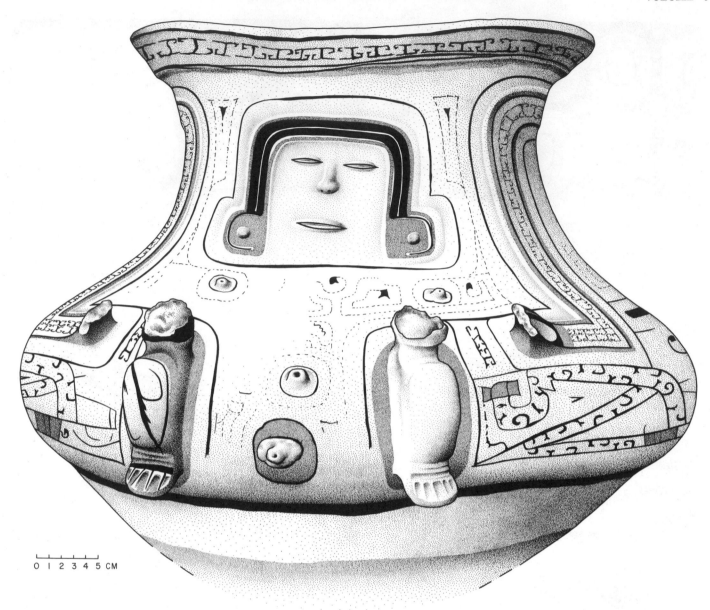

0 1 2 3 4 5 CM

FIGURE 58.—Reconstructed Rocafuerte Painted vessel with anthropomorphic treatment. (Stippling in zones=red, black=black.)

level but not smooth to uneven, leaving distinct parallel gouge marks and intervening ridges.

Small circular punctates may be associated; depth is similar to that of incisions on the same vessel.

A few examples (pl. 69) have thick white paint applied to wide incisions and excised areas, often slopping over onto the margin of the adjacent surface. This inlay tends to flake off, but can usually be distinguished from white slipping subsequent to decoration by its greater thickness, as well as absence from the well preserved portions of the surface.

Motif: Design area may be divided into panels by an undulating line. Excision is employed to cut back trianguloid or stepped zones, frequently leaving a circle in relief at the center. Excision may be limited to

occasional accent in incised designs but more typically is employed to produce 50 percent or more of the pattern.

TEMPORAL DIFFERENCES WITHIN THE TYPE: None observed.

CHRONOLOGICAL POSITION OF THE TYPE: Present throughout the seriated sequence except possibly in the most recent levels (fig. 63).

Tiputini Plain Incised

PASTE: Principally on Napo Plain (p. 58); rarely on Armenia Plain (p. 52) or Tiputini Plain (p. 72); see those type descriptions for details.

SURFACE:

Color: Buff, tan, orange, reddish orange, grayish brown;

uniform or with little variation in tone except where fire clouded.

Treatment: Variation from even and compact but not slick, to irregular with pits, flaws, striations, and protruding temper grains. Decorated surfaces (exterior) may be more poorly smoothed than undecorated interiors.

Hardness: 2.5–3.

FORM:

Rim: Exteriorly thickened, cambered, channel, direct, everted or collared, with flattened or rarely rounded or tapered lip. Size of sample: 63.

Body wall thickness: Range 4–10 mm.; majority 4–6 mm. (except at carination, which may reach 1.8 cm.).

Base: Flat (Forms A, B, and E), rounded (Form C); probably also annular (Form D).

Reconstructed common vessel shapes (figs. 36, 38, 40–41):

Form 12: 36.5 percent.
Form 7: 9.5 percent.
Form 8: 7.9 percent.
Form 1: 7.9 percent.
Form 4: 6.4 percent.
Form 14: 6.4 percent.

Minor vessel shapes (frequency less than 5 percent; figs. 36–41, 44): Forms 3, 5, 9, 10, 11, 13, 15, 16; Rare Form 4.

DECORATION (pl. 70):

Technique: Incision with a single-pointed tool on an unslipped surface. Wide variation in width and depth of lines and in quality of design. Incision width typically 1–2 mm., rarely up to 5 mm.; depth 1–3 mm. with vertical walls. Execution typically sloppy, with thrown up edges and ends, ragged edges, or a "plug" of clay left in the trough at the end of a stroke. Lines are crooked, unequally spaced and unevenly parallel, but junctions are not overshot. Punctates may be associated, either circular (diameter 2 mm.) or rectanguloid (4 by 2 mm. to 4 by 5 mm.). Depth is the same as the associated incised lines.

A few sherds preserve traces of white pigment in the bed of the incision, applied prior to firing. This technique is difficult to distinguish from white slipping in the eroded condition characteristic of most sherds, and may have been more common than evidence now suggests. Sherds combining single- and double-line techniques have been classified under Napo Plain Incised (see p. 59).

Motif: Complicated combinations of straight and curved lines, including coils, concentric triangles, and undulating lines. One example is diagonal checkerboard (pl. 70*h*). A face also occurs only once (pl. 70*a*).

TEMPORAL DIFFERENCES WITHIN THE TYPE: None observed.

CHRONOLOGICAL POSITION OF THE TYPE: Present throughout the seriated sequence in slightly declining frequency (fig. 63).

Tiputini Red Excised

PASTE: Principally on Napo Plain (p. 58), occasionally on Armenia Plain (p. 52), rarely on Tiputini Plain (p. 72); see those type descriptions for details.

SURFACE:

Color: Cream, light tan, light brown to reddish brown. Fire clouding frequent.

Treatment: Generally even, varying from smoothed leaving flaws, pits, and scraping striations to compact and smooth to touch, with the latter in the minority. Decorated surface (exterior) slightly better finished but may retain striations, small pits, and visible temper grains.

Hardness: 2.5.

FORM:

Rim: Direct, cambered, channel or exteriorly thickened (rare), with flat or rounded lip. Size of sample: 64.

Body wall thickness: Range 3–12 mm.; majority 4–9 mm.

Base: Probably rounded (Form C).

Reconstructed common vessel shapes (figs. 36–37, 40):

Form 12: 50.0 percent.
Form 3: 22.2 percent.
Form 5: 6.7 percent.
Form 4: 5.5 percent.

Minor vessel shapes (frequency less than 5 percent; figs. 36–37, 40): Forms 1, 6, 11, 13.

DECORATION (pls. 51*b*, 71–72):

Technique: Incisions and excised zones executed with a single-pointed tool before or after the application of a red slip. Incisions are sharply defined, vertical walled, rectangular in cross-section. Width varies from 1–5 mm., depth from 0.5–3.0 mm., but variation is slight on a single example. Narrower lines are more even in width than wider ones, which often have irregular margins partly resulting from failure of successive tool strokes to coincide. Margins and terminations may be slightly thrown up. Corners are usually rounded; intersections are not overshot. Lines are not equally spaced or evenly parallel.

Excised areas are defined by incised lines, which often remain visible; a few examples are so irregular as to suggest outlining may have been omitted. Excision is gouged out, leaving a very uneven floor in most cases. Depth varies from 1–4 mm. Excised segments are not uniform in size or shape, even when they constitute repeating elements of the design.

Small circular to ovoid punctates are frequently employed.

Eighty-five percent of the examples were red slipped on the exterior prior to incision, the remainder subsequently. Color varies from rich red to reddish orange, often in the form of a thin wash incompletely obliterating the underlying surface.

Motif: Parallel vertical or diagonal lines define panels filled with stepped elements, interlocking or single coils or asymmetrical figures. Larger excised areas often contain a circle with a central punctate.

TEMPORAL DIFFERENCES WITHIN THE TYPE: None observed.

CHRONOLOGICAL POSITION OF THE TYPE: Present throughout the seriated sequence except possibly in the latest levels (fig. 63).

Tiputini Red Excised, White Retouched

PASTE: Predominantly on Napo Plain (p. 58), rarely on Armenia Plain (p. 52) or Tiputini Plain (p. 72); see those type descriptions for details.

SURFACE:

Color: Buff, light tan, grayish tan, orange to reddish orange; relatively uniform shade except where fire clouded.

Treatment: Smoothed, obliterating flaws; sufficient floating to bring enough fine clay particles to surfaces to produce an even, compact surface. Fine brush-like horizontal striations may remain visible. Majority even and smooth to touch.

Hardness: 2.5.

FORM: Same as Tiputini Red Excised (see p. 75). Size of rim sample: 26.

DECORATION (pl. 73 *a–l*):

Technique: Incision, excision and punctation with a single-pointed tool before or after addition of red slip, subsequently white coated. Incision variable in width (1–6 mm.) and depth (0.5–3.0 mm.), but relatively uniform on a single vessel. Lines bold, sharply defined, vertical walled, but not straight or evenly parallel. Edges not dragged or thrown up; intersections not overshot.

Excised zones outlined by incision and then gouged out with short strokes parallel to the longest axis of the zone. Bed is typically left rough, but better done examples have parallel scoring of even depth. Boundary may be jagged or nonsymmetrical. Depth varies from 1–3 mm., and may be equal to or greater than the depth of incised lines on the same vessel.

Circular punctations are 1–4 mm. in diameter, 1–3 mm. deep.

Thin red slip or wash was applied before or after incision to the exterior, including the lip, and sometimes slopping slightly over onto the interior. Rarely, red was applied only to the decorated area, leaving the lower exterior plain. Color varies from rich red to reddish orange depending on thickness and firing.

The final step in decoration was the addition of a white wash or slip to the incisions and excised zones. The material varies from a thick coating with fine crackle lines to a thin wash, which often slops unevenly onto the adjacent surface.

Motif: Similar to Tiputini Red Excised (see pls. 71–72).

TEMPORAL DIFFERENCES WITHIN THE TYPE: None observed.

CHRONOLOGICAL POSITION OF THE TYPE: Present throughout the seriated sequence except possibly in the upper third (fig. 63).

Tiputini Red Incised

PASTE: Predominantly on Napo Plain (p. 58); rarely on Armenia Plain (p. 52) or Tiputini Plain (p. 72); see those type descriptions for details.

SURFACE:

Color (undecorated surfaces): Cream, light tan, light brown, grayish brown, reddish orange; variable over small area because of poorly controlled firing and fire clouding. Dark gray fire clouds common.

Treatment: Even but rarely smoothed sufficiently to eliminate abrasive texture derived from sand temper. Pits and defects rare. Horizontal smoothing striations may be accompanied by a slight ridge.

Hardness: 2.5.

FORM:

Rim: Direct, exteriorly thickened, cambered, channel or everted, with flattened, rounded, or tapered lip. Size of sample: 19.

Body wall thickness: Range 4–10 mm.

Base: Rounded (Form C), possibly also flat (Form A).

Reconstructed common vessel shapes (figs. 36, 40–41):

Form 12: 52.8 percent.
Form 4: 21.1 percent.
Form 1: 10.5 percent.
Form 3: 10.5 percent.
Form 15: 5.3 percent.

DECORATION (pl. 74 *a–i*):

Technique: Medium to broad incisions executed with a single-pointed tool before or after application of a red slip. Width varies considerably (1–4 mm.) within the type, but is relatively uniform on a single vessel. Depth is between 1–2 mm.; also with little variation on a single example. Depth is not correlated with width, and the widest lines may be at either end of the range. Circular or elongated punctations may be associated. Execution is typically sloppy, with ragged or thrown up margins, unequal spacing and poor parallelism. Corners tend toward rounding. Intersections are not overshot.

A red slip was applied typically after incision but occasionally before. Where well preserved, the color is rich red to reddish orange. Streakiness may result from uneven application. Where applied after incision, beds of incisions are evenly coated suggesting a relatively liquid condition. Red may slop unevenly over the lip onto the interior of the rim, but does not cover the interior.

Tiputini Red Incised, white retouched variety occurs on a few sherds, where a white coating was applied to the incisions, often slopping over onto the adjacent surface along the margin (pl. 74 *j–o*). When applied thickly, the pigment develops fine crackle and tends to flake off especially when applied over red slip.

Motif: Parallel lines changing direction at 90 degree angles to produce hooks and rectanguloid figures, sometimes with a central dash or punctation.

TEMPORAL DIFFERENCES WITHIN THE TYPE: None observed.

CHRONOLOGICAL DISTRIBUTION OF THE TYPE: Absent from the upper third of the seriated sequence (fig. 63).

Tiputini White Excised

PASTE AND SURFACE: On Napo Plain (p. 58); see that type description for details.

FORM:

Rim: Cambered with flat lip. Size of sample: 3.

Body wall thickness: 5 mm.

Base: Rounded (Form C).

Reconstructed common vessel shapes (fig. 36): Form 3.
DECORATION (pl. 73 *m–n*):
Technique: Incision and excision with a single-pointed tool prior to coating of the decorated area with a white wash. Execution similar to that of Tiputini Plain Excised (see p. 72).
Motif: Undulating line divides the decorated area into semicircular panels containing a curved stepped line and a circle with a central punctate.
TEMPORAL DIFFERENCES WITHIN THE TYPE: None observed.
CHRONOLOGICAL POSITION OF THE TYPE: Very rare (fig. 63) but given type status to facilitate comparison of the ceramic complex with that of other areas.

Tiputini White Incised

PASTE: All on Napo Plain (p. 58); see that type description for details.
SURFACE:
Color: Orange, tan, reddish brown; dark gray fire clouds frequent.
Treatment: Superficially smoothed leaving tracks parallel to the rim, scratches and other flaws. Sandy texture resulting from protruding temper grains.
Hardness: 3.
FORM:
Rim: Channel or exteriorly thickened, with flat or tapered lip. Size of sample: 5.
Body wall thickness: Range 3.5–7.0 mm., increasing to 2.7 cm. at carination.
Base: Probably rounded (Form C).
Reconstructed common vessel shapes (figs. 36, 38): Forms 4, 7, 8, 9.
DECORATION (pl. 75):
Technique: Incision with a single-pointed tool on a plain surface, subsequently covered with a thin white wash. Incising tool unstandardized so that almost every example differs in width, depth and form of lines. Width 1.5–5.0 mm., typically with little variation on a single sherd; however, one example has lines 1.5 mm. wide adjacent to a zone containing 4 mm. wide grooves. Depth is less than 1 mm. Wide lines tend to be shallow and concave in cross-section, resulting in poor visibility when the surface is uneven. Bed may be smooth or filled with fine parallel striations. Terminations are typically pushed up. Not equally spaced or evenly parallel.

Subsequent to incision, a white coating was applied to the decorated zone. Erosion has reduced evidence to scattered traces on most examples, suggesting that it was never thick or evenly applied. This type is difficult to distinguish from white filled incisions of Tiputini Plain Incised (see p. —).
Motif: Most examples feature a single or interlocking squared coil, sometimes with a punctate at the center.
TEMPORAL DIFFERENCES WITHIN THE TYPE: None observed.
CHRONOLOGICAL DISTRIBUTION OF THE TYPE: Absent from the upper third of the seriated sequence (fig. 63).

Unclassified Decorated

BLACK-ON-RED PAINTING (pl. 76a).—One body sherd is decorated on the exterior with small black figures on a thinly red slipped surface. Open spaces enclosed by black lines were subsequently retouched with red in the style of normal polychrome designs. Paste is Napo Plain. One example from N–P–2, Broadside B.
FINGER-PRESSED LIP.—A large (diameter 36 cm.) deep bowl with outslanting walls has the lip decorated by pressing with the finger, producing a continuous series of deep impressions separated by high ridges and with an undulating or scalloped border resulting from displacement of the clay to the sides. Paste is Napo Plain. One vessel from N–P–3, Test B extension.
FINGER-PRESSED RIM (pl. 76 *b–g*).—Several rim sherds from large vertical walled bowls have decoration on the exterior rim thickening produced by pressing with the finger from left to right, creating a row of shallow, fingertip sized depressions separated by high (5 mm.) curved ridges. The pottery type is Napo Plain or Armenia Plain. Examples from N–P–2, Area 2a and N–P–3, Surface and Test A, and Test B extension.
IMPRESSED RING (pl. 76h).—One fragment of an open bowl with rectanguloid rim lobes has a large ring impressed from the exterior, leaving a conical center. Exterior diameter is 4.3 cm., depth 5–7 mm. There is no distortion of the interior surface because of thickening of the wall in this region. The pottery type is Armenia Plain. From N–P–2, Broadside A.
INCISED LINE (pl. 76o).—One sherd of a bowl with interiorly thickened rim, tapered to a rounded lip and everted. Mouth diameter is 20 cm. Fine sand temper with light orange-red surfaces and traces of a rudimentary polish. Exterior decoration of fine incised lines, 0.5 mm. wide, crooked but evenly spaced with intersections overshot. From N–P–3, Surface.

Trade Pottery

Several sherds from N–P–2 and N–P–3 are distinct in paste, vessel shape and decoration from the ceramic complex of the Napo Phase. They appear to be contemporary with the Napo Phase pottery, rather than to result from later intrusion; if so, they must have originated from trade.

The paste is tempered with fine sand sometimes containing abundant mica, visible as pinpoint sparkles on the surface. Other sherds lack the mica. One contains black ash. Surface finish is best on the rim top and upper interior, poorest on the exterior, which remains slightly uneven.

Two principal kinds of decoration are represented:

(1) corrugation, beginning at the rim and extending down the exterior of the neck in a series of fine, horizontal, slightly overlapping coils (pl. 76 *i–m*), or occupying the waist rather than the neck; and (2) parallel, closely spaced incised lines forming bands and zones alternately left plain and filled with trianguloid punctations of distinctive form (pl. 76*n*). Both techniques may occur on different parts of the same vessel. In one case the corrugations are embellished with shallow ovoid punctates (pl. 76*m*); another has diagonal scoring (pl. 76*l*).

Vessel shape is a wide mouthed jar with a prominent rounded or angular shoulder, insloping, vertical or outsloping neck and sharply everted rim with a flat sloping top tapering to a flat or rounded lip. Interior rim diameter is 14–24 cm., with one example having a square rather than circular form (fig. 59).

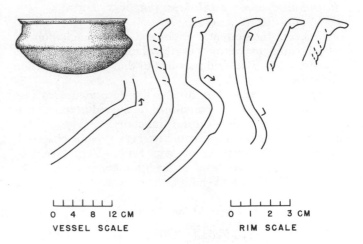

FIGURE 59.—Rim profiles and reconstructed vessel shape of sherds of probable trade origin from Napo Phase sites.

THE SERIATED SEQUENCE AND ITS IMPLICATIONS

The seriated sequence of the Napo Phase is based on trends in popularity of the plain pottery types as indicated by their relative frequencies in the two levels of N–P–2, Cut 1, the only stratigraphic excavation representing the Phase. Analysis showed an increase in the frequency of sand-tempered Napo Plain and decreases in the frequencies of the other two plain types, cariapé-tempered Armenia Plain and charcoal-tempered Tiputini Plain. Fourteen other collections, representing the surface and tests at N–P–2 and five other Napo Phase sites were sufficiently large and unselected to be useful for seriation. The attempt

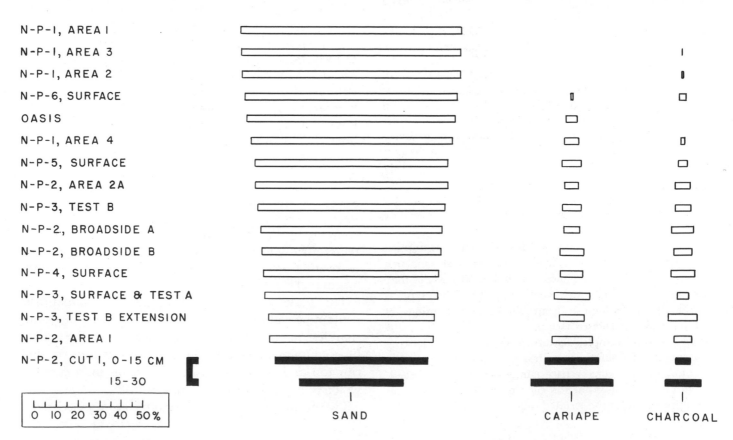

FIGURE 60.—Seriated sequence of Napo Phase sites derived from classification of both plain and decorated sherds by temper.

to interdigitate them into the sequence, however, brought to light several problems. First, the large number of decorated pottery types into which each sample was classified resulted in very small representation of most of the types, making trends difficult to observe. Second, differences in frequency between samples are relatively small, probably because a short length of time is involved. As a consequence, an attempt at seriation did not produce one ordering that was clearly preferable to other possibilities. Many of the samples appeared to fit equally well in several alternative positions.

Two supplemental methods of analysis were employed to evaluate the alternative seriated sequences and determine which was most likely to be reliable. One was the classification of all sherds by temper, regardless of the surface finish, and calculation of the relative frequency of the use of sand, cariapé, and charcoal (Appendix table 9). When the strips were arranged in the order indicated by the percentage distribution in the two levels of N–P–2, Cut 1, namely increasing popularity of sand temper and decreasing popularity of both cariapé temper and charcoal temper, the result is a relatively smooth pattern of change in all three types (fig. 60). A second basis for analysis was provided by the presence of two techniques of incision, one executed with a single- and the other a double- or multiple-pointed tool. All incised and excised sherds were sorted in terms of tool type employed, and both relative and absolute frequency of the two types was calculated for each sample (Appendix table 9). Seriation following the trend exhibited by the two levels of N–P–2, Cut 1, again produced another relatively smooth pattern of change (fig. 61), but resulted

in a different arrangement from that based on temper. Since the reliability of different kinds of traits and size of samples for chronological inference has been debated (e.g. Lathrap, 1964; Evans and Meggers, 1964), this conflicting result is worth analyzing in some detail.

Correlation of the two seriated sequences (fig. 62) shows most of the displacements to be minor. Four collections occupy the same relative position in both sequences (N–P–1, Area 4; N–P–2, Broadside B; N–P–4, Surface; and N–P–2, Cut 1, Level 15–30 cm.), five are shifted upward or downward by only one unit (N–P–1, Area 1; N–P–1, Area 3; Oasis; N–P–2, Broadside A; N–P–3, Test B Extension), and three are shifted upward or downward by two units (N–P–1, Area 2; N–P–2, Area 2A; N–P–3, Surface and Test A). One sample is displaced by three units (N–P–6). These represent more than two-thirds of the collections, and considering that the differences in frequencies determining seriated position are often less than one percent, these discrepancies are insignificant.

The four remaining collections are displaced markedly from one seriated sequence to the other. The practice of seriation is based on the premise that cultural traits change in frequency through time in a systematic manner approximating a bell curve, and all classes of traits should theoretically be expected to produce a similar chronological result. In reality, however, traits differ in their suitability for chronological studies. Some change too slowly to be useful, others are too rare to appear in small samples or to show a clear trend of changing frequency.

Insufficient sample size may explain the larger

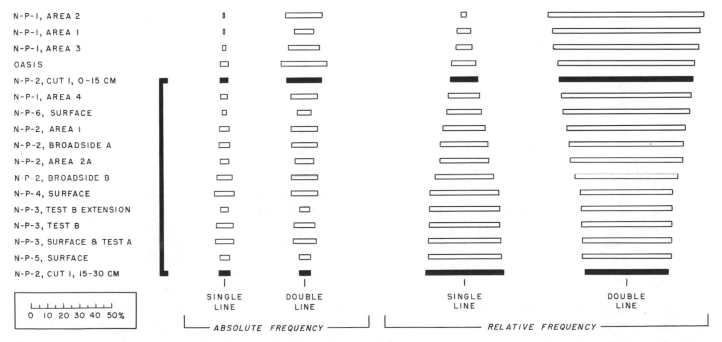

FIGURE 61.—Seriated sequence of Napo Phase sites derived from classification of incised and excised sherds by technique of incision.

discrepancies in the Napo Phase seriation attempts. In all the collections used for seriation, the total sherds available for classification by temper exceed 250 except for one sample totalling 167 sherds (Appendix table 9). Since unselected samples of 100 or more have been shown to be dependable for seriation purposes (Ford, 1949, pp. 35–36), the arrangement based on temper satisfies the requirement of adequate sample size. By contrast, the total number of incised and excised sherds exceeds 100 in only 9 of the 17 seriated collections. While most of the undersized samples agree closely with the result obtained from the larger number of sherds classified by temper, two differ markedly: N–P–2, Area 1, represented by only 57 incised and excised sherds, and N–P–5, with only 38. In these cases, inadequate sample size is the probable explanation for the lack of correspondence

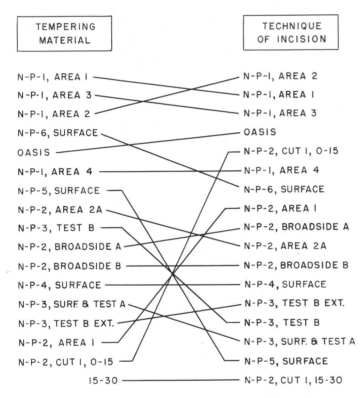

FIGURE 62.—Correlation of seriated sequences of Napo Phase sites based on temper and on technique of incision and excision.

and the result obtained from the larger sample should be the more reliable. The two remaining collections (N–P–2, Cut 1, Level 0–15 cm. and N–P–3, Test B) have sufficiently large samples in both classifications to be considered dependable, so that a choice between them must be based on other considerations.

The relative validity of the two arrangements can be assessed by construction of a third sequence utilizing the pottery types rather than isolated modes of paste or decoration. When this is done, the best fit is achieved when the order indicated by the changing popularity of temper varieties is followed. Trends in the plain types generally parallel those of the temper seriation (cf. figs. 60 and 63), and the two samples showing poorest fit (N–P–5 and N–P–6) have been distorted by surface erosion. In each case, the proportion of Napo Plain is larger and that of Rocafuerte Painted is smaller than expected (fig. 63), indicating that some sherds originally having painted decoration are now plain.

Few of the decorated types show notable or consistent changes in frequency. In all cases, however, the single-line technique represented by the Tiputini Incised and Excised types dies out earlier than the double-line technique represented by the Napo Incised and Excised types. Only one pair of types approaches the ideal pattern of successive dominance, namely, Tiputini Red Incised, which expands and then declines as Napo Red Incised grows more popular. In excised decoration, all slip variants tend to disappear, leaving double-line excision on a plain surface (Napo Plain Excised). Rocafuerte Incised, characterized by incisions painted red subsequent to white slipping of the surface, is absent from the upper third of the existing sequence. Armenia White-on-red and Napo Negative are present throughout, as is Rocafuerte Painted, which is always the most popular decorated type.

All of the plain types are present and relatively common at the beginning of the sequence. At the end, sand temper (Napo Plain) occurs in 99 percent of the sherds and charcoal temper (Tiputini Plain) is represented by the remaining 1 percent (fig. 60). Cariapé tempering ceases to exist shortly before the final levels.

Only one collection made by previous investigators was large enough to be classified and inserted into the seriated sequence. This is the sample of 40 sherds from Oasis in the Museum of the American Indian, Heye Foundation. Analyses on the basis of paste (fig. 60) and technique of incision (fig. 61) place it in a late relative position. The selectivity for decorated sherds made it necessary to correct the sample before it could be seriated into the pottery type sequence. This was done by computing the average frequency of decorated sherds in unselected collections and increasing the total used for percentage calculation to include the equivalent number of plain sherds (Appendix table 8). The result fits rather well into the upper portion of the sequence (fig. 63).

When the attempt is made to detect changes in popularity of vessel shapes, the small size of rim samples must be taken into consideration. Only four collections included more than 100 rims, five had between 50 and 100 rims, and six had less than 50 rims. As a consequence, when the relative frequency of the 20 common forms is calculated and the levels are arranged in seriated sequence, few trends emerge (fig. 64). Most of the forms are present with similar frequency throughout, or exhibit occasional erratic fluctuations attributable to inadequacy of the sample. All forms are present initially and remain in use at the end of the sequence. Possibly significant increases in popularity are exhibited by Forms 1 and 15, but sampling error cannot be ruled out since the two samples occupying the latest positions contain less than 100 rims each.

It should be kept in mind that evidence of chronological orientation for the seriated sequence is limited to the trends exhibited by the two levels of N–P–2, Cut 1. The shallowness of this excavation makes its reliability as a basis for determining the direction of change open to question, and the possibility exists that early and late portions are inverted. Inferences derivable from changes in artifact types or relative antiquity of sites are therefore tentative unless supported by other kinds of evidence.

The three carbon-14 dates do not clearly validate or refute the seriated sequence. Two come from N–P–2 and are not in seriated order, although the difference between them is only 11 years so that their inversion is not likely to be significant. The earliest, from N–P–2, Broadside B, is 782 ± 53 years or A.D. 1168 (P–347); the more recent, from N–P–2, Cut 1, Level 0–15 cm., is 771 ± 51 years or A.D. 1179 (P–269). The third date is from N–P–3, Test B Extension, which seriates intermediate between the other two collections. However, it is considerably more recent than either at 470 ± 180 years or A.D. 1480 (SI–299). All determinations were made from organic carbon extracted from charcoal-tempered sherds of Tiputini Plain, so that there is no obvious basis for rejection of any date on the ground of probable contamination or lack of association with the Napo Phase. The fact that the two earlier dates were furnished by the University of Pennsylvania and the late one by the Smithsonian Institution introduces a possibility that different laboratory procedures may be responsible for the discrepancy. Numerous independently seriated collections show N–P–2 and N–P–3 to be contemporary, so that either the single N–P–3 date or the two N–P–2 dates must be rejected.

In view of the ethnohistorical evidence that the region was uninhabited in 1521, a date of A.D. 1480 seems too recent to correspond to the lower portion of the sequence, in spite of the short duration implied by the relatively small amount of ceramic change that took place. The earlier dates also agree better with the date from Coarí on the Solimões (see pp. 94-95) where ceramic resemblances to the Napo Phase occur.

Several interesting observations can be made when the composition and geographical location of the sites are examined in terms of the seriated sequence. First, quantitative results obtained for samples representing different portions of the same site are so similar as to suggest that the entire area was occupied simultaneously (figs. 28–29, 63). Taken in conjunction with the extremely shallow nature of the refuse deposits, this situation implies the existence of relatively large villages for a brief span of time. Although the site sample is too small to be conclusive, the fact that the two smallest sites (N–P–5 and N–P–6) occupy a relatively late position in the seriated sequence suggests a diminution in village size.

When the geographical location of the individual sites is compared with their seriated position, no clear pattern is evident. When contemporary occupations are considered, however, it can be seen that the three earliest sites (N–P–2, N–P–3, N–P–4) are farther downriver than the three later ones (N–P–5, N–P–6, N–P–1) (fig. 3). The Oasis sample, which seriates late, is the farthest upstream. On the other hand, the small number of sites investigated allows the possibility that this patterning may be fortuitous, and the ambiguous result of attempts to seriate a sherd sample from the Rio Yasuní (see p. 37) lends credence to this view.

Burial urn types and nonceramic artifacts are too rare and accompanied by insufficient provenience data to be analyzed in chronological terms.

Pottery of possible trade origin occurred in sherd collections from three locations at two sites: N–P–2, Broadside A and Area 2, and N–P–3, Test B extension. These collections occupy seriated positions in the early half of the sequence, implying that communication with the makers of the alien ceramics dates from the time of arrival of the Napo Phase in the area.

DIAGNOSTIC FEATURES OF THE NAPO PHASE

Seven habitation sites in the 1956 survey represent the Napo Phase. Six are on the Rio Napo and one on the Rio Tiputini, where the elevation of the bank is sufficient to escape flooding. Occupation refuse is distributed in a relatively narrow strip along the bank, typically varying between 20 and 65 meters wide, erosion by the river having in some cases reduced the original width. Two sites are more than 500 meters in length and the majority exceed 100 meters. All are very shallow and disturbed by recent habitation, so that the seriated sequence is based on trends of ceramic change exhibited by only one stratigraphic excavation of two 15 cm. levels.

There is no direct evidence of subsistence pattern. Numerous potrest fragments relate to cooking practices. Large griddles, some 40 cm. in diameter, suggest the Napo Phase processed bitter manioc according to the same methods used today by South American Tropical Forest Indians. Shallow, flat bottomed basins of similar size perhaps had a related function. Two fragments of what appear to be large manos, if correctly identified, imply the processing of grain. Consideration of the probable highland origin of the Napo Phase suggests that this may have been maize. Fishing and hunting must have contributed importantly to the diet, as well as the gathering of wild plants.

A number of anthropomorphic urns have been collected from habitation sites, while others appear to have been buried in isolated spots. Finds have been accidental and few details are recorded. Bones have been reported in some, and the small size implies that the burial was secondary, although incomplete cremation is also a possibility. The vessels vary in the completeness and realism of anthropomorphic execution, and display considerable variety in rendition of facial features. The surface is painted, sometimes combined with broad incision.

Information on dress and ornament is provided by the anthropomorphic urns (pls. 55–65). Face painting is characteristic, surrounding the eyes and extending over the cheek and in some cases around the mouth. Although similar, the patterns on right and left are never exact mirror images. Ear lobes are sometimes perforated. Hair may be gathered into a long queue down the back. Both arms and legs have bulging areas between constrictions suggesting use of ornamental ligatures. A triangular relief at the center of the chest may represent an ornament. Bodies are nude, but three figures hold small circular shields. One of the shields has geometrical ornamentation, while another is painted with a panpipe having the tubes graduated from both sides toward the center.

The pottery of the Napo Phase has been classified into 4 undecorated and 18 decorated types. Napo Plain, tempered with sand, is by far the most abundant type, constituting 35 percent or more of the sherds in unselected samples. Two minor plain types are Armenia Plain, tempered with cariapé, and Tiputini Plain, tempered with fine charcoal. Napo Red, in which the surface is covered with a fine red slip,

has also been included among undecorated types.

Decoration is by incision, excision, painting, and rarely modeling on a plain surface, frequently combined with a red or white slip. In the most elaborate types, incisions or excisions have been colored to contrast with the surface or slip. Examples include Rocafuerte Incised, in which a white slip was applied after incision and the incision subsequently colored red, and Napo Red Excised, White Retouched, in which the process was reversed so that the excisions and incisions are accented with white after the surface was slipped red. Two easily differentiated varieties of incision reflect use of two kinds of tools, one with a single and the other with a double or multiple end. Different combinations of these two techniques with different kinds of surface treatment account for most of the proliferation of decorated types. The remainder represent several kinds of painting: white-on-red, negative, red-on-white, black-on-white, and polychrome (red and black-on-white). The former two are very rare, while the latter three are variants of Rocafuerte Painted, which is the most popular decorated type.

Napo Phase vessel shapes include several varieties of channel-rimmed bowls, large basins and small open to constricted mouthed vessels with rounded or markedly carinated shoulders. Larger vessels have collared or channel rims. Bases may be flat, rounded or annular. Outline is typically square. All forms and decorative techniques abound in habitation sites. The only form clearly not of domestic use is the anthropomorphic burial urn.

Pottery and stone artifacts are rare. Solid cylindrical potrests, occasionally ornamented with incised and excised patterns, are the most common. The design style on roller stamps of rolling-pin shape suggests that they are probably associated with the Napo Phase, although this has not been confirmed. One small perforated pottery disk may be a spindle whorl. Stone artifacts include pecked and incompletely polished side-notched axes and rare eared axes, chisels, grinding stone fragments, hammerstones, and unshaped rocks used for abrading, hammering, and cutting.

The absolute chronological position of the Napo Phase is attested by three carbon-14 dates. Two place it in the latter half of the 12th century A.D. The third, A.D. 1480, seems too recent to be acceptable. The existence of pottery with zoned punctate decorations and non-Napo Phase vessel shapes at several sites implies trade relations with a group in the Andean foothills to the west with a different ceramic tradition.

The Cotacocha Phase

DESCRIPTION OF SITES AND EXCAVATIONS

This Phase is represented by a small sample of sherds from four sites, most of which were known at the time of collection in the field to be of recent origin. No effort was made to locate more sites, or to accumulate ethnographic material.

N–P–3: Nuevo Rocafuerte

An annular-based bowl with red-banded decoration and cariapé-tempered paste came from the surface, where it had probably been thrown by one of the modern residents after it broke. Its inclusion in the Napo Phase sample was inadvertent, and no effort was made to collect recent pottery from this modern settlement (see pp. 34–35 for detailed description).

N–P–9: Cotacocha

In addition to the Napo Phase material from this site (see p. 36), a large number of Cotacocha Phase sherds were collected. Residents of the house occupying the site were absent at the time of our visit, so that it could not be ascertained whether the pottery was used by them or by prior occupants. The slight amount of surface erosion in comparison with that exhibited

by the Napo Phase sherds is circumstancial evidence of recency.

N–P–14: Latas

A modern house is located on the left bank of the Rio Napo, just below the first rapid (fig. 1). The spot is strategic in river commerce, since portage is required for all cargo intransit upriver (pl. 2a). The land rises considerably a little in from the river bank, and the slopes and summit are under cultivation. Two small sherd concentrations were encountered on the top of the first shelf of terrace, each about 5 meters in diameter. Depth was no greater than 5 cm.

N–P–15: Tiputini Road

An area beside the road connecting Tiputini with the airstrip has been used since the time of the Shell Petroleum Company as a trash dump (same location as N–P–1; see fig. 3). Among the cans and bottles was a broken vessel of Form 1 with red slip on the rim and exterior below the neck, probably discarded by one of the Indian families in the employ of the Company or of the Army base (see pp. 32–33).

ANALYSIS OF MATERIALS

No stone artifacts and only one possible pottery artifact are associated with the Cotacocha Phase. The

latter is a small spool-shaped object from N–P–9, about 4 cm. in diameter at the ends and 2.8 cm. in diameter at the constricted waist. Both faces are concave. The paste is cariapé tempered.

Ceramic Classification

Cotacocha Phase pottery types are based on material from only four sites, two of which produced a single vessel each. In the absence of stratigraphic control, it was not possible to test the relative value of ceramic features for revealing temporal differences. Both temper and firing were consequently used in the classification of plain sherds. This results in two principal sand-tempered plain types: completely oxidized Cotacocha Plain and incompletely oxidized Latas Plain. A few cariapé-tempered sherds have been segregated into an unclassified plain type. Walls are thin and surfaces are not even or polished. Decoration is simple and largely a by-product of construction, consisting as it does of unobliterated coil junctions and fingernail marks left in the process of joining coils. Zoned red slip or red bands also occur. Vessel shapes are few and simple; only circular outlines were recognized.

Type descriptions have been arranged in alphabetical order following description of vessel and base forms. Information on provenience and frequency is provided in Appendix tables 3 and 5.

Reconstructed Vessel Forms

Common Forms

1. Jar with constricted neck and everted rim (fig. 65–1):
   Rim: Insloping to nearly vertical or slightly outsloping and mildly to sharply everted between 1.0 and 2.5 cm. below the lip. Interior of the bend may be rounded or angular; exterior is rounded because of thickening at the bend. Lower edge of the thickening is unobliterated, remaining as a line or elevation. Exterior rim diameter, 18–36 cm.
   Lip: Rounded or flattened.
   Body wall thickness: Range 4–6 mm.
   Base: Pedestal (Form A) or flat (Form B).
2. Wide mouthed jar with vertical rim (fig. 65–2):
   Rim: Insloping, becoming approximately vertical 2.5–3.0 cm. below the lip. Change in direction is angular on the interior and observable as a slight step on the exterior. The effect may be produced with or without thickening. Rim diameter about 32 cm.
   Lip: Rounded.
   Body wall thickness: Range 3.5–5.5 mm.
   Base: Probably flat (Form B) or concave (Form C).
3. Shallow bowl with annular base (fig. 65–3):
   Rim: Upcurving and direct. Diameter 22–24 cm.
   Lip: Rounded.
   Body wall thickness: Range 4–6 mm.
   Base: Annular (Form D).

Minor Rim Forms

1. Nearly vertical rim possibly representing a jar similar to Form 2, with unsmoothed coils on the exterior. Rim diameter 32 cm. (fig. 65–4). The upper coil is decorated with fingertip impressions.
2. Insloping rim, everted 4 cm. below the rounded lip producing a slightly outsloping collar. Rim diameter 32 cm. (fig. 65–5).

Base Forms

Four base forms are distinguishable. Two are correlated with rim forms on complete vessels; the others may be alternatives to any of the three principal forms.
A. Pedestal, the flat bottom making a vertical, steplike junction with the exterior. Pedestal height about 8 mm. Diameter 12 cm. (fig. 65–A).
B. Flat, making an angular junction with the outsloping body wall. The interior is a smooth curve. Diameter 12 cm. (fig. 65–B).
C. Slightly concave and making a rounded junction with the outsloping body wall. A slight convexity is detectible on the interior. Diameter about 10 cm. (fig. 65–C).
D. Annular, flaring, and thickened so as to create a smoothly curving surface on the exterior. A small concavity occurs on the interior. Diameter 6.5 cm., height 2 cm. (fig. 65–3).

Pottery Type Descriptions

Cotacocha Plain

PASTE:
   Method of manufacture: Coiling.
   Temper: Fine angular sand, grain diameter typically less than 0.5 mm. Color predominantly black, with scattered white quartz and golden iron pyrites particles. Abundant, giving speckled appearance to cross-section.
   Texture: Fine grained, often laminated with fine crevasses parallel or diagonal to surface.
   Color: Buff, light orange to tan throughout the cross-section; rarely grayish brown.
SURFACE:
   Color: Light buff, tan, grayish brown, often with a dusty hue. Dark gray to black surfaces rare, although gray spots from fire clouding are typical.
   Treatment: Best finished examples retain pits and unevenness; range like that of Latas Plain. Interior often better smoothed than exterior.
   Hardness: 4.
FORM:
   Rim: Everted and slightly thickened, with rounded or flattened lip. Size of sample: 6.
   Body wall thickness: Range 4–7 mm.
   Base: Flat (Form B) and concave (Form C); probably also pedestal (Form A).
   Reconstructed common vessel shapes (fig. 65): Form 1: 100 percent.

OCCASIONAL DECORATION: Most vessels have minor embellishment of one or more of the following kinds:

1. Unsmoothed coils on neck, either left plain or ornamented on the lower half by a row of fingernail marks (pl. 77 d–e).
2. Fingernail marks on the lower edge of exterior rim thickening, overlapping slightly onto adjacent surface. Rarely, fingertip marks are substituted (pl. 77 a–c).
3. Horizontal row of punctates at base of neck, made with stick or fingernail.

TEMPORAL DIFFERENCES WITHIN THE TYPE: None observable.
CHRONOLOGICAL POSITION OF THE TYPE: No evidence.

Cotacocha Red

PASTE AND SURFACE: On Latas Plain (p. 86) or Unclassified Cariapé-tempered Plain (p. 86); see those descriptions for details.

FORM:

Rim: Direct or everted and exteriorly thickened; rounded lip. Size of sample: 3.
Body wall thickness: Range 4–6 mm.
Base: Pedestal (Form A) or annular (Form D).
Reconstructed common vessel shapes (fig. 65):
Form 3: 66.6 percent (2 vessels).
Form 1: 33.3 percent (1 vessel).

DECORATION:

Technique: Application of a thin red coating to all or part of the surface. Wide color variation from orange to red to reddish brown because of unequal thickness and poorly controlled firing. Application may be before or after striated polishing; in the latter case, slip is duller than adjacent surface.
Motif: Two principal categories occur:

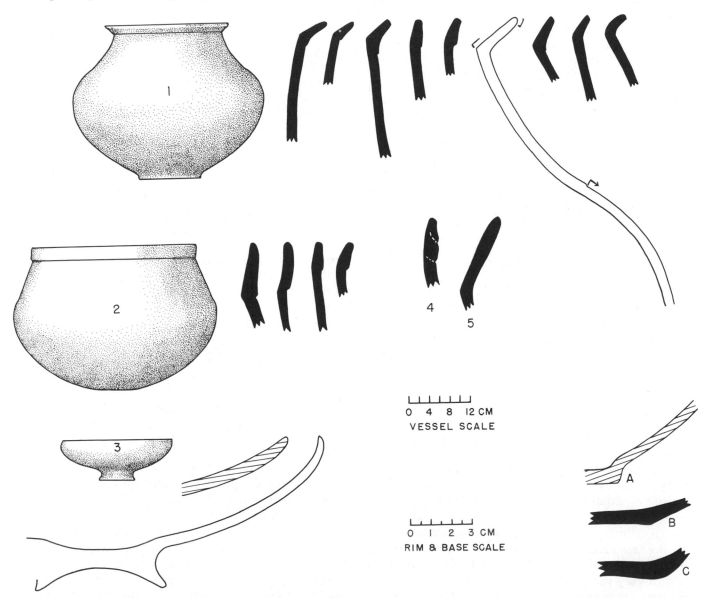

FIGURE 65.—Rim profiles and reconstructed vessel shapes of the Cotacocha Phase. 1–3, Common Forms 1–3. 4–5, Minor Forms 1–2. A–C, Base Forms. Arrows and brackets designate decorated zones. (Black=undecorated, white=decorated, hachure=red slipped.)

1. Slipping of portions of the surface, such as the body and rim leaving the neck bare, characteristic of jars.
2. Curved red bands of finger width filling quadrants, found on bowl interiors.

TEMPORAL DIFFERENCES WITHIN THE TYPE: None observable.

CHRONOLOGICAL POSITION OF THE TYPE: Absent from N–P–14.

Latas Plain

PASTE:

Method of manufacture: Coiling; coils often unobliterated on the exterior for ornamental effect.

Temper: Fine angular sand, grain diameter typically less than 0.5 mm. Color predominantly black, with scattered white quartz and golden iron pyrites particles. Abundant giving speckled appearance to cross-section.

Texture: Fine grained, often laminated with fine crevasses parallel or diagonal to surface.

Color: Typically medium to dark gray throughout the cross-section; rarely light gray. Oxidation may be limited to the surface or penetrate to 2 mm. inward in a band of uniform or fluctuating width along both surfaces.

SURFACE:

Color: Light buff (whitish), light tan, light orange, brownish orange, grayish brown, dark gray to black; color may vary greatly over a small area because of fire clouding. Interior and exterior may be similar shades or at opposite ends of the range.

Treatment: Smoothed superficially leaving unevenness and small defects; sometimes striated polished leaving parallel horizontal smoothing tracks and producing a more compact surface; never polished enough to create luster. Interior tends to be better smoothed than exterior.

Hardness: 4.

FORM:

Rim: Everted and slightly thickened on the exterior, with flattened or rounded lip. Size of sample: 9.

Body wall thickness: Range 3.5–5.0 mm.

Base: Probably pedestal (Form A), flat (Form B), or concave (Form C).

Reconstructed vessel shapes (fig. 65):

Form 2: 55.6 percent.
Form 1: 22.2 percent.
Minor Form 1: 11.1 percent.
Minor Form 2: 11.1 percent.

OCCASIONAL DECORATION (pl. 77 *f–l*): Unobliterated coils and fingernail marks are the same as on Cotacocha Plain (p. 84); see that type description for details.

TEMPORAL DIFFERENCE WITHIN THE TYPE: None observable.

CHRONOLOGICAL POSITION OF THE TYPE: No evidence.

Unclassified Cariapé-tempered Plain

PASTE:

Method of manufacture: Coiling.

Temper: Cariapé, in the form of whitish "bundles" up to 5 mm. long, visible on the surface or in cross-section. Black ash and sand also occur, the latter in smaller proportion than in Cotacocha Plain and Latas Plain.

Texture: Abundant fine air pockets, often occurring at ends of longer temper particles; orientation parallel or perpendicular to surface. Breaks with a very uneven edge.

Color: Dark gray or brown throughout the cross-section, or partly gray and partly brown.

SURFACE:

Color: Tan to dark gray; large black fire clouds.

Treatment: Smoothed leaving broad (about 2 mm. wide) tracks, but with large pits and defects remaining.

Hardness: 2.5.

FORM: Only body sherds are included in the sample; wall thickness 5–10 mm.

TEMPORAL DIFFERENCES WITHIN THE TYPE: None observable.

CHRONOLOGICAL POSITION OF THE TYPE: Absent from N–P–14.

THE SERIATED SEQUENCE AND ITS IMPLICATIONS

The small size and nonstratigraphic origin of pottery samples from Cotacocha Phase sites makes diachronic analysis of the archeological remains impossible (Appendix tables 3 and 5). However, both distributional and historical evidence suggest that the easternmost sites reflect the recent spread of Quechua speaking acculturated Indians down the Napo in very recent times.

Pottery resembling that of the Cotacocha Phase both in vessel shape and in embellishment by un-smoothed coils, fingernail marks and zoned red slip occurs archeologically in the vicinity of Cotundo in the Andean foothills (fig. 1). In this area these elements have some time depth, perhaps extending backward into the pre-European period.

The recent spread of the Quechua language down the Napo has been noted by Ferdon (1950, pp. 4–5). When Alfred Simson travelled in eastern Ecuador before 1886, he found Quechua speaking Indians only as far east as the mouth of the Rio Coca (ibid.).

Since then their area of distribution has extended to the Peruvian border and possibly beyond. Ferdon questions whether this represents peopling of an uninhabited area or displacement of aboriginal pagan groups by Christianized Quechua speakers. Existing archeological evidence favors the former alternative.

DIAGNOSTIC FEATURES OF THE COTACOCHA PHASE

Pottery classified as belonging to the Cotacocha Phase was collected at four locations along the Rio Napo, from Latas to near the Peruvian border, and equates with the historic settlement of the region. The sparsity of sherds and small number of vessels represented reflect both the scattered homestead pattern of modern settlement and the adoption of nonceramic types of containers.

The ceramic complex includes two principal sand-tempered plain types: Cotacocha Plain with completely oxidized firing, and Latas Plain with incompletely oxidized firing. A few cariapé-tempered sherds are associated. Unsmoothed coils and fingernail marks occur on the exterior of most plain vessels. Walls are relatively thin but surfaces are not even or polished. Decoration is restricted to red bands or zones unbounded by incision. Vessel shapes are simple utilitarian forms, including open bowls sometimes with annular base, and globular-bodied jars with insloping to vertical neck and everted rim.

The only artifact associated with the Cotacocha Phase is a spool-shaped object of cariapé-tempered pottery of unknown use.

The Rio Napo Cultural Sequence and Its Implications

An attempt to trace the origin and affiliations of the archeological phases identified on the Rio Napo and its tributaries is a fascinating and frustrating task. It is fascinating because two of the four phases can be equated with complexes that are widely dispersed over northern South America; it is frustrating because so little is known of vast regions, and hypotheses regarding paths of diffusion must be erected on the flimsiest of evidence. Even in the present limited state of knowledge, however, a picture can be sketched that may serve to focus attention on areas where archeological investigation is urgently needed.

The time that man first set foot on the eastern Ecuadorian lowlands may always be a matter of inference from evidence in the adjacent highlands rather than local finds. The combination of dense vegetation, intermittently flooded terrain, riverbank erosion, sediment deposition and dike formation, and availability of perishable material for tools suggests that the probability of preceramic sites being preserved, much less discovered, is infinitesimal. However, it seems reasonable to assume that hunters explored the lowlands along with the highlands as they peopled the continent at least 10,000 years ago and perhaps much earlier.

THE YASUNÍ PHASE

The archeological record on the Rio Napo begins with the introduction of pottery making. The earliest known ceramic complex belongs to the Yasuní Phase, and although negative evidence is never conclusive, its affiliations to early Formative complexes in the Andean region make it likely that it represents the first sedentary pottery-making immigrant group to settle on the banks of the Rio Napo. A single carbon-14 date places this occupation at 2000 ± 90 years ago, or 50 B.C. (SI–300). Two habitation sites were investigated, both shallow and relatively small in area.

A considerable number of distinctive elements characterize the ceramic complex and are useful for tracing the affiliations of the Yasuní Phase. In decoration, these consist of zoned incision (subdivided into fine cross hachure, broad cross hachure, fine parallel hachure, broad outline, patterns of narrow bands or irregular zones) on the flat rim top or exterior wall, broad-line incision, zoned punctation, dot-ended line, dotted line or drag-and-jab punctation, rim lobing, applique rib, nicked rim, and zoned red. Vessel shape details include Yasuní Phase Common Forms 1–9 and features such as angular carination, rounded shoulder, sublabial flange, and annular base.

Examination of the geographical occurrence of these diagnostic Yasuní Phase traits of decoration and vessel shape reveals a remarkable pattern. Complexes possessing a large number of the traits in question (fig. 66) are Waira-jirca and Tutishcainyo, located in the highlands and eastern lowlands of Peru, respectively; Macas in eastern Ecuador; Puerto Hormiga on the Caribbean coast of Colombia; El Mayal and Rio Guapo styles on the Venezuelan coast, and the Jauarí and Ananatuba Phases on the

CERAMIC TRAITS	Puerto Hormiga	Waira-jirca	Jauarí	Ananatuba	Rio Guapo	El Mayal	Tutishcainyo	Macas	Yasuní
COMPLEXES									
DECORATION									
Applique rib							x		x
Broad-line incision	x	x	x	x	x	x	x	x	x
Dot ended line	x	?				x	x		x
Dotted line	x						x		x
Excision	x	x							
Nicked rim				x	x	x	x	x	x
Nicked shoulder							x		x
Rim adornos	x			x	x	x			
Rim lobing	x				x	x	x		x
Zoned incision:									
Fine cross hachure			x	x	x	x	x	x	
Broad cross hachure	x			x			x	x	
Fine parallel hachure	x	x	x	x	x		x		x
Narrow bands	x	x	x	?			x	x	?
Irregular zones	x	x	x	x	x	x	x	x	x
Broad-line border	x	x	x	x	x	x	x	x	x
On flat rim top				x		x	x	x	?
Zoned punctation	x	x							
Zoned red		x					x	x	
VESSEL SHAPE									
Yasuní Phase Forms									
1				x			x		x
2	x			x	x		x		x
3									x
4				x			x		x
5				?					x
6							x	x	x
7							x		x
8							x		x
9								x	x
Bottle		x			x	x	x		?
"Tecomate"	x	x	x	x	x	x			
Angular shoulder				x		x	x		?
Rounded shoulder				x	x	x	x		x
Waist flange							x		
Sublabial flange							x		x
OTHER FEATURES									
Shell temper				x	x		x		
Tubular pipe				x	x				
Shell midden	x		x		x	x			

FIGURE 66.—Occurrence of Yasuní Phase ceramic traits of decoration and vessel shape in other complexes representing the Zoned Hachure Horizon Style (X=present; ?=identification uncertain). Information is derived from the following sources: Macas, Bushnell, 1946; Tutishcainyo, Lathrap, 1962; Waira-jirca, Izumi and Sono, 1963; Puerto Hormiga, Reichel-Dolmatoff, 1965b; Rio Guapo and El Mayal, Cruxent and Rouse, 1958; Jauarí, Hilbert, 1959a; Ananatuba, Meggers and Evans, 1957.

lower Amazon. Only Macas, in the southeastern Ecuadorian highlands, is in relatively close geographical proximity (fig. 67). Except on the Venezuelan coast, each complex is believed to be the earliest in the local ceramic sequence, and where carbon-14 dates have been obtained, they support this placement. The greatest antiquity has been established at Puerto Hormiga, Colombia, with five dates ranging from 4502 ± 250 (I–1123) to 5040 ± 70 (SI–153) years ago (Reichel-Dolmatoff, 1965b, p. 53) or 2552 to 3090 B.C. Next in antiquity is the Waira-jirca Phase at Kotosh, Peru dated between 3180 ± 130 (N–69–2) and 3800 ± 110 (GAK–262) years ago or 1230 to 1850 B.C. A charcoal sample from an Ananatuba Phase site, collected by Mario F. Simões (n.d.), has been dated at 2930 ± 200 (SI–385) years or 980 B.C. The two Venezuelan occurrences, El Mayal and Rio Guapo, are placed by Cruxent and Rouse (1958, pp. 101, 121) in late Period II on stylistic grounds. A carbon–14 date for El Mayal gave 1795 ± 80 (Y–297) years ago or A.D. 155 (op. cit. p. 15).

In 1961, in an attempt to reconstruct on a broad scale the prehistory of the Tropical Forest Area, we proposed the existence of a Zoned Hachure Horizon Style represented by the Tutishcainyo, Yasuní, Jauarí, and Ananatuba complexes (Meggers and Evans, 1961, pp. 375–378). In the absence of carbon-14 dates, and unaware of the existence of the Waira-jirca and Puerto Hormiga complexes, we postulated an Andean origin for this style. More recent information now permits a reexamination of its possible origin and dissemination.

If these complexes are derived from the north coast of South America, as the priority of the Puerto Hormiga dates implies, their wide geographical and chronological separation would be expected to result in stylistic differences. This is indeed the case. However, the patterning of these differences does not coincide with the obvious natural routes connecting known sites. A brief review will illustrate the problem.

Puerto Hormiga pottery, which is dated so much earlier than the other members of this group that it constitutes a potential source of the tradition, combines zoned hachure and broad-line incision with adornos of an incipient Barrancoid style. This combination of traits makes Puerto Hormiga (or a complex derived from it) a logical predecessor for both the southern and eastern representatives. On the Venezuelan coast by the time of El Mayal, zoned hachure is a minor decorated technique and modeling has become dominant (Cruxent and Rouse, 1958, pl. 44). The minimum lapse of some 2700 years between El Mayal and Puerto Hormiga allows sufficient time for much alteration both through cultural drift and through influence from local Venezuelan ceramic styles, so that the survival of zoned hachure and other traits relating to the Yasuní Phase even to a minor degree is rather remarkable. This tradition continues into the lesser Antilles, where zoned hachure and adornos are major elements in the earliest ceramic complex, appearing about the beginning of the Christian era (Bullen, 1965, p. 240).

Diffusion toward the south and the Peruvian highlands appears to have been accompanied by cultural drift in the opposite direction to that along the Venezuelan coast. In the Waira-jirca Phase, modeling is rudimentary or absent and zoned hachure has become the dominant decorative technique (pl. 78 a–l). The Puerto Hormiga trait of applying red pigment to incisions subsequent to firing is frequently used to enhance zones of hachure. Excision has also been retained as a minor decorative technique. Typical Waira-jirca Phase vessel shapes are rounded jars with constricted mouths like those of Puerto Hormiga.

When the effort is made to fit the Tropical Forest occurrences into this dichotomy, the pattern becomes less distinct. Along the lower Amazon, for example, the Jauarí Phase combines bulbous-eyed rim adornos with zoned hachure, aligning it with the Caribbean complexes. This affiliation is strengthened by the fact that the site is a shell midden (as are Puerto Hormiga, Rio Guapo, and El Mayal), and by the presence of tubular pipes, which also occur at Rio Guapo and El Mayal. By contrast, the Ananatuba Phase on Marajó Island at the mouth of the Amazon lacks both modeling and tubular pipes, although the zoned hachure decoration is identical in technique and motif to that of Jauarí Phase ceramics (cf. Meggers and Evans, 1957, pls. 38–41, and Hilbert, 1959a, pp. 13, 15). This situation suggests that the Jauarí Phase is earlier and that the absence of certain traits from the Ananatuba Phase is the result of simplification during diffusion, a frequently observed effect. These traits set the lower Amazonian occurrences apart from those in the west, and suggest that their relationship may be an indirect one, stemming from remote common ancestry, rather than a direct one resulting from west to east diffusion down the Amazon. If the carbon-14 dates are accepted, the greater antiquity of the Ananatuba Phase also rules out derivation from the western lowland complexes (Tutishcunyo and Yasuní).

The three eastern Andean complexes form a somewhat more consistent unit. Although the Tutishcainyo and Yasuní Phases are at least 850 kilometers apart in a direct line, and much more widely separated if natural river routes between them are considered (fig. 67), resemblances in both vessel shape and decoration are numerous. Similarities in decorative elements are particularly striking, considering the

poor surface condition of the Yasuní Phase material. Duplications include parallel stepped lines, drag-and-jab ("dotted") lines, incision terminating in punctation, a row of nicks at the lower edge of the decorated zone, sublabial flange with nicked edge, squared coils, and of course zoned hachure (pl. 78 m–t; table C; Lathrap, 1958, fig. 1). Vessel shapes are more divergent since the strongly carinated shoulders and broad flanges characteristic of the Tutishcainyo complex do not appear to occur in the Yasuní Phase. However, Yasuní Phase Forms 1, 2, 4, and 8 (and possibly 6 and 7) resemble Tutishcainyo vessel shapes, and rims of Yasuní Phase Rare Forms 1, 2, 5, 6, and 8 are represented in the Early Tutishcainyo sample (Lathrap, 1962, table 142).

TABLE C.—*Occurrence of Yasuní Phase decorative elements in Tutishcainyo Phase pottery* (figures refer to Lathrap, 1962)

Traits	Phases		
	Yasuní	Early Tutishcainyo	Late Tutishcainyo
Parallel stepped lines	x	Fig. 31 f–h	Fig. 50c
Drag and jab lines	x	Fig. 23 e, 25	Fig. 43 f, h
Squared coil	x	Fig. 29c	Fig. 41g
Elongated rectangular zones created by vertical connections between straight parallel lines	x	Fig. 25	
Incision terminating in punctate	x	Fig. 28 d–e	
Horizontal parallel lines on rim exterior	x		Fig. 41 d, f
Nicks on lower rim thickening	x		Fig. 41d
Row of nicks at lower edge of decorated zone	x		Fig. 44k
Vertical applique ribs	x		Fig. 44 d–f
Sublabial flange with nicked decoration	x		Fig. 46l
Protuberances at shoulder	x		Fig. 41 h–j

When the chronological distribution of the shared traits in the Tutishcainyo sequence is examined (table C), the closest resemblance is with the Late Tutishcainyo complex. Although there are no carbon-14 dates available for Late Tutishcainyo, its antiquity has been estimated by Lathrap (1965) as prior to 1000 B.C. The Yasuní Phase date of 50 B.C. (SI–300) is considerably more recent than might be expected in view of the numerous similarities between the pottery of the two complexes.

The most accessible source for the Tutishcainyo ceramic complex is the Waira-jirca Phase, the earliest component of the stratigraphic sequence established at Kotosh in the central Peruvian highlands (fig. 67). However, although numerous detailed correspondences can be observed in the zoned-hachure tech-

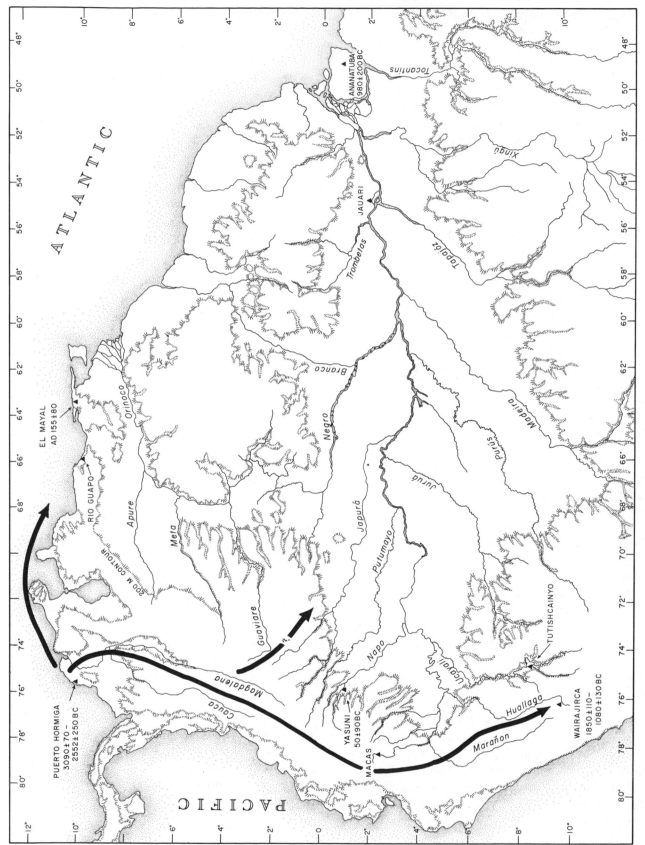

FIGURE 67.—Map of northern South America, showing the location of sites representing the Zoned Hachure Horizon Style.

nique and motif, vessel shapes are less similar. Also, characteristic Tutishcainyo Phase decorative techniques, such as ornamental rim treatment and drag-and-jab or "dotted" lines substituting for incision, are absent from Waira-jirca Phase pottery. A pronounced difference in application of zoned hachure exists in the emphasis on discrete rectanguloid panels on Tutishcainyo pottery, while Waira-jirca designs are dominated by continuous narrow bands (Izumi and Sono, 1963, pls. 81–83). Characteristic features of Tutishcainyo Phase vessel shapes, such as broad horizontal rims and flanges (Lathrap, 1962, figs. 20–29), are not represented in Waira-jirca Phase ceramics. These differences imply the existence of a time gap between the two phases. The Waira-jirca Phase has been dated by carbon-14 between 3180 ± 130 (N–69–2) and 3800 ± 110 (GAK–262) years ago, or 1230–1850 B.C. One date for a complex at site PAC–14 on the Rio Nazaratequi, originally said to have affinities with Late Tutishcainyo, is 1346 ± 110 years or A.D. 604 (P–995), while another sample from 30 centimeters deeper in the same excavation gave 2620 ± 100 years of 670 B.C. (Y–1546). Lathrap (pers. commun.) subsequently rejected these dates as relevant to Tutishcainyo, and continues to support an antiquity of some 4000 years (Lathrap, 1967 p. 17) for the latter. Although speculation will continue until dates for the Tutishcainyo Phase are obtained, the amount of divergence from Waira-jirca suggests that it may be more recent than has been supposed.

The affiliations between Yasuní Phase and Macas pottery are more difficult to evaluate because of deficiencies in the size and condition of both samples. A majority of the Macas sherds is decorated with zoned red, which cannot be identified on Yasuní Phase pottery because of the eroded condition of the surfaces. However, many decorative features are shared and Macas vessel shapes also emphasize everted or exteriorly thickened flat-topped rims, often with lobed lips (Bushnell, 1946, fig. 1 a–o; Collier and Murra, 1943, pl. 7).

An attempt to trace affiliations of Yasuní Phase pottery with other Ecuadorian complexes is inhibited by the vacuum that exists in the data from the highlands for the early time period. On the Ecuadorian Pacific coast, similarities can be noted between some of the Yasuní Phase rim forms and those of the Machalilla Phase. The most significant may be Yasuní Phase Form 9, which has an unusual cambered rim like that of Machalilla Phase Generalized Form 14 (Meggers, Evans, and Estrada, 1965, p.

142). However, the more characteristic flat-topped and exteriorly thickened Yasuní Phase rim varieties are not present on the coast in this early period, and decoration is also different. Zoned hachure occurs in coastal Formative complexes, it is true, but it is executed with a single width of line, setting it apart from the broad border and fine hachure diagnostic of the Yasuní Phase and of the Zoned Hachure Horizon Style in general. Zoning of the latter kind appears in the pottery of Period D of the Valdivia Phase, also on the Ecuadorian coast (Meggers, Evans, and Estrada, 1965, pls. 113 1–s; 114 a–p), but the relatively late date in comparison to that on the north coast of Colombia suggests that this may be derived from a highland representative of the Zoned Hachure Horizon Style rather than serving as a possible source.

This review of the distribution of decoration by zoned hachure, in which the border incisions are wider than those employed for texturing, raises more problems than it resolves. Clusterings of associated elements, particularly vessel shape, as well as carbon-14 dates now available, permit recognition of two paths of diffusion from a north Colombian center. One of these moved southward, probably through the Andean highlands, reaching the Huallaga valley after a lapse of about a millenium (fig. 67). Another moved more slowly eastward along the Venezuelan coast, surviving in places along the eastern coast and in the Lesser Antilles after more than two and a half millenia. Postulation of a third emination either southeastward from the north Colombian center or splitting off from one of the other paths seems necessary to account for the relatively great age of the lower Amazonian Ananatuba Phase, as well as its trait inventory, which deviates from those of the more recent representatives of the two principal disseminations. Although one can speculate that its introduction may have proceeded down the Japurá or the Negro, such hypotheses are essentially meaningless. It is obvious that the distribution of the Zoned Hachure Horizon Style cannot be interpreted satisfactorily until additional evidence has accumulated from portions of northern South America intervening between known occurrences, and a larger number of carbon-14 dates becomes available. The fact that no pottery of this horizon style is included in Nimuendajú's sherd samples from more than 75 sites on the middle and lower Amazon, however, suggests that filling of the distributional gaps may not be an easy task.

THE TIVACUNDO PHASE

A gap of five centuries separates the carbon-14 date for the Yasuní Phase occupation of the Rio Napo from that of the next pottery-making group identified by our survey. This is the Tivacundo Phase, represented at two small sites on the Rio Tiputini. One of these, N–P–8, has been reduced to a remnant by cutting of the river bank, although a site of the Napo Phase (N–P–6) a few meters away is still largely intact (fig. 15). Before carbon-14 dates were obtained, this circumstance was interpreted as evidence that the Tivacundo Phase occupation was the earlier of the two, an inference also supported by the greater degree of deterioration of Tivacundo Phase pottery surfaces. This relative chronology has been confirmed by a carbon-14 date of 1440 ± 70 years or A.D. 510 (SI–330) obtained for N–P–7, the more recent of the two Tivacundo Phase sites in the seriated sequence.

The affiliations of the Tivacundo Phase are obscure. The zoned red decoration is similar in technique to that reported from Macas and the southern Ecuadorian highlands, but details of execution and motif are different. The relatively broad-line incision used to define red zones on Macas sherds contrasts with the extremely fine incision characteristic of Tivacundo Phase decoration. The painting of a red band on top of some fine incisions is a Tivacundo Phase characteristic conceptually similar to the red-retouched incision of the Napo Phase, but in the latter case red was applied to the bed of broader lines. Vessel shapes are unrelated to those of any other complex so far described in the region. Simple rounded bowls and neckless jars are typical, as is a slight modification of the rim giving the effect of beading. Oval as well as circular outline occurs. In spite of the distinctive character of both vessel shape and decoration, no comparable material can be cited either from the highlands or from the lowlands.

THE NAPO PHASE

Identification of the Napo Phase as the third or next to latest in the relative chronological sequence on the Rio Napo is based on circumstantial evidence and carbon-14 dating. The former consists of the physical location of N–P–6 with relation to N–P–8, which has just been reviewed, and the lesser degree of deterioration exhibited by sherd surfaces in comparison to samples of Yasuní and Tivacundo Phase pottery, implying a briefer exposure to the deleterious effects of alternately soaked and baked acid soils. The carbon-14 dates, obtained from carbon extracted from sherds of Tiputini Plain (Evans and Meggers, 1962). are in agreement with this relative position. The two most acceptable are 782 ± 53 years or A.D. 1168 (P–347) and 771 ± 51 years or A.D. 1179 (P–269). The third, which seems too recent (see p. 81), is 470 ± 180 years or A.D. 1480 (SI–299).

The seriated sequence of Napo Phase sites indicates that the ceramic complex was introduced into eastern lowland Ecuador in a fully developed condition. Since all of the decorative variants and vessel shapes are present in the earliest levels (figs. 63–64), all can be used for tracing the origin of the Phase. However, the task is complicated by lack of evidence from the adjacent lowlands. No archeological remains have been described between eastern Ecuador and the vicinity of Tefé, Brazil, some 1900 kilometers downriver or about 1200 kilometers in a straight line (fig. 68), although Lathrap (1967) has reported discovery of several sites around an ox-bow lake on the right bank of the Amazon a little upstream from the Colombian town of Letitia. A similar void extends 850 kilometers to the south, as far as Pucallpa on the Rio Ucayali in the eastern Peruvian lowlands. The entire eastern portion of Colombia is also virtually unknown archeologically.

The highland situation is not much better. While the north highlands of Peru are poorly reported, what has been described fails to include diagnostic Napo Phase elements. Highland Ecuador has also been superficially investigated, but Jijon y Caamaño who had a lifetime of familiarity with the archeology once observed (1951, p. 377) that "the civilization on the upper Napo, near the junction with the Curaray, is completely distinct from those of the Ecuadorian highlands and coast." By contrast, although the highlands of Colombia are also poorly known, existing data attest the presence of many Napo Phase characteristics. These are best represented in the Quimbaya region of the upper Rio Cauca (figs. 68, 79; Cubillos and Bedoya, 1954; Duque, 1963a). A lesser number occur in the San Agustín area. Traits include sand temper, details of vessel shape such as thickened carination, square outline, annular base, anthropomorphic treatment, and possibly channel rim, and decorative techniques such as excision, white retouch, single-line incision, red and black-on-white painting, negative painting and white-on-red painting. Urn burial becomes a typical method of disposal of the dead throughout Colombia by 1000 A.D. (Reichel-Dolmatoff, 1965a, p. 136), and is reported several centuries earlier in the San Agustín region (Duque, 1963b, fig. opp. p. 106). Anthropomorphic urns often have limbs modeled in the round to show swellings resulting from ligatures like those of Napo Phase examples. A vessel from Manizales (Uhle, 1889, pl. 2, fig. 9) resembles Napo Phase Form 6. Unfortunately, these traits are poorly defined both temporally and spacially, although present knowledge suggests that they are all extant at a sufficiently early time to antedate the Napo Phase. Their area of distribution does not appear to extend to the southern Colombian highlands.

By the time of its arrival in eastern Ecuador, the Napo Phase had acquired several ceramic features not reported in the Colombian highlands. Most distinctive of these is tempering with cariapé, obtained by burning the siliceous bark of certain species of trees. Other additions of possible non-highland origin include collared rims, lobed rims, grooving, double-line incision, and the production of pseudo-negative designs by positive painting. The application of a white slip or wash subsequent to incision is also unreported in the highlands, along with red retouch of incisions on a previously white slipped surface. Several of these traits are widespread in the Amazon basin; others are of limited distribution, if present evidence can be relied upon (fig. 68). Their incorporation into the Napo Phase complex is significant in that it suggests an indirect route from the highlands to the Rio Napo, an implication also inherent in the northerly distribution of Napo-like traits in the Colombian highlands.

Tracing of this route is impeded by the absence of information from eastern Colombia and the upper Amazon. Most of the Napo Phase traits have been reported on the middle Amazon between the Rio Japurá and the Rio Negro, but here two features absent in the Napo Phase are characteristically associated—adornos and flanges. A small collection of sherds from the Rio Güepí, a tributary of the Rio Putumayo (fig. 3), incorporates the temper variants characteristic of the Napo Phase (cariapé, black ash, and sand) as well as sherd temper, which makes its appearance on the Amazon at Manacapurú. Un-

fortunately, the only decorated technique represented is red slip (table D). Although the chronological position of this collection is unidentified, it demonstrates that cariapé tempering was employed in south central Colombia. Whether the Napo Phase incised and excised techniques also occur on the upper Putumayo has not yet been established.

TABLE D.—*Frequency of temper varieties in a sherd collection from the Rio Güepí.*

Temper	Surface treatment	
	Plain	Red slipped
Cariapé	74	6
Charcoal	13	4
Sand	5	–
Sherd	1	–
TOTAL	93	10

Most of the ceramic traits diagnostic of the Napo Phase occur along the middle Amazon between the Rio Japurá and the Rio Tapajóz and on the island of Marajó (fig. 68), a distribution that led to the formulation of the Polychrome Horizon Style (Meggers and Evans, 1961, pp. 379–381). Except for limited excavation by Hilbert, documentation is principally in the form of complete vessels and decorated sherds collected over the past century and deposited in museums around the world. Provenience identification is often vague. Where a specific place name is provided, it may be impossible to find on a map. In some cases, several collections with the same provenience are so different in content that they must represent different sites or archeological phases. Other collections incorporate a range of decorative techniques and vessel shapes indicative of mixture, but whether this is the result of reoccupation of the site, amalgamation of different cultural traditions, or careless methods of collection in which samples were mixed by the collector cannot be determined without systematic fieldwork. These inadequacies in contextural data make it necessary to restrict this review to the occurrence of Napo Phase traits, ignoring associated features.

Evidence of the relative or absolute chronological position of these complexes along the Amazon is minimal. Hilbert's work in the Manaus area and that of Meggers and Evans on Marajó, places the Guarita and Marajoara Phases late but prior to European contact (Meggers and Evans, 1961, pp. 379–381). The only available carbon-14 date derives from Hilbert's work at Coarí (Evans and Meggers, 1962, p. 244). Organic temper, in this case spicules of fresh-water sponge or cauixí, extracted from a sample of sherds, gave an age of 800 ± 47 years or A.D. 1150 (P–373). This is nearly contemporary with the earliest Napo Phase date of A.D. 1168 (P–347).

Major locations from which Napo Phase (Polychrome Horizon Style) traits have been reported will be reviewed in alphabetical order. Locations are shown on figure 68 and traits are summarized on figure 79, where the arrangement is in geographical order from west to east.

Beruri, Rio Purús

ARCHEOLOGICAL REMAINS.—Two vessels in the custody of the Instituto Geográfico e Histórico do Amazonas, Manaus, are from Beruri near the mouth of the Rio Purús. One is an anthropomorphic urn with a flat bottom, rounded shoulders, tall concave-walled neck, and slightly everted rim. The surface is badly eroded and retains no traces of slip or ornamentation. The lid has the form of a rounded bowl whose mouth diameter coincides with that of the jar rim. One side bears an anthropomorphic face framed by a relief band; eyes and nose are also relief (mouth area is broken off). The lid surface retains traces of white slip. Due to inability to remove specimens from the exhibit case, the measurements are approximate. Jar height is about 38 cm.; lid height about 10 cm.

The second vessel is a deep bowl mounted on a tall ring base. The sides of the bowl are flattened producing a squarish outline. The exterior was decorated with broad (5–8 mm. wide) grooves prior to the addition of a white slip. Traces of black painting remain between the grooves. The pattern includes a stylized

face with eyes and nose in low relief. Total height is about 24.5 cm.

REFERENCES.—None.

Boca do Xavier, Rio Urubú

ARCHEOLOGICAL REMAINS.—A collection of about 100 sherds from the lower Rio Urubú, a small tributary of the left bank of the Amazon (fig. 68), was deposited by Nimuendajú in the Göteborg Museum. A variety of decorative techniques of non-Napo Phase affiliation are represented, but a few sherds represent waist flanges with grooved decoration like that reported from other middle Amazonian locations. Surfaces are typically red or white slipped subsequent to incision. Incision with a single- or double-pointed tool also occurs, as do small adornos. Broad everted rims and flanges may be lobed. Temper is cariapé or cauixí.

REFERENCES.—None.

Coarí Region

ARCHEOLOGICAL REMAINS.—The ceramic complex in the vicinity of Coarí, on the right bank of the Amazon (fig. 68), has been defined by Hilbert (n.d.). Detailed analysis of sherd samples from stratigraphic tests reveals many similarities to Napo Phase pottery. Cariapé, cauixí, and charcoal temper occur; sand was not employed. Decoration is predominantly grooved (pl. 79 *b–f, h–i*), with the surface sometimes subsequently white (pl. 79*a*) or red slipped. Other techniques include single-line incision (pl. 79 *l–m*), excision and painting (red-on-white, black-on-white,

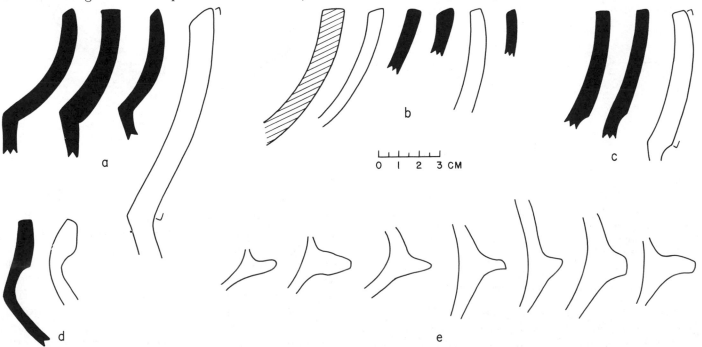

FIGURE 69.—Rim and body profiles of sherds from the Coarí region. (Courtesy Peter Paul Hilbert; black=undecorated, white=decorated, hachure=red slipped.)

red and orange-on-white, red and black-on-white; 79 *g, j–k*), Adornos are rare. Painted designs are poorly preserved but several suggest the pseudo-negative technique.

A number of features of vessel shape duplicate those of the Napo Phase. Among these are channel rims (fig. 69*a*; Napo Phase Form 10), collared rims (fig. 69*c*; Napo Phase Form 16), shallow bowls with direct rim (fig. 69*b*; Napo Phase Form 12) and vessels with a thickened carination or, more typically, a waist flange (fig. 69*e*; Napo Phase Forms 7–10), usually with a notched edge. Exteriorly thickened rims (fig. 69*d*), probably associated with the flanges, resemble Napo Phase Form 7. The flat lip characteristic of vessels from the Coarí region is also paralleled in the Napo Phase. Base forms include all Napo Phase varieties. Although the small size of most sherds makes contour difficult to recognize with certainty, one base suggests a square outline.

Other sources add little to the details furnished by Hilbert's work. However, a small globular vessel illustrated by Cruls (1942, pl. 12, lower left) is of interest because it possesses a square orifice. The exterior is covered with grooved decoration.

REFERENCES.—Cruls, 1942, p. 213 and pl. 12; Hanke, 1959, pp. 43–50 and figs. 15–27; Hilbert, n.d.

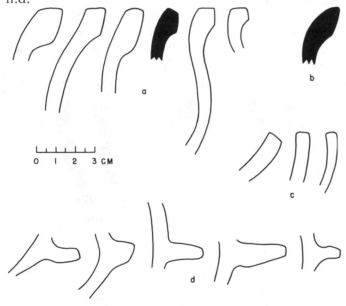

FIGURE 70.—Rim and body profiles of sherds from the Guarita Phase. (Courtesy Peter Paul Hilbert; black=undecorated, white=decorated.)

Guarita Phase (Manaus)

ARCHEOLOGICAL REMAINS.—Construction of an oil refinery near Manaus has destroyed a site belonging to the Polychrome Horizon Style. Hilbert (1959b) was able to make two small stratigraphic tests in a remnant of the site, and a surface collection. The site area was reported to have been 200–300 meters in diameter. Guarita Phase pottery is cauixí or cariapé tempered. Decoration is by grooving (pl. 80 *a–j*) prior to addition of a white slip, polychrome painting (red and black-on-white, red and orange-on-white), red-on-white painting, and less commonly, incision with a single- or double-pointed tool. Polychrome painting may embellish grooved designs. Adornos are rare.

Vessel shape characteristics include broad everted rims (pl. 80*k*), sometimes with lobes, and prominent waist flanges with notched or plain edges (fig. 70*d*; pl. 80 *l–m*). Thickened carination is rare. Some sherds appear to represent vessels with flattened sides, but truly square examples have not been noted. Shallow bowls with flat lip (fig. 70*c*) and rims of Napo Phase Forms 7 and 8 can be recognized (fig. 70 *a–b*).

REFERENCES.—Hilbert, 1959b; Métraux, 1930, pp. 154–165.

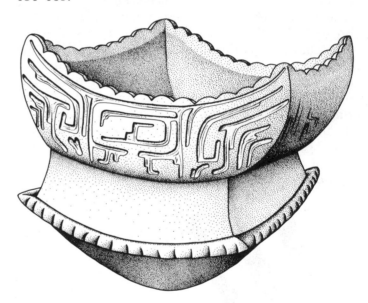

FIGURE 71.—Excised vessel from Ilha dos Muras. (After Barbosa Rodrigues, 1891, pl. 8–1.)

Ilha dos Muras

ARCHEOLOGICAL REMAINS.—Two complete vessels described and illustrated in the last century by Barbosa Rodrigues combine typical Napo Phase characteristics with alien elements. They originate from Ilha dos Muras, just above the mouth of the Rio Negro (fig. 68). One is a square basin with a tall pedestal base, the exterior of which is covered with excised decoration more reminiscent of the Marajoara Phase than of the Napo Phase examples. The description suggests it may be red slipped and white retouched. The second is a square vessel with a channel rim rising to peaks at the corners, a flange or thickened carination, and a pointed bottom (fig. 71). The exterior of the collar is covered with excision resembling that on Napo Phase examples (e.g., fig. 47).

REFERENCES.—Barbosa Rodrigues, 1891–1892, pp. 28–32 and pl. 8, figs. 1 and 2.

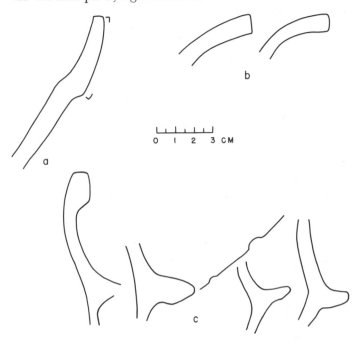

FIGURE 72.—Rim and flange profiles of decorated sherds from Itacoatiara, Guajará (Museu Paulista, São Paulo).

Itacoatiara

ARCHEOLOGICAL REMAINS.—Hilbert has investigated a large habitation site underlying the western half of the town of Itacoatiara, on the left bank of the Amazon about 100 kilometers below Miracanguera (fig. 68). The aboriginal occupation area extends for about 800 meters along the bank and about 200 meters inland. The pottery is cauixí tempered, and decorated with single-line (pl. 81 *j–k*) and double-line incision (pl. 81 *l–p*), grooving (pl. 81 *q–r*), excision (pl. 81 *a–f*), painting (red and black or red and orange-on-white) and modeling in the form of small zoomorphic or geometric adornos. Some examples are white slipped after incision (pl. 81 *g–i*). Fine incisions may be filled with red or yellow pigment. Vessel shapes have little in common with Napo Phase forms, but broad everted rims, sometimes lobed, occur (fig. 72*b*), along with vestigial channel forms (fig. 72*a*). A single hollow rim represents the westernmost reported occurrence of this form. Waist flanges are common (fig. 72*c*).

An anthropomorphic urn illustrated by Netto (1885, pl. 5A, fig. 3) resembles examples from the nearby site of Miracanguera. It has a low pedestal base, wide rounded shoulders and slightly concave walls. A specially made bowl-like lid covers the orifice. A stylized face on the upper side of the neck is the only anthropomorphic detail. The exterior is white slipped and probably was polychrome painted.

Two large sherd collections were made at Itacoatiara by Harald Schultz in 1955 and deposited in the Museu Paulista, São Paulo, Brazil. One, from Barrio Colónia, consists predominantly of adornos and sherds decorated by finely incised lines, although certain traits of the Polychrome Horizon Style are represented (such as excision, double-line incision, and white slipping). The other collection, labeled "Itacoatiara, Guajará", includes grooving, excision, single-line and double-line incision, red-on-white painting, and white slipping subsequent to grooving, as well as ring impression, dentate stamping, and punctation. In both samples, tempering is cauixí.

REFERENCES.—Hilbert, 1959b; Netto, 1885, p. 548 and pl. 5A, fig. 3.

Rio Japurá

ARCHEOLOGICAL REMAINS.—Potsherds and complete vessels are reported to occur at a number of locations along the Rio Japurá, but none is identified with sufficient precision to permit location on a map. Hanke visited several sites between the mouth and the Colombian border. Most of the illustrated sherds are geometric and zoomorphic rim adornos. However, a number of Napo Phase characteristics are associated, including grooved decoration, lobed rim treatment, waist flanges, black-on-white painting, single-line incision and possibly double-line incision (although the drawings are not clear). Broad everted rims are typical.

An anthropomorphic urn from the lower Japurá above Maparí has been described by Métraux. The stylized face resembles that of some Napo Phase urns, as does the general vessel form (cf. fig. 68).* Limbs are absent. The orifice is covered with a bowl-shaped lid made for the purpose. The jar exterior is white slipped and a broad red band encircles the waist. Height is 42 cm., maximum diameter 37.5 cm., and body wall thickness 1 cm. Hilbert (1962b, p. 465), who later visited the Maparí site, reports the ceramic complex to be "a cauixí tempered ware with painting in red and black on white, grooving and flanges around the area of maximum body diameter by open bowls. Modeling is rare and seems to be limited to an-

---

* The Amazonian distribution of this style of anthropomorphic vessel has been reviewed by Imbelloni (1950, p. 148, footnote 83), who suggests that the diffusion proceeded from east to west.

thropomorphic burial urns." No other sites of this tradition were found by Hilbert in a survey extending upstream for 350 kilometers, although he found it characteristic "in most of the sites around the mouth of the Japurá as well as around Tefé" (ibid.).

Another collection of sherds from various locations along the Rio Japurá was made by A. Melchoir and deposited in the Koninklijk Instituut voor de Tropen in Holland (Feriz, 1963, pp. 150–151). Particularly interesting is a rim lobe with anthropomorphic eye treatment, and grooved and polychrome decoration reminiscent of Rocafuerte Incised designs on the flaring walls of basins of Form 14 (frontispiece; pl. 42; op. cit., fig. 13). This sherd was obtained 350 kilometers above the mouth of the Japurá (op. cit., p. 168). Other fragments exhibit such Napo Phase elements as square outline (op. cit., figs. 3, 9) and thickened carination (op. cit., figs. 9–10). One location specifically mentioned is a site on the bank of Lago Amaná, some distance inland from the left bank of the Japurá near the mouth (fig. 68). Burial urns were observed eroding out of the ground (op. cit., fig. 1), and a fragment of face (op. cit., fig. 11) suggests that some may have been anthropomorphic. A rim sherd with excised decoration on the exterior and a "not quite circular opening" was obtained in the vicinity (op. cit., p. 165 and fig. 5). Adornos also occur (op. cit., figs. 19–22).

REFERENCES.—Feriz, 1963; Hanke, 1959, pp. 51–60 and figs. 28–43; Hilbert, 1962b; Métraux, 1930, pp. 165–166 and fig. 35.

Lago Araça Region

ARCHEOLOGICAL REMAINS.—A surface collection made by Hilbert at Lago Araça, about 80 kilometers west of Codajas on the left bank of the Amazon (fig. 68), incorporates a number of traits allying it with the complex at Coarí, and more remotely with the Napo Phase. Cauixí temper predominates over cariapé, while a few sherds contain charcoal or clay (crushed sherd?). Decorated techniques include double-line incision, excision, grooving, and single-line incision. Slipping is not reported and red painting is rare.

Among Napo Phase elements of vessel shape, channel rims (fig. 73a) and collared rims (fig. 73c) are rare. A few rims resemble Napo Phase Forms 7 and 8 (fig. 73b) and are probably associated with body sherds showing thickened carination (fig. 73d) or waist flanges (fig. 73d). Numerous sherds represent square vessels, some with rounded rather than flat sides, but one exhibits the pointed corners and concave sides of some Napo Phase examples. Grooved decora-

tion frequently extends onto the flange, terminating in notches on the edge.

A small rounded jar with a slightly everted rim, decorated on the exterior with incision and excision, has been reported by Barbosa Rodrigues from "above Cudayas," possibly from the same site investigated by Hilbert. It is tempered with cauixí.

REFERENCES.—Barbosa Rodrigues, 1877; Hilbert, n.d.

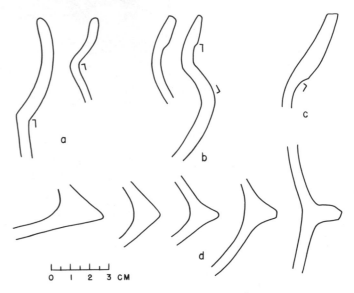

FIGURE 73.—Rim and body profiles of decorated sherds from the Lago Araça region (Courtesy Peter Paul Hilbert). Brackets designate decorated zones.

Rio Madeira

ARCHEOLOGICAL REMAINS.—Two small pottery samples collected by Nimuendajú and separately cataloged in the Göteborg Museum both seem from the description to be from Guajará on the lower Rio Madeira (fig. 68). One sample contains six sherds, all cauixí tempered, exhibiting flanges, a large rim lobe and grooved decoration. The other sample totals ten sherds, principally zoomorphic and anthropomorphic adornos, sometimes accompanied by incision. Sherd tempering is characteristic. A fragment of a cylindrical stamp is included.

Several anthropomorphic urns of the style associated with Miracanguera but attributed to sites on the lower Rio Madeira are in the collection of the Instituto Geográfico e Histórico do Amazonas, Manaus. One, from the Rio Ipixuna, has a flaring pedestal base, angular shoulder and insloping walls free of anatomical detail (pl. 89c). The head forms the lid, and bears an anthropomorphic face framed by a relief band. Nose and mouth are low relief; eyes are narrow horizontal incisions. Eyes and mouth are outlined with paint, which also ornaments the rest of the face. The vessel is covered with a polished white slip and painted with black lines in the pseudo-negative technique. Jar height is about 21 cm., lid height about 7 cm. Another with similar painted decoration (pl. 89d) is of unknown provenience.

Three other urns in the same collection are from Nova Olinda. One is very similar both in form and anthropomorphic treatment to that from the Rio Ipixuna. Another has a flaring base, low rounded shoulders, and a tall vertical-walled neck (pl. 89b). The surface of this neck was decorated with broad (4–5 mm. wide) grooves before the application of a thick white slip, which filled and rendered almost invisible the grooved decoration. Its presence is now revealed by the eroded condition of the surface. The head, which forms the lid, has an elaborate relief band framing the face. The glass exhibit case could not be opened so measurements are approximate. Jar height is about 45 cm., lid height about 17 cm. The third vessel has lost the head-lid. Anthropomorphic detail on the body is relatively realistic, including low relief arms, high relief lower legs and free modeled feet. Breasts are low nubbins, navel a raised ring with a depressed center, and genitalia a triangular relief. Traces of a complicated pattern in fine and medium reddish brown lines remain on the white slipped surface. Relief is bordered by broad red bands. Jar height is about 54 cm.

REFERENCES.—None.

Manacapurú

ARCHEOLOGICAL REMAINS.—The modern settlement of Manacapurú is on the left bank of the Solimões above the mouth of the Rio Negro (fig. 68). Hilbert undertook a small stratigraphic test here, which produced more than 2000 sherds. Cauixí is the principal temper, but cariapé and crushed sherd also occur. Decoration includes grooving, single-line and double-line incision, and red-on-white (rarely, red and orange-on-white) painting. Some examples were red slipped prior to incision. Vessel shapes are simple and not reminiscent of Napo Phase forms.

Other collections from the Manacapurú region, however, show closer affiliations to the Napo Phase. Hanke investigated four locations, which are not separately identified in the sherd sample deposited in the Museu Paulista. This sample includes grooved, excised, single-line incised and painted (red and black-on-white) decoration, as well as lobed rims, and zoomorphic and anthropomorphic adornos. Red or white slipping occurs subsequent to grooving. Temper is sherd, cariapé, or cauixí. Thickened

carinations and flanges with notched ornamentation are typical. Some vessels are noncircular. Hanke (1959, p. 41) reports the existence of secondary urn burial.

Additional evidence comes from decorated sherds deposited by Harald Schultz and Geraldo Pinheiro in the Museu Paulista. Included are fragments with typical Napo Phase decoration, both in technique and motif, among them single-line and double-line incision (pl. 82 g–h, j), excision (pl. 82 c–d, f), black-on-white

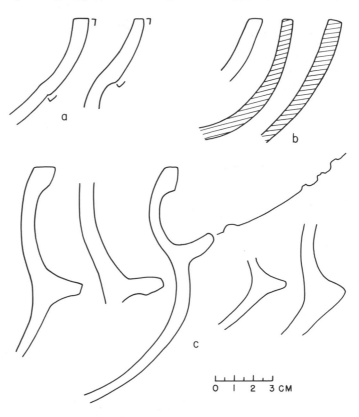

FIGURE 74.—Rim and body profiles of sherds from Manacapurú (Museu Paulista, São Paulo). Brackets designate decorated zones. (White=decorated, hachure=red slipped.)

(pl. 82l), and polychrome (red and black-on-white) painting (pl. 82k). Other Napo Phase characteristics include red or white slipping subsequent to grooving or incision (pls. 82 a–b, e, i, 83a), and a tendency to square shape (pl. 83b). Several specimens have prominent flanges (fig. 74c; pls. 82 b, e, 83a). Flat and cylindrical stamps with deeply grooved or excised designs are associated. A number of features of vessel shape duplicate those of the Napo Phase. Among these are channel rims (fig. 74a), shallow bowls with direct rims (fig. 74b), exteriorly thickened rims (fig. 74c) associated with waist flanges, and both plain and lobed waist flanges (fig. 74c; pls. 82 b, e, 83a).

REFERENCES.—Hanke, 1959, pp. 37–43 and figs. 1–14; Hilbert, n.d.

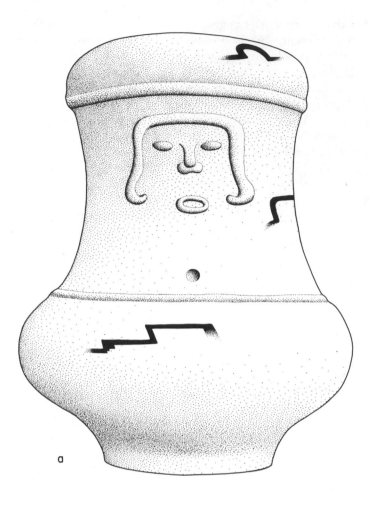

FIGURE 75.—Anthropomorphic urns with painted decoration from Miracanguera. Measurements not provided on original drawings. *a*, Anthropomorphic urn with face on neck and with a lid. *b*, Jar with face on flange and with a pedestal base. (After Barbosa Rodrigues, 1891, pls. 3–1 and 3–4.)

Marajoara Phase (Marajó)

ARCHEOLOGICAL REMAINS.—Numerous sites on the eastern half of the island of Marajó at the mouth of the Amazon (fig. 68) have produced a ceramic complex that has long commanded attention (Meggers and Evans, 1957, pp. 259–324) because of the variety and complexity of decoration (pls. 84–87, 88*b*). The existence of large samples from stratigraphic testing (ibid.; Hilbert, 1952; Figueiredo and Simões, 1963), as well as numerous surface sherds and complete vessels, permits more accurate identification of Napo Phase traits than is possible in any other part of the Amazon basin. Few of the features selected for distributional analysis are absent (fig. 79). These are decoration by double-line incision,* grooving, negative painting, white-on-red painting, and white slipping subsequent to incision; channel and collared rims, waist flanges, and anthropomorphic urns with the separable head serving as the lid. Tempering is by crushed sherd. Although cariapé has been reported by Mordini (1947, p. 640) in some sherds from Pacoval, this identification has not been verified by other observers. It is interesting because of the association of cariapé with the Polychrome Horizon Style farther up the Amazon, and because of the relatively early position of Pacoval in the Marajoara Phase seriated sequence (Meggers and Evans, 1957, fig. 141). Complete vessels from Pacoval exhibit other survivals of traits more common upriver, such as flattening of the sides of circular bowls (pl. 86) and modeling of limbs with swollen calves on anthropomorphic jars (pl. 88*b*).

REFERENCES.—Figueiredo and Simões, 1963; Hilbert, 1952; Meggers and Evans, 1957, pp. 259–404; Mordini, 1947; Palmatary, 1950.

Miracanguera

ARCHEOLOGICAL REMAINS.—One of the earliest sites to be reported from the middle Amazon is Miracanguera, on the left bank approximately opposite the mouth of the Rio Madeira (fig. 68), where Barbosa Rodrigues collected numerous burial urns nearly a century ago. At that time the cemetery was inundated during the rainy season, and when the water receded "on the beach, thousands of potsherds attest the great number of burial urns destroyed by the collapse of the bank, to be carried in fragments and interred in the bottom of the river" (Barbosa Rodriques, 1892, p. 2). The urns are typically large jars with flat,

---

* Guajará Incised, a late Marajoara Phase decorated type, employs a different kind of double-line incision from that characterizing the Napo Phase.

annular or pedestal base, low rounded shoulders and insloping neck (figs. 75–76; pl. 89a). Anthropomorphic details include stylized arms and legs, often partly in the round, and a face either on the neck (fig. 75a), on the lid (pl. 89a) or on a lobe extending vertically from the rim (fig. 75b). The surface is white slipped and painted with red and black. One example in the

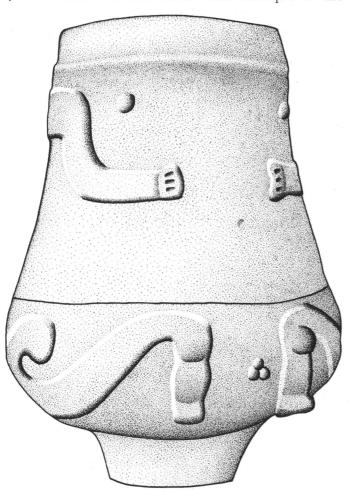

FIGURE 76.—Anthropomorphic urn from Miracanguera. Measurement not provided on original. (After Barbosa Rodrigues, 1891, pl. 2–8.)

Museu Paulista (pl. 88a) of slightly different style, is painted in the pseudo-negative technique typical of the Napo Phase. Other decorative techniques include grooving, with the surface subsequently white slipped and the grooves painted with red, single-line incision, and adornos. Napo Phase vessel shapes include shallow bowls with flat lip, channel rims, and small vessels with exteriorly thickened rims and waist flanges or thickened carination. Ovoid or boat shapes occur, but square vessels have not been reported. Zoomorphic forms combine painting and modeled animal heads and tails (fig. 77).

REFERENCES.—Barbosa Rodrigues, 1891–1892; Nordenskiöld, 1930, pp. 22–3 and pl. xxvi, f.

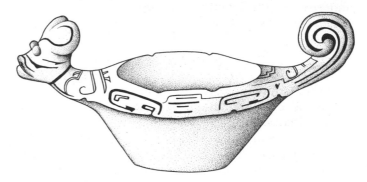

FIGURE 77.—Zoomorphic vessel from Miracanguera with red and black-on-white painted decoration. Length from nose to tail circa 24 cm. (After Barbosa Rodrigues, 1891, pl. 3–7.)

Mocajatuba, Rio Urubú

ARCHEOLOGICAL REMAINS.—Nimuendajú collected 157 sherds from an island in Lago Saracá on the lower course of the Rio Urubú (fig. 68), which are now in the collections of the Göteborg Museum. Although the complex generally relates more closely to that at Itacoatiara than to more typical members of the Polychrome Horizon Style, it incorporates such elements as excision, single-line and double-line incision, red and orange-on-white and red-on-white painting, red-retouched incision on a white slipped surface, and small adornos. Some fine incisions are white filled. Broad horizontal rims, sometimes lobed, occur but flanges are unrepresented. There is one annular base. Several rim adornos appear to be from the corners of square bowls. Temper is cariapé or cauixí.

REFERENCES.—None.

Nazaré dos Patos

ARCHEOLOGICAL REMAINS.—Samples in the Göteborg Museum, collected by Nimuendajú from three sites on the lower Rio Tocantins, contain a number of Polychrome Horizon Style features. The largest sample, some 350 sherds, is from Nazaré dos Patos, on the right bank (fig. 68). A remarkably large number of Napo Phase decorative techniques are present, including grooving typically done with a double-pointed or serrated tool (pl. 90 a–h) and excision (pl. 90 i–j) associated with plain, white or red slipped surfaces, and sometimes red or white retouched. Surface erosion sometimes makes it uncertain whether a white slip was applied after grooving (pl. 90f, h) or the cuts were white filled. Grooving is rare, as is red-on-white painting. Adornos are typically small. Temper is predominantly sand, and rarely cariapé. Elements of vessel shape include broad everted rims with lobed or irregular lip, hollow rims, and slightly thickened carinations.

REFERENCES.—None.

Rio Padauirí

ARCHEOLOGICAL REMAINS.—One fragmentary vessel in the collection of the Museu Paraense Emilio Goeldi is attributed to the Rio Padauirí, an affluent of the left bank of the Rio Negro (fig. 68). It has a prominently thickened carination and grooved decoration covers the upper wall. This is the northernmost reported occurrence of these traits in the Amazon basin.

REFERENCES.—None.

Paurá

ARCHEOLOGICAL REMAINS.—A collection of 84 sherds in the Göteborg Museum, acquired by Nimuendajú from Paurá on the left bank of the Amazon below the mouth of the Rio Uatumá (fig. 68), is of interest principally for the presence of several broad everted rims with excised decoration (pl. 91 a–c). Single-line incision prior to red slipping of the surface, and small adornos are also typical. Some vessels have annular bases. Tempering is cauixí or cariapé.

REFERENCES.—None.

Poço do Jaburú

ARCHEOLOGICAL REMAINS.—A small sample of decorated sherds in the Museu Paulista was collected from Poço do Jaburú, tentatively placed in the vicinity of Anamã on the left bank of the Solimões below the mouth of the Rio Purús (fig. 68). All are cauixí tempered. Decorative techniques include excision, grooving, single-line incision on a plain or red slipped surface, double-line incision and red-on-white painting. Thickened carination and flanges are typical.

REFERENCES.—None.

Ponta Negra, Rio Negro

ARCHEOLOGICAL REMAINS.—While in Manaus in 1966, we were able to visit a site on the left bank of the Rio Negro just below the mouth of the Igarapé Taruma (fig. 68). Surface sherds extended along the summit of the bank for about 650 meters, and inland to a maximum of 150 meters. Elevation of the bank above river level in June, at the beginning of the dry season, was about 15 meters. The habitation deposit has been badly disturbed by excavation of sand for road construction, but original depth appears not to have exceeded 10 cm. The soil is white sand, discolored gray in the occupation layer.

A large surface collection was made. Temper is sand or cariapé. Decorative techniques and vessel shapes indicate this site to belong to the Guarita Phase. Decoration is by single-line incision, painting (red-on-white, black-on-white, or red and black-on-white), or grooving, with the latter predominant. Grooved designs were often subsequently white or red slipped, and sometimes embellished with black-on-white painted decoration. Vessel shapes include Napo Phase Forms 1 (fig. 78a), 7 (fig. 78b), 8 (fig. 78c), 10 (fig. 78e), 11 (fig. 78f), 12 (fig.78g), and 14 (fig. 78i), and Rare Forms 2 and 4. A common rim may have evolved from Napo Phase Form 9, with a flat upper surface replacing the channel (fig. 78d). Other similarities to Napo Phase vessel shapes include the annular base, lobed rim, noncircular outline, thickened carination and waist flange (fig. 78h).

Although the Polychrome Horizon Style has been guess-dated prior to European contact (Meggers and Evans, 1961, fig. 7), several blue and white glass "seed" beads were collected from the surface of Ponta Negra. Association is not conclusive since fragments of European china, tile, and glass were also collected from the surface, indicating reoccupation in recent times.

REFERENCES.—None.

Pontão, Rio Urubú

ARCHEOLOGICAL REMAINS.—The Göteborg Museum has 59 sherds collected by Nimuendajú from a site on the north shore of Lago Saracá on the lower Rio Urubú (fig. 68), probably representing the same complex as at Mocajutuba. Temper is cauixí. Decoration includes excision (pl. 91f), single-line and double-line incision (pl. 91e), grooving (pl. 91g), red and black-on-white painting, and small adornos. Vessel shape details include broad everted rims, often lobed, flanges, and possibly square outline.

REFERENCES.—None.

Santarem Area

ARCHEOLOGICAL REMAINS.—The Göteborg Museum collections made by Nimuendajú, represent a number of localities around Santarem, which produced typical Santarem style ceramics. However, a few sherds appear to belong to the Polychrome Horizon, suggesting that there may be sites of this occupation in the area. Diagnostic features include single-line (pl. 92 h–l) and double-line incision (pl. 92 a–g), red and black-on-white painting, broad everted rims, flanges, thickened carinations, and annular bases. One lobed rim has an incised design with a touch of excision. Adornos are abundant. All types of temper are present: sand, crushed sherd, cariapé, and cauixí. A fragment of a vessel with excised decoration and a flange is illustrated by Feriz (1963, fig. 14).

REFERENCES.—Feriz, 1963.

Tauaquera, Rio Anibá

ARCHEOLOGICAL REMAINS.—Two small collections deposited by Nimuendajú in the Göteborg Museum are from Tauaquera, on the left bank of the Rio Anibá near its mouth (fig. 68). Although cataloged separately, they may be from the same location. Each contains 35 sherds. Temper is sand, sherd, cariapé, or cauixí. Decoration includes excision (pl. 91*d*), grooving, incision with a single-pointed tool, and adornos. Broad everted rims and one hollow rim occur. Other sherds are decorated with relief and punctation, which do not form part of the Polychrome Horizon Style.

REFERENCES.—None.

Tefé Region

ARCHEOLOGICAL REMAINS.—Several kinds of decorated sherds are reported from the vicinity of the confluence of the Rio Tefé and the right bank of the Amazon (fig. 68). An anthropomorphic head about 11 cm. high, broken off at the neck, is interpreted by Métraux (1930, pp. 146–147 and fig. 1) as a figurine because of the absence of an opening in the top. Its size suggests, however, that it may represent an urn with the orifice in the bottom like many Napo Phase examples. The surface is white slipped but no traces of painting are noted except touches of red on the mouth and ears. Other pottery from this region described by Métraux consists of anthropomorphic and zoomorphic adornos.

Two vessels, one complete and one fragmentary, originate from Lago Macupy, located by Hébert (1907, p. 185) "near the Japurá" and by Métraux (1930, pl 152) on the Rio Tefé. The fragment represents an anthropomorphic seated vessel with limbs modeled in the round and hands on the knees. The head is superficially demarcated from the rounded

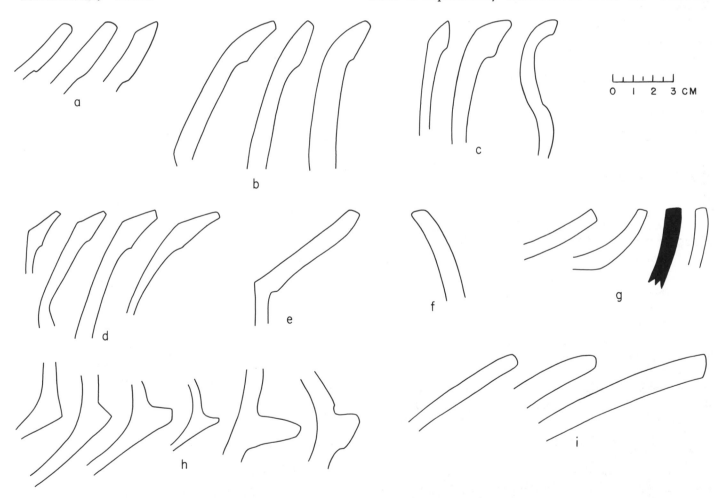

FIGURE 78.—Rim and body profiles of sherds from Ponta Negra, Rio Negro. (Black=undecorated, white=decorated.)

body, and features are crudely modeled. Sex is male. The other vessel is an ovoid jar with constricted neck and everted rim. The shoulder is decorated with a pattern of concentric diamonds and coils executed by broad deep grooves. Small zones of punctation are associated, possibly previously excised (Métraux, 1930, pl. II).

A number of sherds from the Tefé region in the Koninklijk Instituut vor de Tropen in Holland have been described by Feriz (1963). Napo Phase features include excision (op. cit., pp. 170–171 and figs. 26–7), red-on-white painting (op. cit., p. 171 and fig. 28), and an anthropomorphic face framed by an elevated band (op. cit., fig. 12). Several different sites are represented, some of which also produced adornos (op. cit., figs. 17–18).

Two collections made by Harald Schultz from the Rio Tefé are in the Museu Paulista. One, from Abial, Lago Tefé, includes white slipped, excised (pl. 93 a–c) and grooved (pl. 93 d–h) decorative techniques. The other, from Boca de Tefé, includes single- and double-line incision, excision, grooving, red-on-white painting, and rim adornos. All sherds are cauixí tempered.

REFERENCES.—Feriz, 1963; Hanke, 1959, p. 51; Hébert, 1907; Hilbert, 1962a; Métraux, 1930.

Significance of the Distributional Pattern

When the occurrences of the principal Napo Phase ceramic features of temper, decoration, and form are arranged in geographical order (fig. 79), a pattern of west to east diffusion emerges. In order to show this more clearly, the traits have been divided into three general groups: (1) those present in highland Colombia and in the Napo Phase; (2) those not reported for highland Colombia but present in the Napo Phase; and (3) those absent in the Napo Phase but associated with the Polychrome Horizon Style along the Amazon. Within each of these groups, traits have been arranged in order of increasing downriver occurrence.

Evaluation of the distributional pattern must take into consideration the incompleteness of the data, which probably accounts for the spotty occurrence of many traits between the Rio Napo and the island of Marajó. At these two extremes, the ceramic complex is known from large and systematically collected and analyzed samples, whereas the intervening sites are often represented by a few complete vessels or a handful of selected sherds, and even these may not be described in detail. Decorative effects such as white slipping subsequent to incision, red retouch of incisions, white retouch of incision or

excision, or color of painted designs often cannot be detected on illustrations and are rarely described. In consideration of such factors, it is probably safe to assume that most, if not all, of the traits would have less broken distributions if the evidence were more complete. It is also predictable that many traits now in Group 2 will be reported from highland Colombia when the pottery there is better known and has been better described.

In spite of the distance separating the Rio Napo from the island of Marajó in the mouth of the Amazon, resemblances between Napo Phase and Marajoara Phase ceramics are numerous and striking. Similarities extend beyond duplication of nearly all decorative techniques, to details of motif (Meggers and Evans, 1958, figs. 3–5). The correspondence is heightened by the absence or extreme rarity in these two complexes of two prominent features associated with the Polychrome Horizon Style throughout the middle Amazon: adornos and flanges. The obtrusive grooved decoration of the intervening area is also little in evidence.

Marajoara Phase pottery, although employing the same range of decorative techniques, is far more elaborate than that of the Napo Phase. This is evident not only in greater complexity of execution and more complete coverage of the vessel surface, but also in the more frequent juxtaposition of different techniques on the same vessel. In the Napo Phase, even painting is rarely combined with other techniques, whereas Marajoara Phase bowls with incised or excised exteriors are typically painted on the interior. Other Marajoara Phase vessels may have one type of decoration on the rim and another on the body. Napo Phase pottery is primitive by comparison.

Vessel shapes diverge more than does decoration. Although several of the common Napo Phase rim profiles occur on Marajoara Phase vessels (such as Forms 1, 7, and 8), they are not typical. The Napo Phase channel and collared rims are absent, and a rounded lip is characteristic. While exaggerated thickening of the carination is a distinctive Napo Phase specialization, thickening of the angle on Marajoara Phase shouldered vessels is relatively slight. Another Napo Phase diagnostic, the square shape, is so weakly manifested by Marajoara Phase bowls as to be easily overlooked unless attention is called to it (pl. 86). The anthropomorphic urns of the two phases are noncomparable in most respects, although one Marajoara Phase example (pl. 88b) is reminiscent of the Napo Phase style. Marajoara Phase specializations, such as stools and tangas, have not been reported in eastern Ecuador.

Even at the present incomplete stage of investigation, the distributional evidence indicates that the

CERAMIC TRAITS	HIGH-LANDS		LOWLANDS																					
	Quimbaya	San Agustín	Río Güepi	Napo Phase	Río Japurá	Tefé región	Coarí region	Araça region	Berurí, Rio Purús	Manacapurú	Ilha dos Muras	Ponta Negra	Guarita Phase (Manaus)	Guajará, Nova Olinda, Río Ipixuna	Miracanguera	Itacoatiara	Boca do Xavier	Tauaquera	Mocajatuba	Pontão	Paurá	Santarem region	Marajoara Phase	Nazaré dos Patos
GROUP 1																								
Negative painting	X	X	X																					
White-on-red painting	X		X																					
Anthropomorphic urn, Type B	X		X		?																			
Channel rim	?	?	X				X	X	X				X											
Grooving	?		X	X	X	X	X	X	X	X	X	X	X	X	X	X	X	X		X				X
Sand temper	X	X	X	X						X								X			X			X
Square outline	X	X	X	X	X			?	X	X	X	X	X				?	?			?			
Anthropomorphic urn, limbs in full round	X		X		X										X						X			
Thickened carination	X	X	X	X		X	X		X	X	X	X										X	X	X
Annular base	X		X			X		X			X	X		X		X	X		X	X	X		X	?
Incision, white retouched	X	X	X															X					X	?
Red and black-on-white painting	X	X	X	?		X		X		X	X			X	X			X				X	X	
Red-on-white painting		?	X	X	X	X		X		X	X	X			X			X					X	X
Single-line incision	X	X	X	X		X	X		X	X	X	X	X	X	X	X	X	X	X	X	X	X	X	X
Excision	X		X			X	X	X		X	X					X		X	X	X	X	X	X	X
Excision, white retouched	?		X						?														X	X
Broad everted rim bowl		X	X	X		X		X		X	X				X	X	X	X	X	X	X	X	X	X
Anthropomorphic urn, limbs absent or stylized	X		X	X				X					X		X	X						X		
GROUP 2																								
Black ash temper			X	X			X	X																
"Collared" rim			X				X	X		X														
Anthropomorphic urn, head-lid			X						X					X	X									
Double-line incision			X	?	X	?	X		X		X			X	X		X	X			X			X
Cariapé temper	X	X				X	X		X		X	X	X		X	X	X	X		X	X		?	X
White slipped after incision			X			X			X	X		X	X		X	X								X
Lobed rim			X	X		X		X		X	X	X		X	X	X		X	X	X	X	X	X	X
"Pseudo-negative" painting			X			X					X	X										X		
Red retouched incision on white slip			X	?									?		X			X					X	X
GROUP 3																								
Body flange			X			X	X		X		X	X	X		X	X			X		X			
Adornos			X	X	X				X		X	X	X	X		X	X	X	X	X	X	X	X	X
Cauixí temper					X	X	X		X		X	X	X	X	X	X	X	X	X					
Red and orange-on-white painting					X				X		X			X				X				X		
Sherd temper	X							?		X				X			X					X	X	
Hollow rim																	X		X			X	X	X

FIGURE 79.—Occurrence of Napo Phase ceramic traits of decoration and vessel shape in Colombia and Brazil. Sites are arranged in geographical order, from west to east. (X=present, ?=identification uncertain.) Information is derived principally from Museum collections, see pp. 95–104 for sources.

spread of the Polychrome Horizon Style cannot be interpreted as a simple down-river movement. Combinations of decorative technique and vessel shape are different in eastern Ecuador, on the middle Amazon, and on Marajó Island, implying either complicated diffusion patterns or temporal differences or both. While some degree of error may be introduced by mixed surface collections, other variations between sherd samples are clearly the result of amalgamation of the Polychrome Horizon Style with preexisting or subsequent local or neighboring ceramic styles. The variation in frequency and elaboration of anthropomorphic and zoomorphic adornos may be one effect of such differential acculturation. Other differences may reflect multiple routes of diffusion. The fact that the headwater tributaries of the Japurá (Caquetá) and Içá (Putumayo) tend to converge in the southeastern mountains of Colombia (fig. 68) makes them all potentially accessible for movements out of the southern highlands. Several are known to have been used by recent colonists (Chaves, 1945, map facing p. 582), and there is some evidence of earlier intrusions into the lowlands (Silva Celis, 1963). Variations in speed of transmittal and amount of acculturation from previously existing pottery-making groups along the way would be expected to create complexes of variable content by the time the Amazon was reached. Detailed sequences of ceramic change

are needed throughout the northwestern lowlands to evaluate this theoretical possibility.

The fate of the Napo Phase in eastern Ecuador is also a matter of speculation at present. It might be inferred on the basis of the sequence derived from the seriation of pottery types that the group was moving upriver (see pp. 78–81), and that continuation in this direction brought closer proximity and perhaps ultimately amalgamation with groups living in the Andean foothills. A square vessel from Avila (Porras, 1961, fig. 17–13) and a few diagnostic Napo Phase sherds collected by Pedro I. Porras from Loreto on the Rio Suno (fig. 1) could be explained in this way (pl. 94 *j–k*). On the other hand, the Loreto material includes sherds of a type also encountered in a few Napo Phase sites, where it was identified as of trade origin (cf. pls. 94 *a–i* and 76 *i–n*). The evidence is thus not conclusive as it bears on the fate of the Napo Phase.

The report by Donald Lathrap (1965, p. 10) of a ceramic complex in eastern Peru "closely related to the well known style of the Rio Napo in Ecuador," suggests another possibility. This complex, known as the Caimito Phase, was identified at several large habitation sites on the borders of Lago Imariacocha, southeast of Pucallpa (fig. 68). A carbon-14 date of A.D. 1320 ± 60 (Y–1544) places these remains sufficiently later than those of the Napo Phase to suggest a derivation from eastern Ecuador.

EUROPEAN DISCOVERY AND THE COTACOCHA PHASE

In the year 1541, when the Rio Napo moved into the sphere of history, it was uninhabited. This situation wrought much hardship on the men who accompanied Orellana on his inadvertent voyage of exploration, which became the first descent of the Amazon. Although the exact route of the expedition and locus of particular events are subject to differences of interpretation (e.g., Heaton, 1934; Millares, 1955; Reyes y Reyes, 1942; Rodríguez, 1955), the general picture is clear: no settlements were encountered between the mouth of the Rio Coca and one day's travel above the mouth of the Rio Curaray.

Along the Rio Coca, the Spaniards found Indian villages (Ortiguera, *in* Heaton, 1934, p. 314), where

> thanks to trinkets and to trade-offerings of salt, which a mong them is prized highly, and to iron axes and iron machetes, they began to bring . . . food in the form of many kinds of fish and maize and yucca and sweet potatoes and other food products that were to be had in the land. . . . they [the Spaniards] went out to fish the river, where they caught a

> great deal of fish, because it was very well stocked with it, an they killed with their arquebuses many turkeys and ducks.

The appearance of the Indians resembled that of more recent groups throughout the eastern montaña (Ortiguera, *in* Heaton, 1934, p. 315):

> The people dwelling along this river have faces with very regular features and have good physiques, and are dressed, wearing cloaks and tunics handpainted in various designs and colors, and the women have clothes with the same painted designs. Among the men there were some who wore gold medal-like pieces on their breasts, and the women [wore] ear-hoops of the same [metal] hanging from their ears, and other pieces hanging from their noses and throats. The weapons which they have are "macanas," which are sticks cut from black palm-trees, long like broadswords, having both edges and a point, which [weapons] they handle prettily and nimbly, and spears to be thrown.

Continuing downriver, the Spaniards entered the uninhabited area and began to suffer from lack of provisions. On the basis of information that a village was to be encountered at a distance of four day's travel, Pizarro decided to send a party for supplies. The plight in which failure to find the village placed the search party is vividly described by one of its members (Robles et al., *in* Heaton, 1934, p. 258):

> . . . the expedition of exploration . . . left . . . to go in search of maize down the river at the river junction concerning which information was at hand, which junction everybody, and the Governor [Pizarro] in particular, said might be at a distance of something like a four days' journey at the most; and we, coming in search of the said maize [undertook this journey] without food or supplies, eating roots, herbs, [and] very dangerous unknown fruits, and harassed by this shortage [of food] we journeyed on for nine days, all through uninhabited territory, and at the end of them God Our Lord having pity [on us], He saw fit to place in our path a village where [upon investigation] in it, we found a certain supply of maize; and from the great hunger thus endured there died several Spaniards, and those of us who were spared became quite ill from the said suffering, because . . . it was very great, not only as a consequence of not eating but also because of the constant rowing from sun to sun, for this alone was sufficient to kill us. . . .

Regarding the starvation, Carvajal (*in* Heaton, 1934, p. 408) is more explicit:

> . . . we were in great danger of death because of excessive hunger that we were enduring. . . . lacking other victuals, we were eating leather from the seats and bows of saddles, and also the leather from game of the chests or hampers whose covering was made out of it, in which we were transporting the little clothing and bedding that we had, and a few tapir skins, not to mention the soles and [even whole] shoes that could be found among the members of the party; and, though there was no sauce other than hunger itself, this latter created in them a taste. . . .

The village that offered the Spaniards salvation from their desperate situation was located a little upstream from the mouth of the Rio Curaray. This identification derives from Carvajal's description (*in* Heaton, 1934, p. 412) of a large tributary passed on the first day's journey after their departure, which "emptied in with such a great onrush and force . . . we barely escaped drowning in getting past the junction of the rivers in a great jam of logs which the current had brought down." Only the Curaray is large enough to create these conditions.

The lower Rio Napo produced a few small villages, but the unsavory reputations of the Spaniards preceded them and the houses were usually found deserted or even burned by the Indians. Starvation was again becoming a serious threat when they emerged from the Napo into the Amazon.

In 1651, the banks of the Napo were still unpopulated above its junction with the Aguarico (de la Cruz, 1900, p. 35). Subsequently, they have been settled by Quechua-speaking Indians, the makers of the Cotacocha Phase pottery. Whether these colonists came from the highlands, where similar pottery has been reported in the Loja basin (Jijón y Caamaño, 1951, pp. 231–233, figs. 254–6), or the eastern foothills, where ceramic resemblances also occur (Porras, 1961, pl. 15), has not been determined. It is possible, as Ferdon has noted (1950, pp. 4–5), that the diffusion of the Quechua language and the ceramic style reflects progressive Christianization of the Indians rather than population movement; on the other hand, the gap that seems to exist in the archeological sequence and the testimony of Orellana's men argue for intrusion of people in post-Spanish times.

Houses of the modern residents are typically scattered at wide intervals along the rivet banks, while their garden clearings occupy inland locations visible from the air (pl. 1*b*). Toward the Peruvian border, some of the land has been cleared for pasture (pls. 6, 13). Rice and cotton have been introduced as cash crops. Nuevo Rocafuerte, an administrative center founded after the 1942 border crisis, and the army base at Tiputini are the two principal settlements. Both are supported by the Ecuadorian national government. A mission at Nuevo Rocafuerte, also with the aid of external resources, propagates the Catholic religion. This latest culture to invade the Rio Napo thus differs from earlier ones in being independent of local resources for survival. Incorporation of the Rio Napo region into the political framework of a modern nation may have broken the pattern of intermittent occupancy that appears to have characterized it throughout prehistoric time. Only the future will tell.

HYPOTHETICAL RECONSTRUCTION OF AMAZONIAN PREHISTORY

The pattern of intermittent occupancy exhibited by pottery-making groups on the Rio Napo is of interest because it contrasts strongly with the evolutionary continuum characteristic during the prehistoric period in the highland and coastal portions of Ecuador.

There, although influences passed to and fro, and the interplay of culture and environment shaped the products in different ways, the thread of continuity can be detected. Continuity is also the dominant pattern elsewhere in the Andean highlands. By contrast, discontinuity (i.e., a sequence of intrusive complexes) has been reported from other parts of the Amazonian lowlands, including Marajó Island (Meggers and Evans, 1957), along the middle Amazon (Hilbert, n.d.) and to judge from preliminary accounts, in eastern Peru (Lathrap, 1965).

A case can be made for the existence of a correlation between these contrasting highland Andean and lowland Amazonian patterns of cultural development and the principal geographical characteristics of the two areas. It has been pointed out (e.g., Reichel-Dolmatoff, 1965, pp. 28, 82) that the geographical diversity of the Andes created multiple ecological niches requiring subsistence specialization for most efficient use. The effect was centripetal in the sense that increasingly efficient exploitation of a local environment correspondingly diminished the possibilities of successful transplantation to a different ecological niche. The centripetal effect was enhanced, or at least not offset, by the existence of mountain ranges, deserts, swamps, and other kinds of natural barriers between regions.

In the Amazonian lowlands, the situation is reversed, and a centrifugal effect develops. Differences in climate and topography are minimal over nearly half a continent, producing a relatively high degree of uniformity in soil, vegetation, and fauna. Similar subsistence techniques are almost equally effective in the Guianas, the upper Xingú or eastern Peru, and local resources requiring specialized technology are few. Sedentariness is actively discouraged by rapidly impoverished soils, while the vast network of navigable rivers encourages mobility. The consequence, apparently, was a semisedentary way of life, characterized not only by frequent resettlement, but by migration, which spread languages and cultural elements from one edge of the lowland tropical forest to the other.

Although few complete sequences are available for the tropical lowlands, existing data suggest two kinds of archeological situations, and their geographical distribution can be explained by the centrifugal hypothesis. One is the already mentioned succession of distinct ceramic complexes of non-homogeneous origin. The other is the presence of a single ceramic complex of long or short duration. When the known occurrences of these two kinds of situations are plotted on a map (fig. 80), it is evident that the areas in which a sequence of archeological phases has been reported are adjacent to the eastern slope of the Andes in Ecuador and Peru, and along the middle and lower Amazon. On the Ucayali and its tributaries, Lathrap (1965, p. 12) reports twelve ceramic complexes, which he places in chronological order on stratigraphic evidence. Our work

has identified a sequence with four independent phases along the Rio Napo in Ecuador. Five successive phases have been recognized on the island of Marajó (Meggers and Evans, 1957; Simões, 1966). Although investigation has been less intensive along the middle and lower Amazon, Hilbert's (1955, 1959 a, b), stratigraphic work and surface collections made by Nimuendajú and others from a large sample of sites attest to the existence of local chronologies composed of several phases of differing content, implying diversified origin.

The presence of a single archeological ceramic phase has been reported from several other parts of the lowlands, all peripheral to the Amazon River. The Rupununi Phase of the interior savanna of Guyana (formerly British Guiana) and adjacent Brazil, and the Taruma Phase of the upper Essequibo river are post-European arrivals in their respective areas (Evans and Meggers, 1960). A similar situation is described by Simões (1967) on the upper Xingú, where pottery also appears to be of relatively recent introduction. Hilbert (1962b, p. 465) encountered remains of a single phase in a 350 km. segment of the Rio Japurá. Survey of parts of the upper Orinoco, Ventuari, and Manipiare rivers in southern Venezuela produced evidence of two geographically isolated archeological phases, each accounting for all the sites discovered in their respective areas (Evans, Meggers, and Cruxent, 1960).

The greater antiquity of pottery making, and the higher level of general cultural development characteristic of the Andean area throughout the aboriginal period, make it seem probable that the primary direction of diffusion was from west to east. The occurrence of multiple phases adjacent to the Andes and along the main course of the Amazon, and single phase occupations in peripheral regions seems consistent with such a hypothesis. With the passage of time, new immigrant groups would have found on the banks of the Amazon more settlements representing greater cultural variety. The ceramic evidence indicates that amalgamation, acculturation, assimilation, displacement, or even extinction were alternative results at different times and places. As population density increased, the centrifugal effect of the lowland environment would be expected to manifest itself in the dispersal of pottery-making groups up the tributaries to the north and south. The diminishing time depth for ceramic-using phases in these marginal areas and relative rarity of multiphase sequences is what would be expected to result from such a process.

Although this reconstruction of Amazonian prehistory is supported by relatively little archeological evidence, it is interesting to note that a generally similar conclusion has been proposed by Noble on the

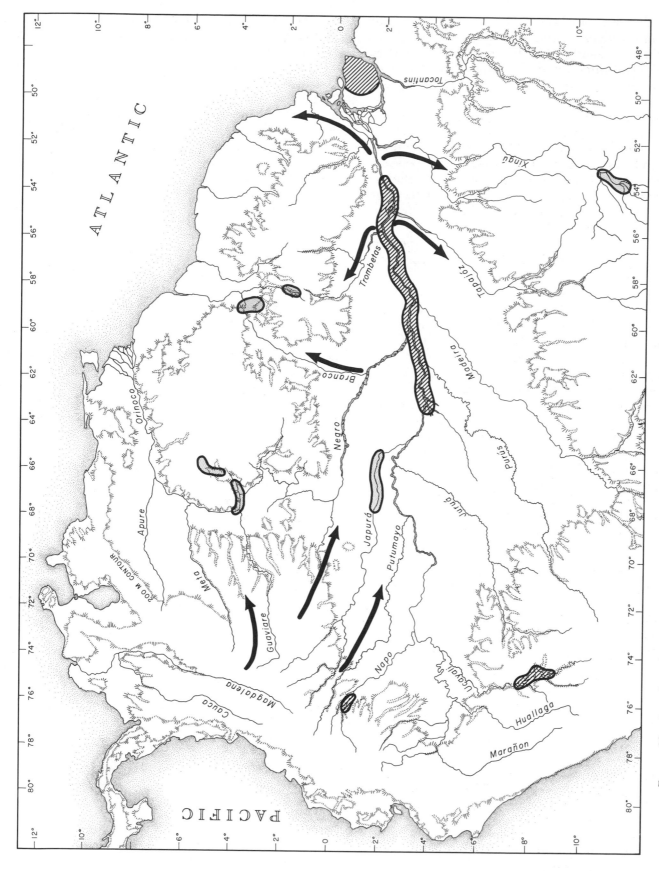

FIGURE 80.—Location of regions with multiple phase (hachure) and single phase (stipple) occupations in the Amazon basin and periphery, and some postulated routes of migration and diffusion.

basis of linguistic analysis. His reconstruction of the origin and differentiation of Arawakan languages leads him to conclude that "this most likely occurred near the headwaters of the Ucayali and Madre de Dios in what is now southeast Peru some 3500 to 5000 years ago" (Noble, 1965, p. 107). In Noble's view, "the most divergent Tupian languages are also distributed in such a way as to suggest that they developed here" (op. cit., p. 109). Unfortunately, even the minimal estimate for the Arawakan dispersal is earlier than any known ceramic complex, including the Zoned Hachure Horizon Style. Even if the date were sufficiently recent, however, the reconstructed phylogeny of the Arawakan family (op. cit., p. 108) and the modern distribution of Arawakan speakers (op. cit., map) fails to coincide with known occurrences of any pottery style or complex of ceramic traits.

The relatively small amount of work that has been done, both in archeology and linguistics, makes it likely that even the most generalized reconstructions of Amazonian prehistory will be modified by future work. A few basic themes seem visible, but most of the variations are unknown. If the foregoing hypothesis about the centrifugal effect of the ecological setting is correct, the archeological picture is likely to become more complicated with further investigations. As a consequence, it will probably be many decades before we begin to achieve full understanding of the manner in which natural factors affected colonization of the Amazonian lowlands by man.

In the meantime, attempts to generalize are justifiable principally because they offer guidelines for research. Along the Rio Napo, the combination of poverty of the soil and widespread flooding creates a habitat with little subsistence potential either for gatherers or for cultivators. How widespread is this ecological situation over the Amazonian lowlands? On the Rio Napo, archeological evidence has led to the inference that the area was colonized by at least four groups probably representing varying levels of sociopolitical complexity. The briefness of their residence suggests that whatever the initial expectations may have been, the subsistence potential did not meet them. The only solution was to move on. Although the word "determinism" has long been avoided by anthropologists, present evidence from archeology, geography, soil science, and ecology suggests that the environment of the Rio Napo determined an intermittent pattern of prehistoric human settlement along its margins. Whether the introduction of new ingredients, such as crops of Old World origin or future technological advances, can disrupt the present ecological balance and create conditions more favorable for human exploitation is yet to be explored. For the past and present, it can be stated with reasonable confidence that, given the natural conditions and the native American food plants, the effect on human habitation was predictable, which is to say inevitable. Whether this combination of factors is common or rare over the lowlands as a whole is the crucial question. The vastness of the area involved and the paucity of investigations in all fields of science underway or in prospect suggest that the answer may be long in coming.

Literature Cited

BARBOSA RODRIGUES, JOÃO
    1877. Arte ceramica. Antiguidades do Amazonas, vol. 2, pp. 2–23. Rio de Janeiro.
    1891–1892. Antiguidades do Amazonas. Vellosia, vol. 2 (1885–1888), pp. 1–40 and vol. 4
            (1885–1888), plates.

BULLEN, RIPLEY P.
    1965. Archaeological chronology of Grenada. American Antiquity, vol. 31, pp. 237–241.

BUSHNELL, G. H. S.
    1946. An archaeological collection from Macas, on the eastern slopes of the Ecuadorian Andes.
            Man, 1946, no. 2, pp. 2–6.

CARVAJAL, GASPAR DE
    See Heaton, H. C.; Millares, Jorge; Reyes y Reyes, Raul.

CHAVES CH., MILCIADES
    1945. La colonización de la Comisaría del Putumayo: un problema etno-económico-geográfico
            de importancia nacional. Bol. Arqueología, vol. 1, pp. 567–598. Bogotá.

COLLIER, DONALD, AND MURRA, JOHN V.
    1943. Survey and excavations in southern Ecuador. Field Museum of Natural History,
            Anthropological Series, vol. 35. Chicago.

CRULS, GASTÃO
    1942. Arqueologia amazônica. Rev. Serviço do Patrimônio Histórico e Artístico Nacional,
            vol. 6, pp. 169–220. Rio de Janeiro.

CRUXENT, JOSÉ M., and ROUSE, IRVING
    1958. An archeological chronology of Venezuela. Social Science Monographs VI. Pan
            American Union, Washington, D.C.

CUBILLOS, JULIO CESAR, and BEDOYA, VICTOR A.
    1954. Arqueología de las riberas del Río Magdalena, Espinal-Tolima. Rev. Colombiana de
            Antropología, vol. 2, no. 2, pp. 115–144. Bogotá.

DE LA CRUZ, LAUREANO
    1900. Nuevo descubrimiento del Rio de Marañon llamado de las Amazonas, hecho por la
            religión de San Francisco, año de 1651. Madrid.

DUQUE GOMEZ, LUIS
    1963a. Los Quimbayas; Reseña etno-histórica y arqueológica. Historia de Pereira. Bogotá.
    1963b. Reseña arqueológica de San Agustín. Instituto Colombiano de Antropología. Bogotá.

EVANS, CLIFFORD; and MEGGERS, BETTY J.
    1960. Archeological investigations in British Guiana. Bur. American Ethnol. Bull. 177.
            Washington, D.C.
    1962. Use of organic temper for carbon 14 dating in lowland South America. American
            Antiquity, vol. 28, pp. 243–245.
    1964. British Guiana archaeology: a return to the original interpretation. American Antiquity,
            vol. 30, pp. 83–84.

EVANS, CLIFFORD; MEGGERS, BETTY J.; and CRUXENT, JOSÉ M.
    1960. Preliminary results of archeological investigations along the Orinoco and Ventuari
            Rivers, Venezuela. Actas del 33 Congreso Internacional de Americanistas, vol. 2,
            pp. 359–369. San José, Costa Rica.

FERDON, EDWIN N., Jr.
  1950. Studies in Ecuadorian geography. Monographs of the School of American Research, no. 15. Santa Fe.
FERIZ, H.
  1963. The ceramics of Tefé-Amaná; a contribution to the archaeology of the Amazon. Ethnos 1963, nos. 2–4, pp. 147–176.
FIGUEIREDO, NAPOLEÃO, and SIMÕES, MÁRIO F.
  1963. Contribuição á arqueologia da fase marajoara. Rev. Museu Paulista, vol. 14, pp. 455–470. Sãn Paulo.
FORD, JAMES A.
  1949. Cultural dating of prehistoric sites in Virú Valley, Peru. American Museum of Natural History Anthropological Papers, vol. 43, part 1, no. 2. New York.
GILLIN, JOHN
  1936. An urn from the Rio Aguarico, eastern Ecuador. American Anthropologist, vol. 38, pp. 469–470.
HANKE, WANDA
  1959. Archäologische Funde im oberen Amazonasgebiet. Archiv für Völkerkunde, vol. 14, pp. 31–66.
HEATON, H. D., Editor
  1934. The Discovery of the Amazon, according to the account of Friar Gaspar de Carvajal and other documents. American Geographical Society Special Publ. no. 17. New York.
HÉBERT, J.
  1907. Survivances décoratives au Brésil. Journ. Soc. Américanistes de Paris, vol. 4, pp. 185–191.
HILBERT, PETER PAUL
  1952. Contribuição à arqueologia da ilha de Marajó. Instituto de Antropologia e Etnologia do Pará, publ. 5. Belem.
  1955. A cerâmica arqueológica do região do Oriximiná. Instituto de Antropologia e Etnologia do Pará, publ. 9. Belem.
  1959a. Achados arqueológicos num sambaqui do baixo Amazonas. Instituto de Antropologia e Etnologia do Pará, publ. 10. Belem.
  1959b. Preliminary results of archeological investigations in the vicinity of the mouth of the Rio Negro, Amazonas. Actas del 33 Congreso Internacional de Americanistas, Tomo II, pp. 370–377. San José, Costa Rica.
  1962a. New stratigraphic evidence of culture change on the Middle Amazon (Solimões). Akten des 34 Internationalen Amerikanisten-kongresses, Wien, 1960, pp. 471–476.
  1962b. Preliminary results of archeological research on the Japurá River, Middle Amazon. Akten des 34 Internationalen Amerikanisten-kongresses, Wien, 1960, pp. 465–470.
  n.d. Archäologische Untersuchungen am mittleren Amazonas. Marburger Studien zur Völkerkunde, Band 1, Dietrich Reimer Verlag, Berlin (in press).
IMBELLONI, J.
  1950. La extraña terracota de Rurrenabaque (noreste de Bolivia) en la arqueología de Sudamérica. Runa, vol. 3, parts 1–2, pp. 71–169. Buenos Aires.
IZUMI, SEIICHI, and SONO, TOSHIHIKO
  1963. Andes 2: Excavations at Kotosh, Peru, 1960. Tokyo.
JIJÓN Y CAAMAÑO, JACINTO
  1951. Antropología prehispánica del Ecuador, Resumen, 1945. Quito.
LATHRAP, DONALD W.
  1958. The cultural sequence at Yarinacocha, eastern Peru. American Antiquity, vol. 23, pp. 379–388.
  1962. Yarinacocha: Stratigraphic excavations in the Peruvian Montaña. Unpublished Ph.D. Dissertation, Harvard University.
  1964. An alternative seriation of the Mabaruma Phase, northwestern British Guiana. American Antiquity, vol. 29, pp. 353–359.
  1965. Investigaciones en la selva peruana, 1964–5. Bol. Museu Nacional de Antropología y Arqueología, año 1, no. 4, pp. 9–12. Pueblo Libre, Lima.
  1967. Report on the continuing program of research on the culture history of the upper Amazon basin. Dept. Anthropology, Univ. Illinois, Urbana (multilithed).

MEGGERS, BETTY J. and EVANS, CLIFFORD
    1957. Archeological investigations at the mouth of the Amazon. Bur. American Ethnology
        Bull. 167. Washington, D.C.
    1958. Archeological evidence of a prehistoric migration from the Rio Napo to the mouth of the
        Amazon. *In* Migrations in New World Culture History, Raymond H. Thompson,
        Editor, University of Arizona Social Science Bull. 27, pp. 9–19. Tucson.
    1961. An experimental formulation of horizon styles in the Tropical Forest Area of South
        America. *In* Essays in Pre-Columbian Art and Archaeology, Samuel K. Lothrop
        and others, pp. 372–388. Cambridge, Mass.
MEGGERS, BETTY J.; EVANS, CLIFFORD; and ESTRADA, EMILIO
    1965. Early Formative period of coastal Ecuador: The Valdivia and Machalilla phases. Smith-
        sonian Contrib. Anthropology, vol. 1. Washington, D.C.
MÉTRAUX, ALFRED
    1930. Contribution à l'étude de l'archéologie du cours supérieur et moyen de l'Amazone. Rev.
        Museo de la Plata, vol. 32, pp. 145–185.
MILLARES, JORGE HERNÁNDEZ, editor
    1955. Relación del nuevo descubrimiento del famoso río Grande de las Amazonas, por Fray
        Gaspar de Carvajal, O.P. Edición, introducción y notas de Jorge Hernández Millares.
        Fondo de Cultura Económica, México-Buenos Aires.
MORDINI, ANTONIO
    1947. L'île de Marajo (bas Amason): un problème archéologique à resoudre. Actes du 28
        Congrès International des Américanistes, pp. 637–642. Paris.
NETTO, LADISLAU
    1885. Investigações sobre a arqueologia brazileira. Archivos do Museu Nacional do Rio de
        Janeiro, vol. 6, pp. 257–554.
NOBLE, G. KINGSLEY
    1965. Proto-Arawakan and its descendants. International Journ. American Linguistics, vol.
        31, no. 3, part II.
NORDENSKIÖLD, ERLAND
    1930. L'archéologie du bassin de l'Amazone. Ars Americana, vol. 1. Paris.
PALMATARY, HELEN C.
    1950. The pottery of Marajó Island, Brazil. Trans. American Philosophical Soc., n.s., vol.
        39, part 3. Philadelphia.
PORRAS G., PEDRO I.
    1961. Contribución al estudio de la arqueología e historia de los valles Quijos y Misagualli
        (Alto Napo) en la región oriental del Ecuador, S.A. Quito.
REICHEL-DOLMATOFF, GERARDO
    1965a. Colombia: Ancient Peoples and Places, vol. 44. London and New York.
    1965b. Excavaciones arqueológicas en Puerto Hormiga (Departamento de Bolivar). Publ.
        Universidad de Los Andes, Antropología 2. Bogotá.
REYES Y REYES, RAUL, editor
    1942. Relación del nuevo descubrimiento del famosa Río Grande que descubrió por muy
        gran ventura el Capitán Francisco de Orellana, por P. Gaspar de Carvajal. Biblioteca
        Amazonas, vol. 1. Quito.
RODRÍGUEZ FABREGAT, E.
    1955. Pasión e crónica del Amazonas. Buenos Aires.
SILVA CELIS, ELIÉCER
    1963. Movimiento de la civilización agustiniana por el alto Amazonas. Rev. Colombiana
        de Antropologia, vol. 12, pp. 389–399. Bogotá.
SIMÕES, MÁRIO F.
    1966. Resultados preliminares de uma prospecção arqueológica na região dos Rios Goiapí
        e Camará (Ilha de Marajó). Atas do Simpósio sôbre a Biota Amazônica, vol. 2,
        pp. 207–224. Rio de Janeiro.
    1967. Considerações preliminares sôbre a arqueologia do Alto Xingú, Mato Grosso. Programa
        Nacional de Pesquisas Arqueológicas: Resultados Preliminares do Primeiro Ano
        1965–66. Museu Paraense Emilio Goeldi, Publicações Avulsas No. 6, pp. 129–151.
        Belém.
    n.d. The Castanheira site: New evidence on the antiquity and history of the Ananatuba
        phase (Marajó Island, Brazil). American Antiquity (in press).

Tosi, Joseph A., Jr.
    1960. Zonas de vida natural en el Peru. Instituto Interamericano de Ciencias Agrícolas de
          la OEA, Zona Andina, Bol. Técnico no. 5. Lima.
Uhle, Max
    1889. Kultur und Industrie Südamerikanischer Völker. Vol. 1, Alte Zeit. Berlin.
    1921. Los principios de la civilización en la sierra peruana. Bol. Academia Nacional de
          Historia, vol. 1 (1920) pp. 44–56. Quito.
Wolf, Theodore
    1933. Geography and geology of Ecuador. Toronto.

APPENDIX

TABLES 1–11

TABLE 1.—*Frequency of vessel forms of Yasuní Phase*

Vessel Forms	N–P–10: Puerto Miranda Hill																	N–P–11: Puerto Miranda Bank				Totals of each Form	
	Miranda Plain		Yasuní Plain		Miranda Modeled		Yasuní Incised		Yasuní Incised and Punctate		Yasuní Nicked		Yasuní Red		Yasuní Zoned Hachure				Miranda Plain		Yasuní Plain			
	No.	%	No.	%	No.	%	No.	%	No.	%	No.	%	No.	%	No.	%			No.	%	No.	%	No.	%
Common Form																								
1	8	10.2	5	5.1	—	—	—	—	—	—	—	—	—	—	—	—			3	23.1	1	25.0	17	8.0
2	11	14.1	1	1.0	—	—	4	50.0	—	—	—	—	—	—	1	20.0			—	—	1	25.0	17	8.0
3	7	9.0	1	1.0	—	—	—	—	—	—	—	—	—	—	—	—			—	—	—	—	8	3.8
4	8	10.2	11	11.2	—	—	—	—	—	—	—	—	—	—	1	20.0			4	30.7	—	—	24	11.4
5	6	7.7	12	12.2	—	—	—	—	—	—	1	33.3	1	100.0	—	—			1	7.7	2	50.0	22	10.4
6	5	6.4	37	37.8	—	—	1	12.5	—	—	—	—	—	—	—	—			1	7.7	—	—	44	20.8
7	3	3.8	9	9.2	—	—	3	37.5	1	50.0	—	—	—	—	—	—			—	—	—	—	16	7.6
8	17	21.8	15	15.3	—	—	—	—	—	—	—	—	—	—	—	—			—	—	—	—	32	15.2
9	3	3.9	5	5.2	—	—	—	—	—	—	—	—	—	—	—	—			—	—	—	—	8	3.8
Rare Form																								
1	—	—	—	—	—	—	—	—	—	—	—	—	—	—	1	20.0			—	—	—	—	1	0.5
2	—	—	—	—	—	—	—	—	—	—	1	33.3	—	—	—	—			—	—	—	—	1	0.5
3	3	3.9	—	—	—	—	—	—	—	—	—	—	—	—	—	—			—	—	—	—	3	1.4
4	—	—	—	—	—	—	—	—	—	—	—	—	—	—	1	20.0			—	—	—	—	1	0.5
5	—	—	—	—	—	—	—	—	—	—	1	33.3	—	—	—	—			—	—	—	—	1	0.5
6	—	—	1	1.0	—	—	—	—	—	—	—	—	—	—	—	—			—	—	—	—	1	0.5
7	—	—	—	—	1	100.0	—	—	—	—	—	—	—	—	—	—			—	—	—	—	1	0.5
8	1	1.3	—	—	—	—	—	—	—	—	—	—	—	—	—	—			—	—	—	—	1	0.5
9	—	—	—	—	—	—	—	—	—	—	—	—	—	—	—	—			1	7.7	—	—	1	0.5
10	—	—	—	—	—	—	—	—	1	50.0	—	—	—	—	1	20.0			—	—	—	—	2	0.9
Unclass.	6	7.7	1	1.0	—	—	—	—	—	—	—	—	—	—	—	—			3	23.1	—	—	10	4.7
TOTALS	78	100.0	98	100.0	1	100.0	8	100.0	2	100.0	3	99.9	1	100.0	5	100.0			13	100.0	4	100.0	211	100.0
Base Forms																								
A	—	—	—	—	—	—	—	—	—	—	—	—	—	—	—	—			2	50.0	—	—	2	20.0
B	—	—	1	16.6	—	—	—	—	—	—	—	—	—	—	—	—			2	50.0	—	—	3	30.0
C	—	—	3	50.0	—	—	—	—	—	—	—	—	—	—	—	—			—	—	—	—	3	30.0
D	—	—	2	33.4	—	—	—	—	—	—	—	—	—	—	—	—			—	—	—	—	2	20.0
TOTALS	—	—	6	100.0	—	—	—	—	—	—	—	—	—	—	—	—			4	100.0	—	—	10	100.0

TABLE 2.—*Frequency of pottery types at sites of the Yasuní Phase*

Pottery Types		Surface and Tests			
		N–P–10: Puerto Miranda Hill		N–P–11: Puerto Miranda Bank	
		No.	%	No.	%
PLAIN	Miranda Plain				
	Yasuní Plain	621	45. 5	27	77. 2
		688	50. 3	8	12. 8
DECORATED	Miranda Modeled	5	0.4	–	–
	Yasuní Incised	27	2.0	–	–
	Yasuní Incised and Punctate .	5	0.4	–	–
	Yasuní Nicked	5	0.4	–	–
	Yasuní Red	7	0.5	–	–
	Yasuní Zoned Hachure . . .	7	0.5	–	–
	GRAND TOTALS	1365	100. 0	35	100. 0
	SUBTOTALS:				
	Plain types	1309	95. 9	35	100. 0
	Decorated types . . .	56	4. 1	0	–

TABLE 3.—*Frequency of vessel forms of Cotacocha Phase pottery*

Vessel Forms	N–P–3: Nuevo Rocafuerte-Surface		N–P–9: Cotacocha-Surface		N–P–14: Latas-Surface		N–P–15: Tiputini Road-Surface	
	No.	%	No.	%	No.	%	No.	%
Common Form								
1	–	–	9	75.0	1	25.0	1	100.0
2	–	–	1	8.3	–	–	–	–
3	1	100.0	2	16.7	–	–	–	–
Minor Form								
1	–	–	–	–	1	25.0	–	–
2	–	–	–	–	2	50.0	–	–
TOTALS	1	100.0	12	100.0	4	100.0	1	100.0
Base Forms								
A	–	–	–	–	–	–	1	100.0
B	–	–	1	50.0	–	–	–	–
C	–	–	1	50.0	–	–	–	–
D	1	100.0	–	–	–	–	–	–
TOTALS	1	100.0	2	100.0	–	–	1	100.0
Total Sherds	1	–	275	–	92	–	1	–

TABLE 4.—*Frequency of vessel forms of the Tivacundo Phase*

Vessel Forms	N–P–7: Chacra Alfaro				N–P–8: Barranco Alfaro		Totals of each Form
	Surface		Cut 1: Combined Levels		Surface and Tests		
	No.	%	No.	%	No.	%	
Common Form							
1	19	14.6	9	10.7	5	5.2	33
2	36	27.7	23	27.4	7	7.3	66
3	20	15.4	16	19.1	24	25.0	60
4	38	29.2	13	15.5	13	13.5	64
5	–	–	1	1.2	21	21.9	22
6	14	10.8	17	20.2	20	20.7	51
Rare Form							
1	3	2.3	1	1.2	1	1.1	5
2	–	–	–	–	1	1.1	1
3	–	–	–	–	–	–	0
4	–	–	–	–	1	1.1	1
5	–	–	–	–	1	1.1	1
Unclass.	–	–	4	4.7	2	2.0	6
TOTALS	130	100.0	84	100.0	96	100.0	310
Base Forms							
A	2	15.4	3	25.1	3	23.1	8
B	9	69.2	7	58.2	7	53.8	23
B: Perforated	1	7.7	2	16.7	–	–	3
C	1	7.7	–	–	2	15.4	3
D	–	–	–	–	1	7.7	1
E	–	–	–	–	–	–	0
TOTALS	13	100.0	12	100.0	13	100.0	38

TABLE 5.—*Frequency of pottery types at sites of the Cotacocha Phase*

Pottery Types	N–P–3: Nuevo Rocafuerte-Surface		N–P–9: Cotacocha-Surface		N–P–14: Latas-Surface		N–P–15: Tiputini Road-Surface	
	No.	%	No.	%	No.	%	No.	%
Cotacocha Plain .	–	–	134	48.7	5	5.4	–	–
Cotacocha Red .	1	100.0	1	0.3	–	–	1	100.0
Latas Plain . . .	–	–	129	47.0	87	94.6	–	–
Unclassified Cariape-tempered Plain	–	–	11	4.0	–	–	–	–
TOTALS . . .	1	100.0	275	100.0	92	100.0	1	100.0

TABLE 6.—*Frequency of pottery types in surface collections and stratigraphic excavations at sites of the Tivacundo Phase*

		Pottery Types	N-P-7: Chacra Alfaro Surface No.	%	Cut 1 0–8 cm. No.	%	8–16 cm. No.	%	16–24 cm. No.	%	N-P-8: Barranco Alfaro Surface & Tests No.	%
DECORATED		Alfaro Plain	206	24.1	25	25.2	157	26.9	42	26.6	178	32.6
		Chacra Plain	273	32.0	23	23.2	166	28.5	55	34.8	67	12.3
		Tivacundo Plain	278	32.5	45	45.5	237	40.6	51	32.3	65	11.9
		Unclassified Cariape-tempered Plain	–	–	–	–	–	–	–	–	14	2.6
		Unclassified Sand-tempered Plain	42	4.9	–	–	–	–	1	0.6	16	2.9
PLAIN		Tivacundo Incised and Zoned Red	2	0.2	–	–	–	–	–	–	187	34.3
		Tivacundo Red Painted	54	6.3	4	4.1	22	3.8	9	5.7	10	1.8
		Unclassified Decorated	–	–	2	2.0	2	0.2	–	–	9	1.6
		GRAND TOTALS	855	100.0	99	100.0	584	100.0	158	100.0	546	100.0
		SUBTOTALS: Plain types	799	93.4	93	94.0	560	96.0	148	93.6	340	62.2
		Decorated types	56	6.6	6	6.0	24	4.0	10	6.4	206	37.8

TABLE 7.—*Frequency of stone artifacts at sites of the Napo Phase*

Type of Stone Artifact	N-P-1 Area 2	N-P-1 Area 3	N-P-1 Area 4	N-P-2 Areas 1 & 2	N-P-2 Broadside A	N-P-2 Broadside B	N-P-2 Cut 1 0–15 cm.	N-P-2 Cut 1 15–30 cm.	N-P-3 Test B	N-P-3 Test B Extension	N-P-4	N-P-6	Eden	Rio Yasuní	Total of each type
Abrader	–	–	3	–	–	–	1	–	–	–	–	1	–	–	5
Ax (Notched)	–	–	2	4	–	–	–	–	–	–	–	1	1	1	9
Ax (T-shaped or eared)	–	–	–	–	–	–	–	–	–	–	–	1	1	–	2
Chisel	–	–	–	–	–	–	–	–	–	–	–	1	–	–	1
Core	1	–	1	–	–	–	–	–	–	–	–	–	–	1	3
Grinding Stone	–	–	2	–	–	–	–	–	–	–	–	–	–	–	2
Hammerstone	–	1	2	1	1	–	–	–	–	–	–	–	–	–	5
Natural Pebble	3	–	5	1	–	2	–	3	4	3	1	–	–	–	22
Paint Stone	–	–	–	–	–	–	–	–	1	–	–	–	–	–	1
Spall	–	–	–	–	1	–	1	–	1	1	1	–	–	–	5

TABLE 8.—*Frequency of pottery types in surface collections and stratigraphic excavations at sites of the Napo Phase*

	Pottery Types	N–P–1: Tiputini								N–P–2: Nueva Armenia			
		Surface and Tests								Surface and Tests			
		Area 1		Area 2		Area 3		Area 4		Area 1		Area 2	
		No.	%	No.	%	No.	%	No.	%	No.	%	No.	%
PLAIN	Armenia Plain	–	–	–	–	–	–	42	3.9	19	7.5	–	–
	Napo Plain	45	26.9	359	54.2	142	53.1	537	50.0	90	35.9	13	19.1
	Napo Red	5	3.0	27	4.1	25	9.3	97	9.1	29	11.5	1	1.5
	Tiputini Plain	–	–	3	0.4	1	0.4	10	0.9	14	5.5	2	2.9
DECORATED	Armenia White-on-Red	1	0.6	7	1.1	3	1.1	1	0.1	–	–	4	5.9
	Napo Negative	–	–	2	0.3	–	–	–	–	–	–	–	–
	Napo Plain Excised	1	0.6	3	0.4	3	1.1	8	0.7	6	2.4	2	2.9
	Napo Plain Incised	17	10.2	124	18.7	36	13.4	117	10.9	31	12.4	17	25.1
	Napo Red Excised	–	–	–	–	–	–	8	0.7	–	–	–	–
	Napo Red Excised, White Retouched	–	–	–	–	–	–	–	–	–	–	–	–
	Napo Red Incised	2	1.2	22	3.3	14	5.2	35	3.3	3	1.2	2	2.9
	Napo White Excised	–	–	1	0.1	–	–	–	–	–	–	–	–
	Napo White Incised	–	–	3	0.4	–	–	8	0.7	2	0.8	1	1.5
	Rocafuerte Incised	–	–	–	–	–	–	14	1.3	2	0.8	–	–
	Rocafuerte Painted	94	56.3	106	16.0	37	13.8	141	13.1	39	15.6	16	23.5
	Tiputini Plain Excised	–	–	–	–	–	–	9	0.8	7	2.8	4	5.9
	Tiputini Plain Incised	2	1.2	6	0.9	6	2.2	26	2.4	3	1.2	2	2.9
	Tiputini Red Excised	–	–	–	–	–	–	6	0.6	–	–	–	–
	Tiputini Red Excised, White Retouched	–	–	–	–	–	–	3	0.3	2	0.8	2	2.9
	Tiputini Red Incised	–	–	–	–	–	–	10	0.9	3	1.2	–	–
	Tiputini White Excised	–	–	–	–	–	–	–	–	–	–	–	–
	Tiputini White Incised	–	–	–	–	–	–	–	–	–	–	–	–
	Unclassified decorated	–	–	1	0.1	1	0.4	3	0.3	1	0.4	1	1.5
TRADE	Trade pottery	–	–	–	–	–	–	–	–	–	–	1	1.5
	GRAND TOTALS	167	100.0	664	100.0	268	100.0	1073	100.0	251	100.0	68	100.0
	SUBTOTALS:												
	Plain types	50	30.0	389	58.5	168	62.7	686	63.9	152	60.6	16	23.5
	Decorated types	117	70.0	275	41.5	100	37.3	387	36.1	99	19.4	51	75.0
	Trade pottery	0	0.0	0	0.0	0	0.0	0	0.0	0	0.0	1	1.5

TABLE 8.—*Frequency of pottery types in surface collections and stratigraphic excavations at sites of the Napo Phase.*—Continued

Pottery Types	N-P-2: Nueva Armenia—Continued										N-P-3: Nuevo Rocafuerte	
	Surface and Tests		Broadside A		Broadside B		Cut 1				Surface and Test A	
	Area 2a		No.	%	No.	%	0–15 cm.		15–30 cm.			
	No.	%					No.	%	No.	%	No.	%
PLAIN												
Armenia Plain	15	2.7	104	3.6	87	4.7	235	12.3	148	23.3	47	10.1
Napo Plain	279	51.1	1325	45.5	682	36.8	827	43.4	203	32.0	172	36.9
Napo Red	44	8.1	259	8.9	132	7.1	118	6.2	42	6.6	51	10.9
Tiputini Plain	14	2.6	207	7.1	86	4.6	79	4.1	96	15.6	12	2.6
DECORATED												
Armenia White-on-Red	6	1.1	21	0.7	58	3.1	5	0.3	3	0.4	1	0.2
Napo Negative	–	–	1	0.1	–	–	5	0.3	1	0.1	–	–
Napo Plain Excised	9	1.6	21	0.7	29	1.6	25	1.3	7	1.1	7	1.5
Napo Plain Incised	41	7.5	292	10.1	194	10.4	353	18.5	23	3.6	46	9.9
Napo Red Excised	1	0.2	25	0.8	10	0.5	17	0.9	1	0.1	3	0.6
Napo Red Excised, White Re-touched	1	0.2	11	0.4	4	0.2	1	0.1	–	–	1	0.2
Napo Red Incised	6	1.1	27	0.9	15	0.9	–	–	–	–	10	2.1
Napo White Excised	–	–	–	–	2	0.1	–	–	–	–	–	–
Napo White Incised	8	1.5	92	3.2	51	2.7	28	1.4	15	2.4	1	0.2
Rocafuerte Incised	–	–	8	0.3	3	0.2	6	0.4	4	0.6	2	0.4
Rocafuerte Painted	88	16.1	315	10.8	326	17.6	115	6.0	47	7.4	51	10.9
Tiputini Plain Excised	6	1.1	43	1.5	44	2.3	33	1.7	15	2.4	8	1.7
Tiputini Plain Incised	7	1.3	76	2.6	78	4.2	29	1.5	13	2.0	19	4.2
Tiputini Red Excised	11	2.0	41	1.4	14	0.8	29	1.5	8	1.2	5	1.1
Tiputini Red Excised, White Retouched	3	0.5	14	0.5	13	0.7	–	–	6	0.9	2	0.4
Tiputini Red Incised	2	0.4	10	0.3	18	0.9	–	–	1	0.1	20	4.3
Tiputini White Excised	–	–	–	–	2	0.1	–	–	–	–	–	–
Tiputini White Incised	–	–	10	0.3	6	0.3	–	–	–	–	1	0.2
Unclassified decorated	5	0.9	3	0.1	4	0.2	2	0.1	2	0.2	7	1.5
TRADE												
Trade pottery	–	–	6	0.2	–	–	–	–	–	–	–	–
GRAND TOTALS	546	100.0	2911	100.0	1858	100.0	1907	100.0	635	100.0	466	100.0
SUBTOTALS:												
Plain types	352	64.6	1895	65.1	987	53.1	1259	66.0	489	77.0	282	60.5
Decorated types	194	35.4	1010	34.7	871	46.9	648	34.0	146	23.0	184	39.5
Trade pottery	0	0.0	6	0.2	0	0.0	0	0.0	0	0.0	0	0.0

TABLE 8.—*Frequency of pottery types in surface collections and stratigraphic excavations at sites of the Napo Phase.*—Continued

| | Pottery Types | N–P–3: Nuevo Rocafuerte—Continued | | | | N–P–4: Bello Horizonte | | N–P–5: Florencia | | N–P–6: Puerto Alfaro | | Oasis | |
| | | Test B | | Test B— Extension | | Surface and Tests | | Surface and Tests | | Surface and Tests | | Surface | |
		No.	%	No.	%	No.	%	No.	%	No.	%	No.	%
PLAIN	Armenia Plain	26	5.4	59	8.0	21	4.6	11	3.9	6	0.6		
	Napo Plain	232	47.8	310	41.9	173	38.1	185	67.1	775	79.3	58	61.8
	Napo Red	27	5.6	10	1.3	48	10.6	10	3.6	51	5.2		
	Tiputini Plain	16	3.3	62	8.4	19	4.2	11	3.9	19	2.0		
DECORATED	Armenia White-on-Red	3	0.6	8	1.1	9	2.0	1	0.4	2	0.2	–	–
	Napo Negative	–	–	–	–	–	–	–	–	–	–	–	–
	Napo Plain Excised	–	–	1	0.1	11	2.4	–	–	2	0.2	1	1.1
	Napo Plain Incised	44	9.1	36	4.9	51	11.2	15	5.5	53	5.4	16	17.0
	Napo Red Excised	3	0.6	–	–	–	–	–	–	4	0.4	5	5.3
	Napo Red Excised, White Retouched	1	0.2	–	–	–	–	–	–	–	–	1	1.1
	Napo Red Incised	8	1.6	3	0.4	13	2.9	5	1.8	23	2.4	3	3.1
	Napo White Excised	–	–	1	0.1	–	–	–	–	–	–	1	1.1
	Napo White Incised	7	1.4	5	0.7	–	–	1	0.4	–	–	–	–
	Rocafuerte Incised	2	0.4	3	0.4	3	0.6	–	–	–	–	–	–
	Rocafuerte Painted	65	13.4	203	27.4	49	10.8	19	6.9	15	1.5	4	4.2
	Tiputini Plain Excised	3	0.6	2	0.3	2	0.5	–	–	3	0.3	2	2.1
	Tiputini Plain Incised	31	6.4	27	3.6	26	5.7	13	4.7	19	2.0	1	1.1
	Tiputini Red Excised	4	0.8	3	0.4	6	1.3	–	–	–	–	2	2.1
	Tiputini Red Excised, White Retouched	10	2.0	2	0.3	–	–	–	–	–	–	–	–
	Tiputini Red Incised	–	–	1	0.1	23	5.1	2	0.7	1	0.1	–	–
	Tiputini White Excised	–	–	–	–	–	–	–	–	–	–	–	–
	Tiputini White Incised	2	0.4	1	0.1	–	–	2	0.7	–	–	–	–
	Unclassified decorated	2	0.4	3	0.4	–	–	1	0.4	4	0.4	–	–
TRADE	Trade pottery	–	–	1	0.1	–	–	–	–	–	–	–	–
	GRAND TOTALS	486	100.0	741	100.0	454	100.0	276	100.0	977	100.0	94	100.0
	SUBTOTALS:												
	Plain types	301	62.0	441	59.5	261	57.5	217	78.6	851	87.1	58	61.8
	Decorated types	185	38.0	299	40.4	193	42.5	59	21.4	126	12.9	36	38.2
	Trade pottery	0	0.0	1	0.1	0	0.0	0	0.0	0	0.0	0	0.0

TABLE 9.—*Frequency of Napo Phase plain and decorated pottery classified by temper and frequency of incised and excised decoration classified by single- and double-line techniques*

	N–P–1: Tiputini								N–P–2: Nueva Armenia			
	Surface and Tests								Surface and Tests			
	Area 1		Area 2		Area 3		Area 4		Area 1		Area 2	
	No.	%	No.	%	No.	%	No.	%	No.	%	No.	%
Temper of all plain and decorated pottery types:												
Black ash	–	–	6	1.0	1	0.3	22	2.0	20	8.0	2	2.9
Cariapé	–	–	–	–	–	–	70	6.5	46	18.3	7	10.0
Sand	167	100.0	658	99.0	267	99.7	981	91.5	185	73.7	59	87.1
Total sherds per site unit used for percentage calculations	167	100.0	664	100.0	268	100.0	1073	100.0	251	100.0	68	100.0
Motifs of all incised and excised decorated types:												
Single-line	2	9.1	6	3.9	6	10.2	53	24.5	15	26.5	8	26.5
Double-line	20	90.9	147	96.1	53	89.8	163	75.5	42	73.5	22	73.5
Total sherds used for percentage calculations	22	100.0	153	100.0	59	100.0	216	100.0	57	100.0	30	100.0

TABLE 9.—*Frequency of Napo Phase plain and decorated pottery classified by temper and frequency of incised and excised decoration classified by single- and double-line techniques.*—Continued

	N–P–2: Nueva Armenia—Continued										N–P–3: Nuevo Rocafuerte	
	Surface and Tests—Con.		Broadside A		Broadside B		Cut 1				Surface and Test A	
	Area 2a						0–15 cm.		15–30 cm.			
	No.	%	No.	%	No.	%	No.	%	No.	%	No.	%
Temper of all plain and decorated pottery types:												
Black ash	38	6.9	303	10.4	153	8.3	126	6.6	103	16.2	26	5.6
Cariapé	33	6.0	215	7.4	204	10.9	466	24.6	234	36.4	75	16.1
Sand	475	87.1	2393	82.2	1501	80.8	1315	68.8	298	47.4	365	78.3
Total sherds per site unit used for percentage calculations	546	100.0	2911	100.0	1858	100.0	1907	100.0	635	100.0	466	100.0
Motifs of all incised and excised decorated types:												
Single-line.	29	33.2	194	30.2	175	36.5	91	17.8	43	48.2	55	44.8
Double-line	58	66.8	448	69.8	305	63.5	424	82.2	46	51.8	68	55.2
Total sherds used for percentage calculations	87	100.0	642	100.0	480	100.0	515	100.0	89	100.0	123	100.0

TABLE 9.—*Frequency of Napo Phase plain and decorated pottery classified by temper and frequency of incised and excised decoration classified by single- and double-line techniques.*—Continued

| | N-P-3: Nuevo Rocafuerte—Con. | | | | N-P-4: Bello Horizonte | | N-P-5: Florencia | | N-P-6: Puerto Alfaro | |
| | Test B | | Test B—Extension | | Surface and Tests | | Surface and Tests | | Surface and Tests | |
	No.	%	No.	%	No.	%	No.	%	No.	%
Temper of all plain and decorated pottery types:										
Black ash	34	7. 0	100	13. 5	50	10. 6	11	3. 9	27	2. 7
Cariapé	40	8. 3	84	11. 3	46	9. 5	24	8. 7	10	1. 0
Sand	412	84. 7	557	75. 2	358	79. 9	241	87. 4	940	96. 3
Total sherds per site unit used for percentage calculations	486	100. 0	741	100. 0	454	100. 0	276	100. 0	977	100. 0
Motifs of all incised and excised decorated types:										
Single-line	50	44. 3	36	43. 9	57	43. 2	19	47. 5	23	22. 0
Double-line	63	55. 7	46	56. 1	75	56. 8	21	52. 5	82	78. 0
Total sherds used for percentage calculations .	113	100. 0	82	100. 0	132	100. 0	40	100. 0	105	100. 0

TABLE 10.—*Frequency of vessel forms and base forms from surface collections and stratigraphic excavations of the sites used in the seriated sequence of the Napo Phase*

Vessel Forms	N-P-1: Tiputini						N-P-2: Nueva Armenia							
	Surface and Tests						Surface and Tests				Broadside A		Broadside B	
	Area 2		Area 3		Area 4		Area 1		Area 2a					
	No.	%	No.	%	No.	%	No.	%	No.	%	No.	%	No.	%
Common Form														
1	14	17.6	7	28.0	11	8.4	2	6.9	1	1.4	15	4.2	4	1.8
2	–	–	–	–	2	1.5	–	–	2	2.8	6	1.7	1	0.4
3	–	–	–	–	2	1.5	1	3.4	9	12.5	9	2.5	10	4.6
4	1	1.2	–	–	7	5.3	–	–	2	2.8	20	5.6	6	2.7
5	1	1.2	1	4.0	2	1.5	–	–	4	5.6	3	0.9	5	2.3
6	–	–	2	8.0	–	–	5	17.4	–	–	4	1.1	2	0.8
7	2	2.5	–	–	4	3.1	2	6.9	7	9.7	32	9.1	16	7.3
8	2	2.5	–	–	6	4.5	1	3.4	3	4.1	16	4.5	12	5.5
9	1	1.2	–	–	9	6.9	2	6.9	1	1.4	16	4.5	37	16.9
10	3	3.8	1	4.0	4	3.1	–	–	2	2.8	8	2.2	10	4.6
11	2	2.5	1	4.0	4	3.1	2	6.9	8	11.1	18	5.1	13	5.9
12	13	16.3	1	4.0	19	14.5	2	6.9	6	8.3	40	11.3	35	16.2
13	5	6.3	5	20.0	10	7.6	2	6.9	7	9.7	29	8.3	17	7.8
14	4	5.0	–	–	13	9.9	1	3.4	4	5.6	19	5.4	6	2.7
15	15	18.8	2	8.0	4	3.1	–	–	–	–	4	1.1	3	1.3
16	6	7.5	2	8.0	13	9.9	4	13.9	5	6.9	52	14.7	10	4.6
17	6	7.5	1	4.0	12	9.2	1	3.4	9	12.5	46	13.0	29	13.4
18	1	1.2	1	4.0	1	0.8	1	3.4	–	–	5	1.4	–	–
19	1	1.2	–	–	–	–	–	–	–	–	–	–	–	–
20	–	–	–	–	–	–	1	3.4	–	–	3	0.9	–	–
Rare Form														
1	–	–	–	–	–	–	–	–	–	–	–	–	2	0.8
2	–	–	–	–	–	–	–	–	–	–	–	–	–	–
3	–	–	–	–	–	–	–	–	–	–	1	0.3	–	–
4	1	1.2	1	4.0	–	–	–	–	1	1.4	1	0.3	–	–
5	–	–	–	–	1	0.8	–	–	–	–	–	–	–	–
Unclassified	2	2.5	–	–	7	5.3	2	6.9	1	1.4	7	1.9	1	0.4
TOTAL	80	100.0	25	100.0	131	100.0	29	100.0	72	100.0	355	100.0	219	100.0
Base Forms														
A	2	–	1	–	1	–	2	–	4	–	13	–	12	–
B	–	–	–	–	–	–	1	–	–	–	2	–	1	–
C	–	–	–	–	1	–	–	–	1	–	3	–	–	–
D	7	–	2	–	5	–	1	–	1	–	5	–	–	–
E	–	–	–	–	1	–	2	–	–	–	6	–	1	–
TOTAL	9	–	3	–	8	–	6	–	6	–	29	–	14	–
Total Sherds	664	–	268	–	1073	–	251	–	546	–	2911	–	1858	–

TABLE 10.—*Frequency of vessel forms and base forms from surface collections and stratigraphic excavations of the sites used in the seriated sequence of the Napo Phase.*—Continued

Vessel Forms	N–P–2: Nueva Armenia—Con.				N–P–3: Nuevo Rocafuerte						N–P–4: Bello Horizonte	
	Cut 1				Surface and Test A		Test B		Test B—Extension		Surface and Tests	
	0–15 cm.		15–30 cm.									
	No.	%	No.	%	No.	%	No.	%	No.	%	No.	%
Common Form												
1	4	2.4	1	1.5	2	3.4	–	–	–	–	6	13.0
2	3	1.8	–	–	1	1.7	–	–	–	–	–	–
3	6	3.7	3	4.4	2	3.4	5	8.8	–	–	1	2.1
4	5	3.1	–	–	2	3.4	1	1.7	3	4.1	3	6.4
5	2	1.2	1	1.5	–	–	1	1.7	6	8.3	–	–
6	4	2.4	1	1.5	1	1.7	1	1.7	5	6.9	–	–
7	16	9.8	3	4.4	3	5.1	3	5.3	5	6.9	4	8.5
8	1	0.6	5	7.3	2	3.4	2	3.5	5	6.9	3	6.4
9	15	9.1	9	13.2	5	8.5	8	14.1	16	22.3	2	4.2
10	10	6.1	2	3.0	1	1.7	1	1.7	1	1.4	2	4.2
11	13	7.9	7	10.3	6	10.2	1	1.7	2	2.8	1	2.1
12	42	25.7	15	22.0	16	27.0	12	21.1	1	1.4	15	32.0
13	5	3.1	1	1.5	3	5.1	9	16.0	1	1.4	–	–
14	5	3.1	2	3.0	1	1.7	4	7.0	4	5.6	4	8.5
15	–	–	1	1.5	–	–	1	1.7	–	–	1	2.1
16	7	4.2	5	7.3	8	13.6	–	–	12	16.7	2	4.2
17	7	4.2	–	–	4	6.8	6	10.5	9	12.5	–	–
18	6	3.7	3	4.4	–	–	–	–	–	–	1	2.1
19	–	–	–	–	2	3.4	–	–	–	–	–	–
20	–	–	1	1.5	–	–	–	–	1	1.4	–	–
Rare Form												
1	–	–	–	–	–	–	–	–	–	–	–	–
2	–	–	–	–	–	–	–	–	1	1.4	–	–
3	–	–	1	1.5	–	–	–	–	–	–	–	–
4	–	–	–	–	–	–	–	–	–	–	–	–
5	1	0.6	1	1.5	–	–	–	–	–	–	–	–
Unclassified	12	7.3	6	8.7	–	–	2	3.5	–	–	2	4.2
TOTAL	164	100.0	68	100.0	59	100.0	57	100.0	72	100.0	47	100.0
Base Forms												
A	10	–	8	–	5	–	1	–	7	–	2	–
B	2	–	1	–	–	–	–	–	1	–	2	–
C	1	–	–	–	–	–	1	–	–	–	–	–
D	1	–	–	–	3	–	–	–	–	–	1	–
E	3	–	–	–	–	–	–	–	1	–	–	–
TOTAL	17	–	9	–	8	–	2	–	9	–	5	–
Total Sherds	1907	–	635	–	466	–	486	–	741	–	454	–

TABLE 11.—*Frequency of technique variants of Armenia White-on-red, Rocafuerte Incised, and Rocafuerte Painted*

Pottery Types and Technique Variants	N–P–1: Tiputini								N–P–2: Nueva Armenia						Broadside A		Broadside B	
	Surface and Tests								Surface and Tests									
	Area 1		Area 2		Area 3		Area 4		Area 1		Area 2		Area 2a					
	No.	%	No.	%	No.	%	No.	%	No.	%	No.	%	No.	%	No.	%	No.	%
Armenia White-on-red																		
White-on-red	1	0.6	7	1.1	3	1.1	1	0.1	–	–	4	5.9	6	1.1	21	0.7	58	3.1
Black and white-on-red	–	–	–	–	–	–	–	–	–	–	–	–	–	–	–	–	–	–
Rocafuerte Incised																		
White incised, red retouched	–	–	–	–	–	–	9	0.8	–	–	–	–	–	–	3	0.1	2	0.15
White incised and red and black-on-white	–	–	–	–	–	–	5	0.5	2	0.8	–	–	–	–	5	0.2	1	0.05
Rocafuerte Painted																		
Red and black-on-white	92	54.8	67	10.2	35	13.1	116	10.8	30	12.0	13	19.1	54	9.9	231	7.9	257	13.8
Red-on-white	2	1.2	28	4.2	2	0.7	8	0.7	–	–	1	1.5	10	1.8	48	1.7	31	1.6
Black-on-white	–	–	11	1.6	–	–	17	1.6	9	3.6	2	2.9	24	4.4	36	1.2	38	2.1
Total sherds per site unit used for percentage calculations	167	–	664	–	268	–	1073	–	251	–	68	–	546	–	2911	–	1858	–

Table 11.—*Frequency of technique variants of Armenia White-on-red, Rocafuerte Incised, and Rocafuerte Painted.*—Continued

Pottery Types and Technique Variants	N-P-2: Nueva Armenia—Continued Cut 1				N-P-3: Nuevo Rocafuerte						N-P-4: Bello Horizonte Surface and Tests		N-P-5: Florencia Surface and Tests		N-P-6: Puerto Alfaro Surface and Tests		Oasis Surface	
	0–15 cm.		15–30 cm.		Surface and Test A		Test B		Test B—Extension									
	No.	%	No.	%	No.	%	No.	%	No.	%	No.	%	No.	%	No.	%	No.	%
Armenia White-on-red																		
White-on-red	5	0.3	3	0.4	1	0.2	2	0.4	7	1.0	9	2.0	1	0.4	2	0.2	–	–
Black and white-on-red	–	–	–	–	–	–	1	0.2	1	0.1	–	–	–	–	–	–	–	–
Rocafuerte Incised																		
White incised, red retouched	1	0.1	–	–	2	0.4	1	0.2	2	0.3	–	–	–	–	–	–	–	–
White incised and red and black-on-white	5	0.3	4	0.6	–	–	1	0.2	1	0.1	3	0.6	–	–	–	–	–	–
Rocafuerte Painted																		
Red and black-on-white	88	4.6	39	6.1	48	10.3	62	12.8	196	26.5	42	9.3	19	6.9	15	1.5	4	4.2
Red-on-white	27	1.4	1	0.2	2	0.4	2	0.4	3	0.4	1	0.2	–	–	–	–	–	–
Black-on-white	–	–	7	1.1	1	0.2	1	0.2	4	0.5	6	1.3	–	–	–	–	–	–
Total sherds per site unit used for percentage calculations	1907	–	635	–	466	–	486	–	741	–	454	–	276	–	977	–	94	–

Plates 1-94

PLATE 1

Air views of the Rio Napo. *a*, Large sand bars exposed in December. Roofs at N–P–1: Tiputini show as bright spots at the center left; grass covered hills at N–P–2 at center top. *b*, Upper Rio Napo, with modern garden clearings in the foreground.

PLATE 2

Views of the upper Rio Napo. *a*, Looking from Latas toward the right bank across a small rapid. *b*, Low left bank near Santa Rosa strewn with drift trees.

PLATE 3

Views of the Rio Napo. *a*, Left bank near the mouth of the Rio Suno, with Sumaco volcano in the distance. *b*, Low right bank above Armenia Vieja, showing large tree deposited by flood waters. *c*, Looking downstream just below the mouth of the Rio Tiputini, with the cleared hill at N–P–10 visible at the center.

PLATE 4

Decline in water level of the Rio Napo opposite N–P–2 during a six week period in November–December 1956.

PLATE 5

Views of the Rio Napo, showing varieties of modern water transportation. *a*, Poling dugout opposite N–P–2. *b*, Port at Nuevo Rocafuerte. *c*, Small inboard motor launch at the junction of the Rio Napo (right) with the Rio Yasuní (foreground).

PLATE 6

Yasuní Phase sites. *a*, N–P–10 on the summit of a low hill. *b*, N–P–11 (beyond buildings) seen from the hill occupied by N–P–10.

PLATE 7

Views of the Rio Tiputini. *a*, Looking downstream from N–P–6. *b*, Mouth, with left bank of the Rio Napo in the distance.

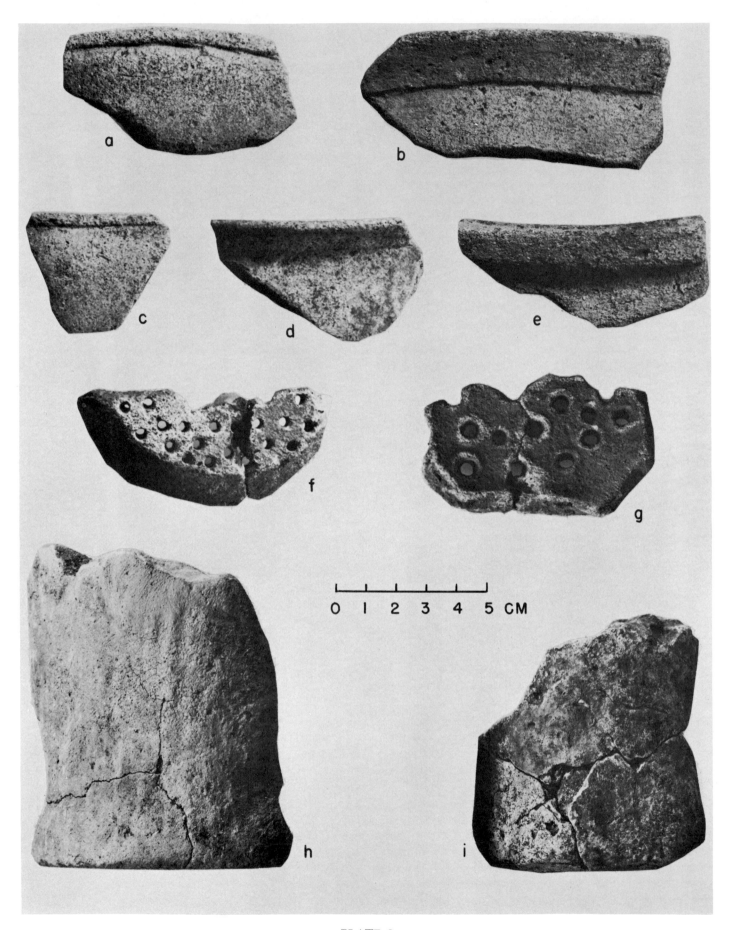

PLATE 8

Tivacundo Phase pottery types and artifacts. *a–e*, Chacra Plain rims. *f–g*, Chacra Plain perforated bases. *h–i*, Potrest fragments.

PLATE 9

Tivacundo Incised and Zoned Red.   *a*, Oval vessel (cf. fig. 23).   *b–d*, Type sherds, Technique 1.   *e*, Type sherds, Technique 2.

PLATE 10

Type sherds of Tivacundo Plain. *a–h*, Rims. *i–j*, Perforated bases.

PLATE 11

Tivacundo Phase pottery types. *a–e*, Tivacundo Red Painted. *f*, Unclassified cariapé-tempered plain.

PLATE 12

Sites of the Napo Phase. *a*, N–P–1: Tiputini, with the original surface elevation visible beneath the porches. *b*, N–P–3: Nuevo Rocafuerte.

PLATE 13

N–P–2: Nueva Armenia, a site of the Napo Phase. *a*, Looking from slightly downstream toward the site (right). *b*, Site area covered with modern buildings, seen from the hill behind.

PLATE 14

Napo Phase site of N–P–2: Nueva Armenia. *a*, Northeast end of the site (Area 2). *b*, Excavation of Cut 1.

PLATE 15

Sites of the Napo Phase. *a*, N–P–4: Bello Horizonte on the high bank at the center. *b*, N–P–5: Florencia, on the level area to the right of the hill.

PLATE 16

Views of the Rio Tiputini.   *a*, Bank occupied by the Napo Phase site of N–P–6.   *b*, Lower bank on the opposite side of the river.

PLATE 17

Potrest fragments from Napo Phase sites. *a–b, d, f–h,* Examples showing exterior surface treatment. *c, e,* Interior texture and manner of fracture.

PLATE 18

Type sherds of Armenia Plain. *a–b*, Rims. *e–h*, Surface treatment. *i–l*, Leaf impressions on exterior of bases.

PLATE 19
Type sherds of Armenia White-on-red.

PLATE 20

Type sherds and complete vessel of Armenia White-on-red. *a–b*, Rare variant painted black and white-on-red. *c*, Vessel of Form 17, from the Rio Aguarico (Peabody Museum of Archaeology and Ethnology, Harvard University).

PLATE 21

Type sherds of Napo Plain.   *a–g*, Rim sherds.   *i–k*, Typical fracture along coil junctions.   *h*, Leaf impression on exterior of base.

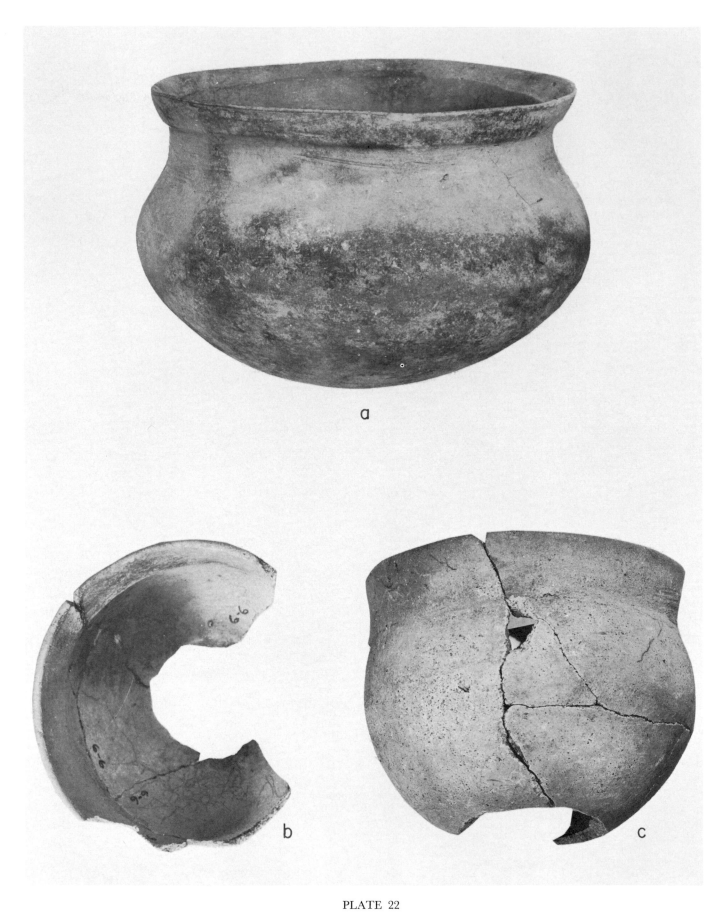

PLATE 22

Complete vessels of Napo Plain. *a*, Form 8, rim diameter 23 cm. *b–c*, Rare Form 1, rim diameter 12 cm. (U.S. National Museum).

PLATE 23
Type sherds of Napo Plain Excised.

PLATE 24
Type sherds of Napo Plain Excised.

PLATE 25

Type sherds of Napo Phase pottery types. *a–c, e,* Napo Plain Excised. *d, f,* Napo Negative.

PLATE 26

Complete vessels of Napo Plain Incised. *a–b*, Form 9. *c–d*, Form 8. *e–f*, Form 7. (U.S. National Museum)

PLATE 27
Type sherds of Napo Plain Incised.

PLATE 28
Type sherds of Napo Plain Incised.

PLATE 29

Type sherds of Napo Plain Incised.

PLATE 30
Type sherds of Napo Plain Incised.

PLATE 31

Type sherds of Napo Plain Incised showing rare combination of single-line and double-line techniques (*a–b*, *d–e*, Heye Foundation).

PLATE 32

Type sherd and bowl of Napo Red Excised.   *a*, Heye Foundation.   *b*, Courtesy Howard S. Strouth.

PLATE 33

Type sherds of Napo Red Excised.

PLATE 34
Type sherds of Napo Red Excised, White Retouched.

PLATE 35
Type sherds of Napo Red Incised.

PLATE 36
Type sherds of Napo White Excised.

PLATE 37
Type sherds of Napo White Incised.

O I 2 3 4 5 CM

PLATE 38

Type sherds of Napo White Incised.

PLATE 39
Type sherds of Napo White Incised.

a

b

PLATE 40
Type sherds of Napo White Incised.

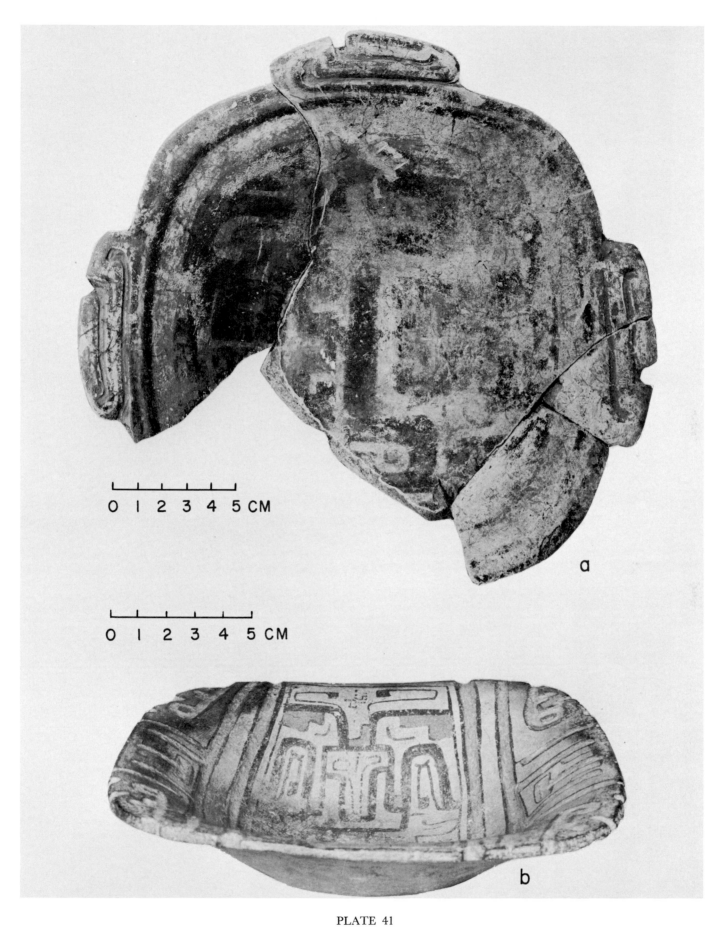

PLATE 41

Bowls of Rocafuerte Incised combined with red and black-on-white painting. *a*, N–P–3, Test B (U.S. National Museum). *b*, Unidentified provenience (American Museum of Natural History).

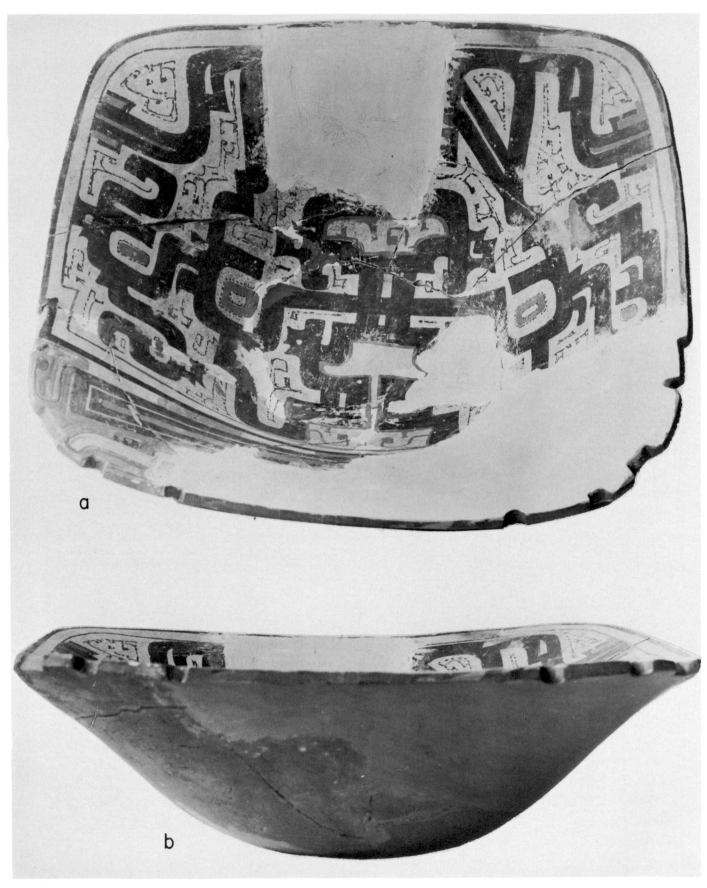

PLATE 42

Basin of Form 14 with Rocafuerte Incised decoration along one side and red and black-on-white painting in Technique 2 on the remainder of the interior. From N–P–2. (Courtesy Museo Arqueológico del Banco Central del Ecuador, Quito.)

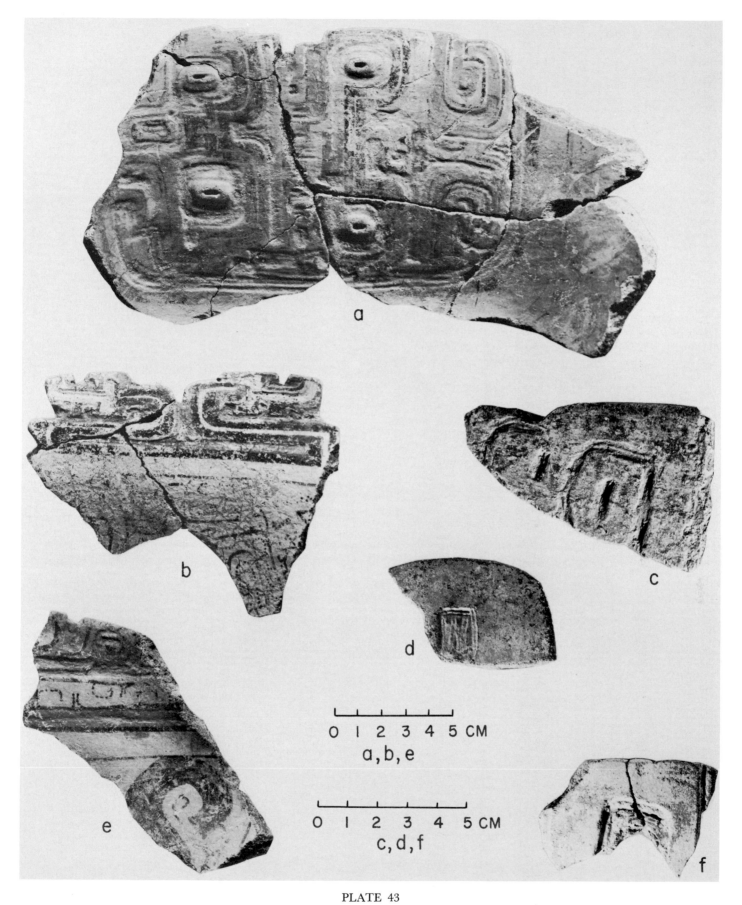

PLATE 43

Type sherds of Rocafuerte Incised. *a–b, e*, Combined with red and black-on-white painting. *c–d, f*, Red paint applied only to incisions.

PLATE 44

Type sherds of Rocafuerte Painted, red-on-white.

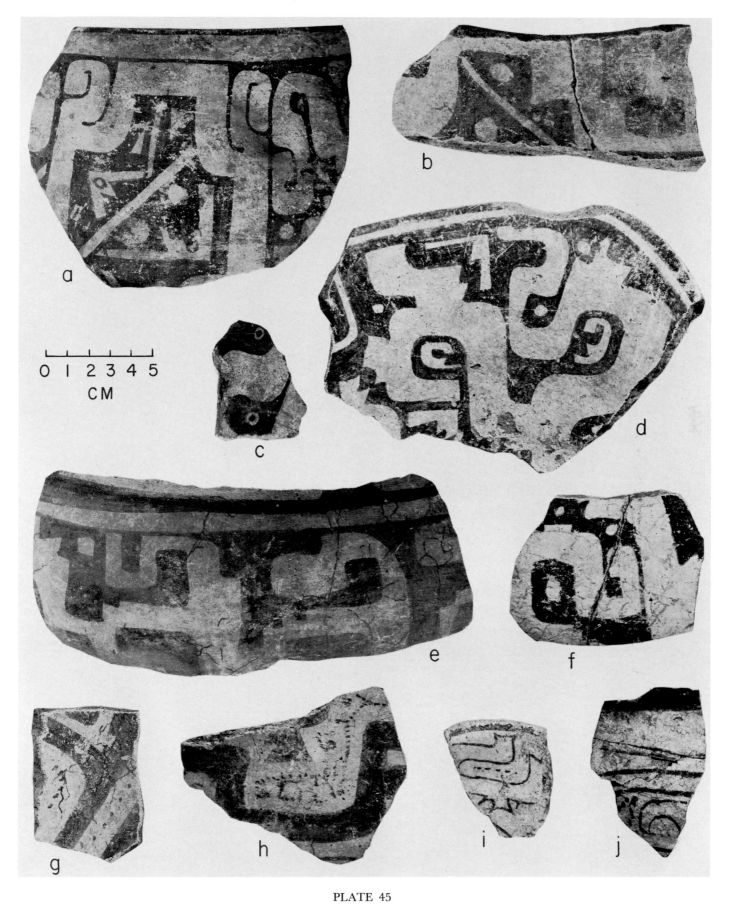

PLATE 45

Type sherds of Rocafuerte Painted, black-on-white. *a–f*, Technique 3. *g–h*, Technique 1. *i–j*, Technique 2.

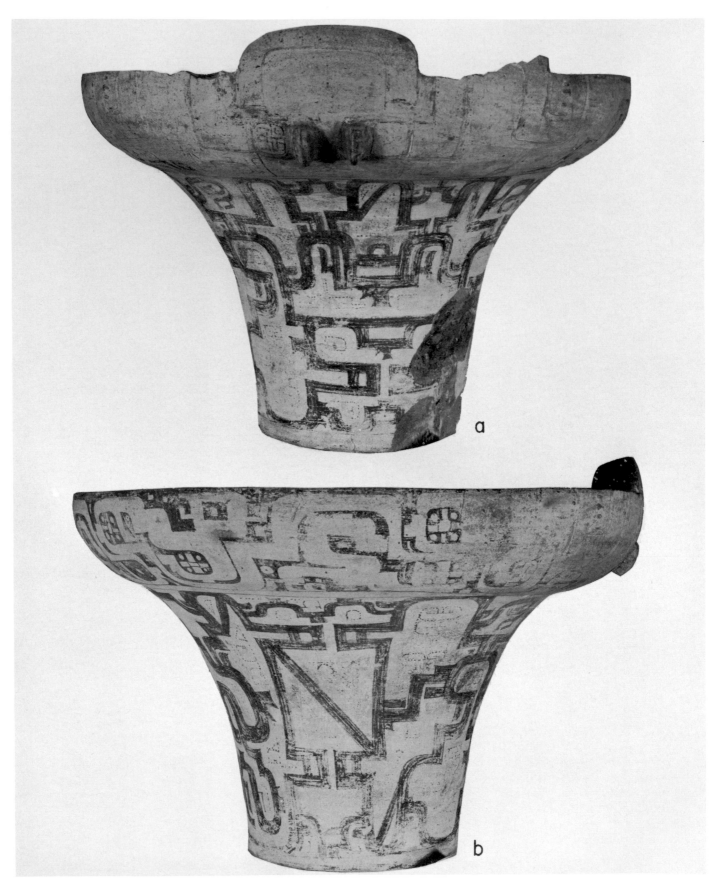

PLATE 46

Rocafuerte Painted vessel of Form 6 from a site on the Rio Aguarico. Painting is red and black-on-white, Technique 1 on the body and black-on white, Technique 3 on the rim (cf. fig. 54). Height 34 cm. (U.S. National Museum).

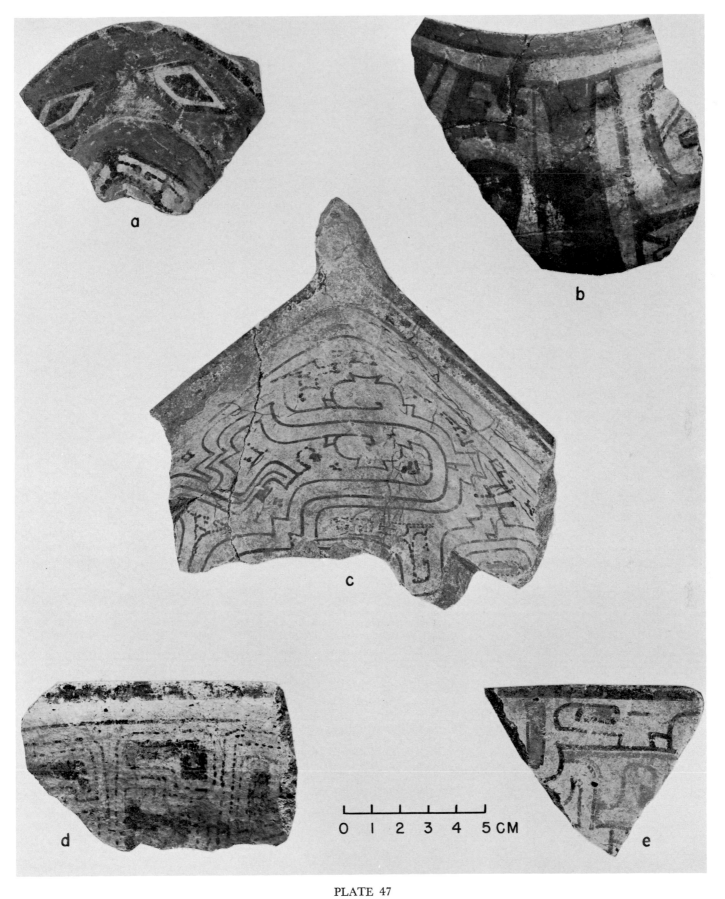

PLATE 47

Type sherds of Rocafuerte Painted, red and black-on-white. *a–b*, Technique 1. *c–d*, Technique 3. *e*, Technique 4.

O 1 2 3 4 5 CM   O 5 CM
a-c, e   d

PLATE 48
Type sherds of Rocafuerte Painted, red and black-on-white, Technique 2.

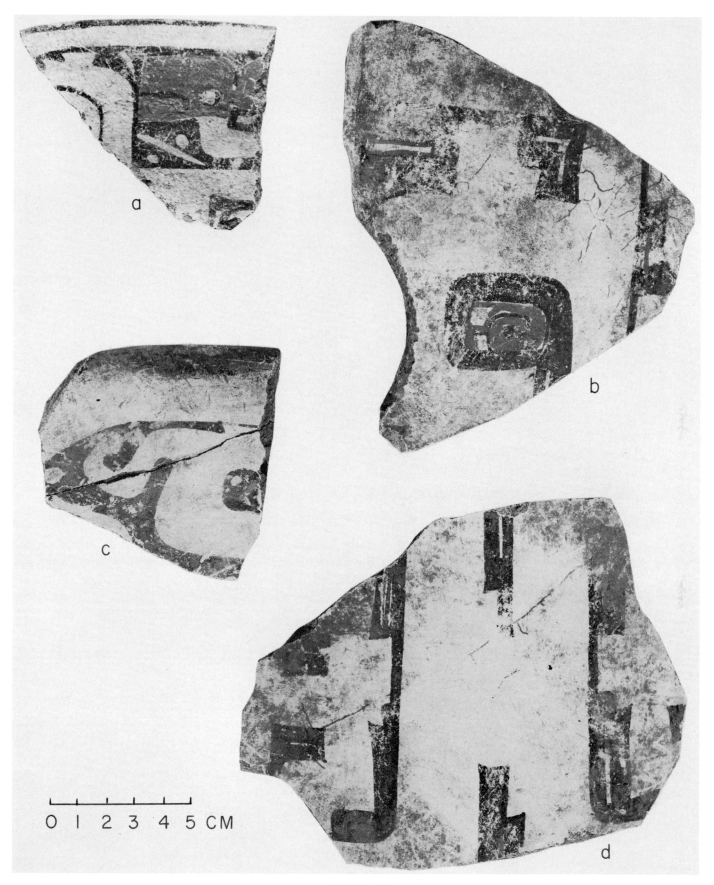

PLATE 49

Type sherds of Rocafuérte Painted, red and black-on-white, Technique 5.

PLATE 50

Vessels of Rocafuerte Painted, black-on-white. *a*, Jar of Form 16 painted in Technique 1. *b*, *d*, Jars of Form 17 painted in Technique 3
c, Jar of Form 17 painted in Technique 3 and supplied with a lid of Form 12 (in Jijón y Caamaño collection, Quito, courtesy of Pedro
I. Porras).

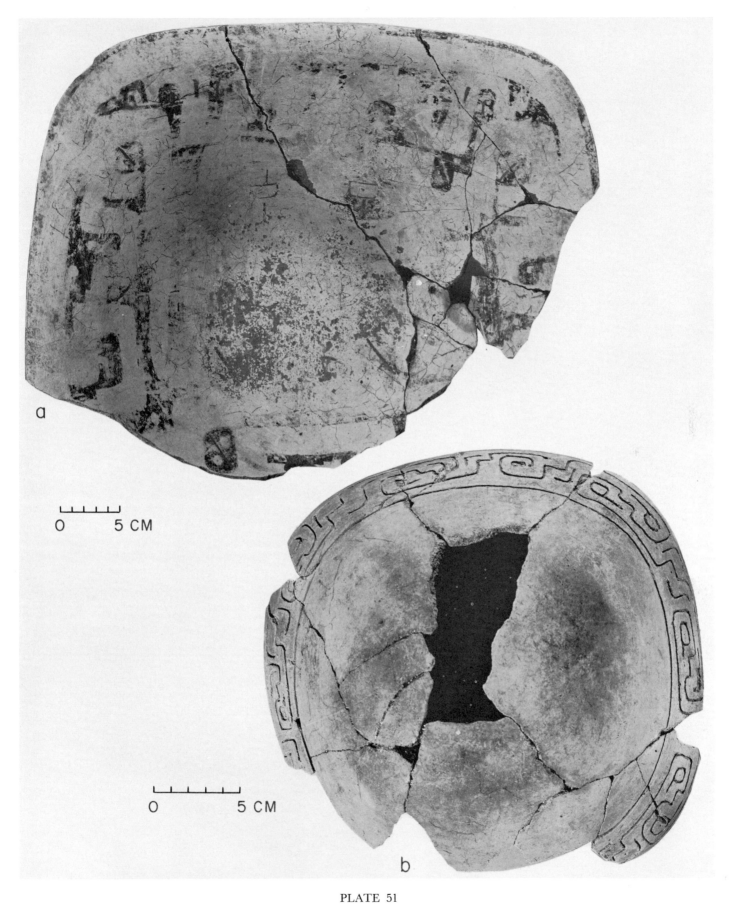

PLATE 51

Partially restored bowls of Napo Phase pottery types. *a*, Rocafuerte Painted, red and black-on-white, Technique 5. *b*, Tiputini Red Excised.

a

0   5   10 CM

b

PLATE 52

Rocafuerte Painted (red and black-on-white) vessel of Form 11 with anthropomorphic treatment (Museo Víctor Emilio Estrada, Guayaquil).

PLATE 53

Rocafuerte Painted (red and black-on-white) vessel of Form 11 with anthropomorphic treatment. (Courtesy of Museo Arqueológico del Banco Central del Ecuador, Quito).

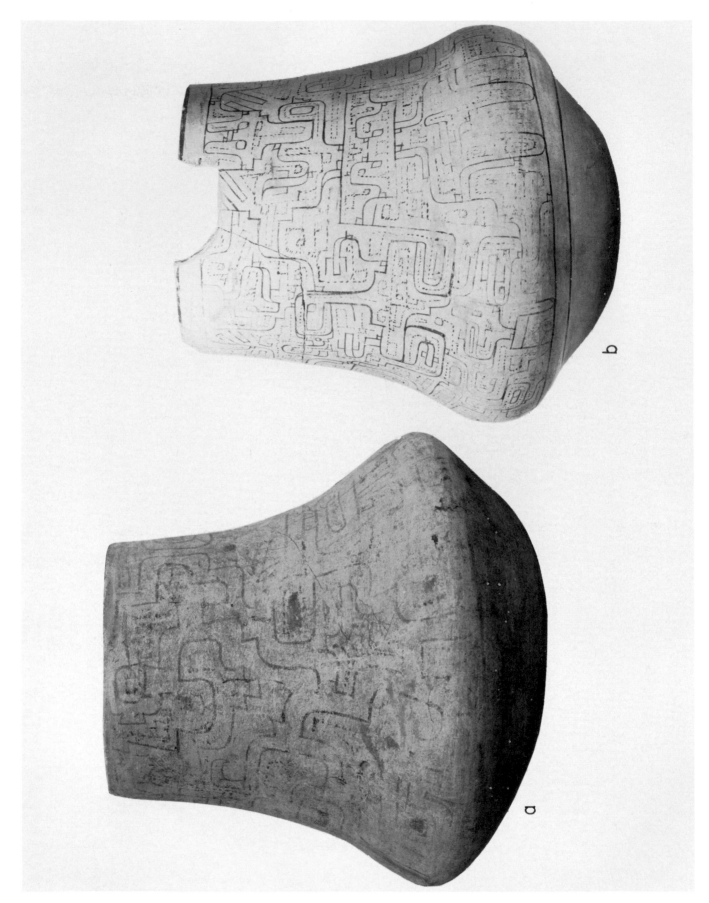

PLATE 54

Vessels of Rocafuerte Painted, Form 17. *a*, Red and black-on-white, Technique 3; height 30.4 cm. (Colegio Militar, Quito). *b*, Black-on-white, Technique 2; height 35.3 cm. (U.S. National Museum).

PLATE 55

Rocafuerte Painted anthropomorphic vessel Type A (Form 21). *a*. Painted red and black-on-white in Technique 2 on rear. *b*, Painted red and black-on-white in Technique 3 on front. Height 38 cm. (After Uhle, 1920, pls. 3–4.) See Table A for detailed description.

PLATE 56

Rocafuerte Painted anthropomorphic vessel Type A, painted red and black-on-white in Technique 2. (Courtesy Jay C. Leff and Brooklyn Museum.) See table A for detailed description.

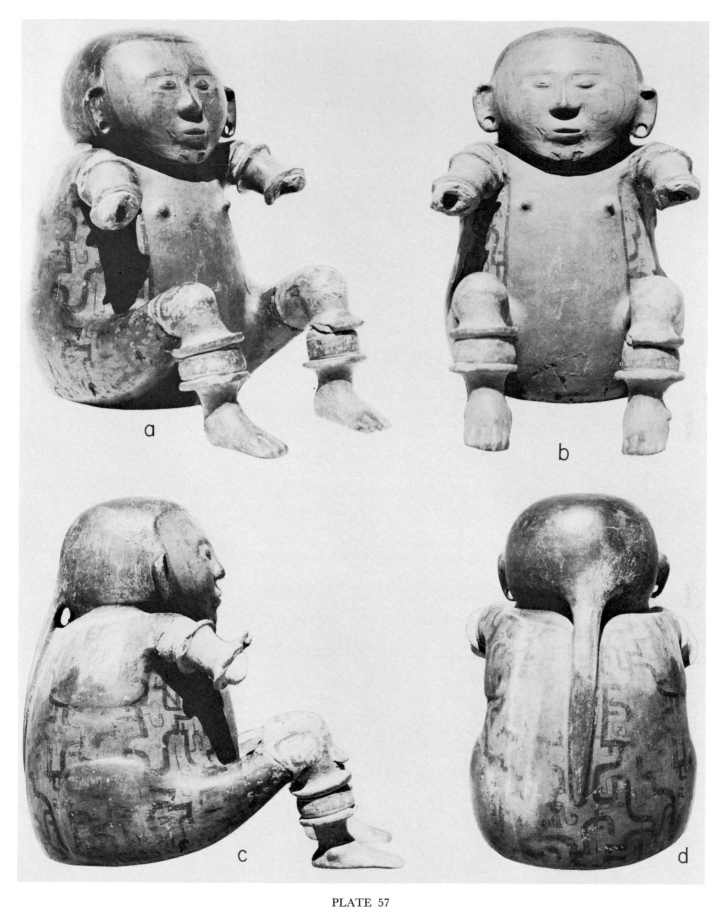

PLATE 57

Rocafuerte Painted anthropomorphic vessel Type B, painted red and black-on-white in Technique 2. (Courtesy Thomas Flannery.)
See table A for detailed description.

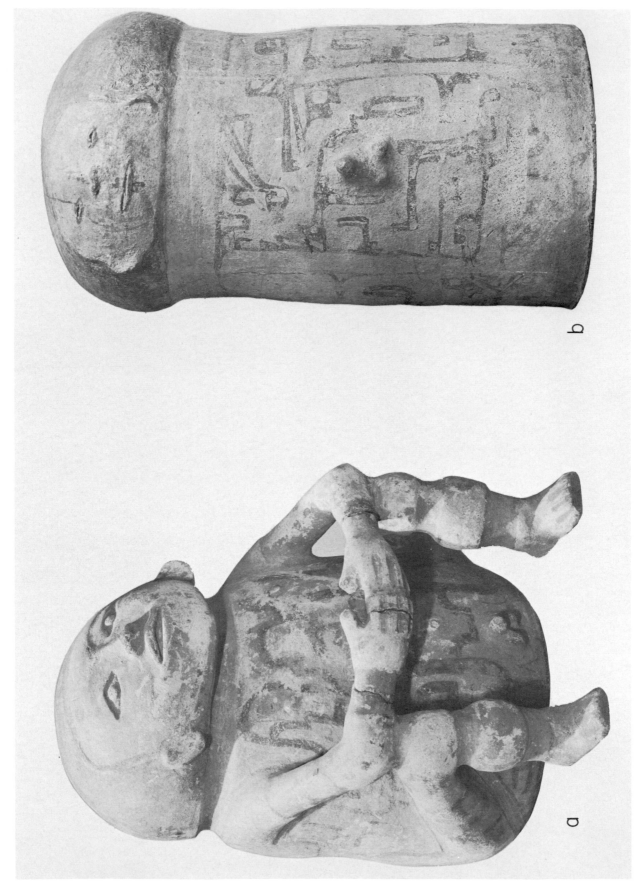

PLATE 58

Rocafuerte Painted anthropomorphic vessels. *a*, Type B, painted red and black-on-white in Technique 2; height 34 cm. (Courtesy Museum of Primitive Art, New York.) *b*, Type B, painted black-on-white in Technique 3; height 36.8 cm. (Courtesy Heye Foundation.) See table A for detailed descriptions.

PLATE 59

Rocafuerte Painted anthropomorphic vessel Type B, with rare grooved decoration between arms and legs (Casa de la Cultura Ecuatoriana, Quito).

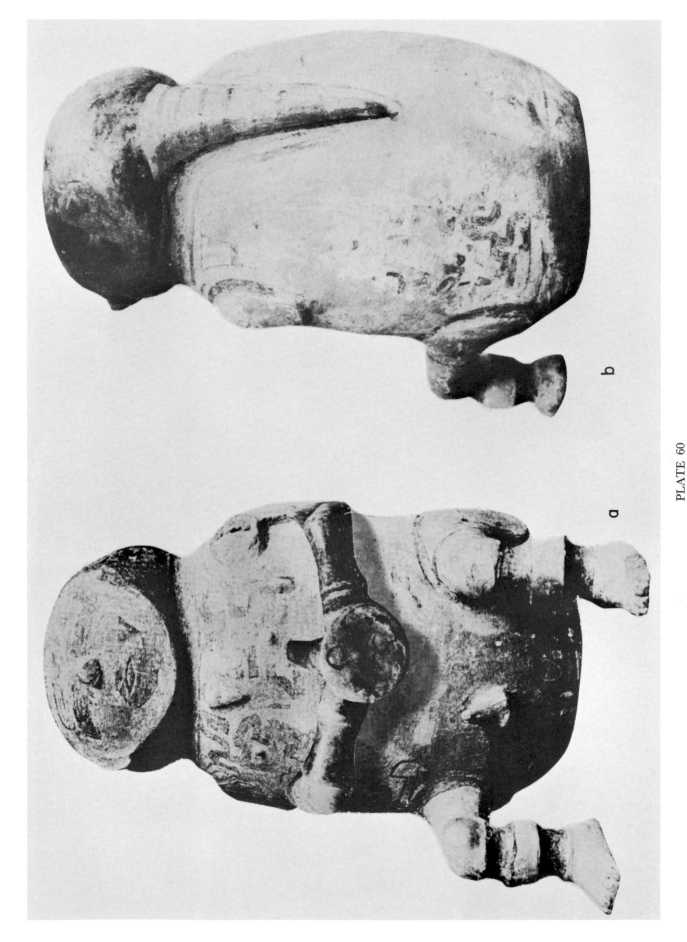

PLATE 60

Rocafuerte Painted anthropomorphic vessel Type B, painted red and black-on-white in Technique 2. (After Uhle, 1921, pls. 1–2; arms photographically restored.) See table A for detailed description.

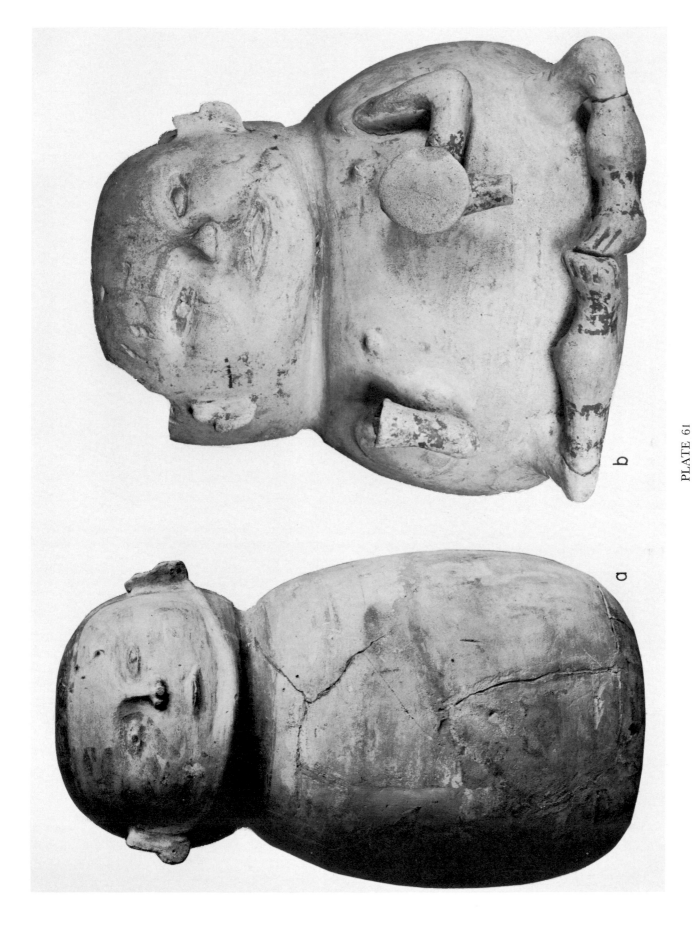

PLATE 61

Rocafuerte Painted anthropomorphic vessels. *a*, Type B, painted red and black-on-white (Musée de l'Homme, Paris). *b*, Type A, painted red-on-white (American Museum of Natural History). See table A for detailed descriptions.

PLATE 62

Rocafuerte Painted anthropomorphic vessels. *a*, Type C, painted red and black-on-white in Techniques 3 (front) and 2 (sides and rear) (American Museum of Natural History.) *b*, Type B, painted red and black-on-white in Technique 3 (Courtesy Alan C. Lapiner). See table A for detailed descriptions.

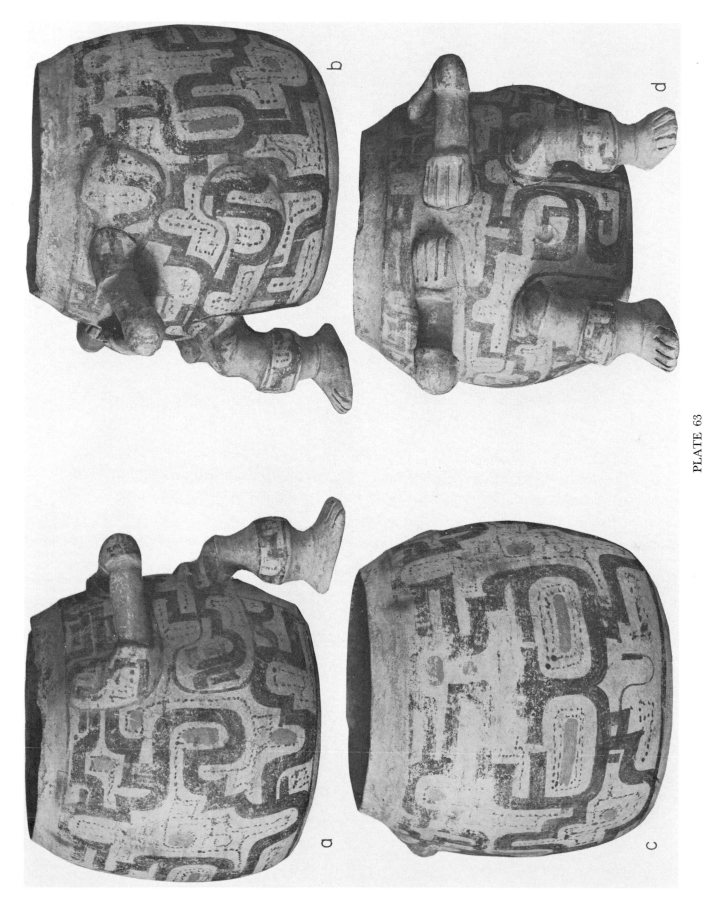

PLATE 63

Rocafuerte Painted anthropomorphic vessel Type C, painted red and black-on-white in Technique 2. (Museo Víctor Emilio Estrada Guayaquil.) See table A for detailed description.

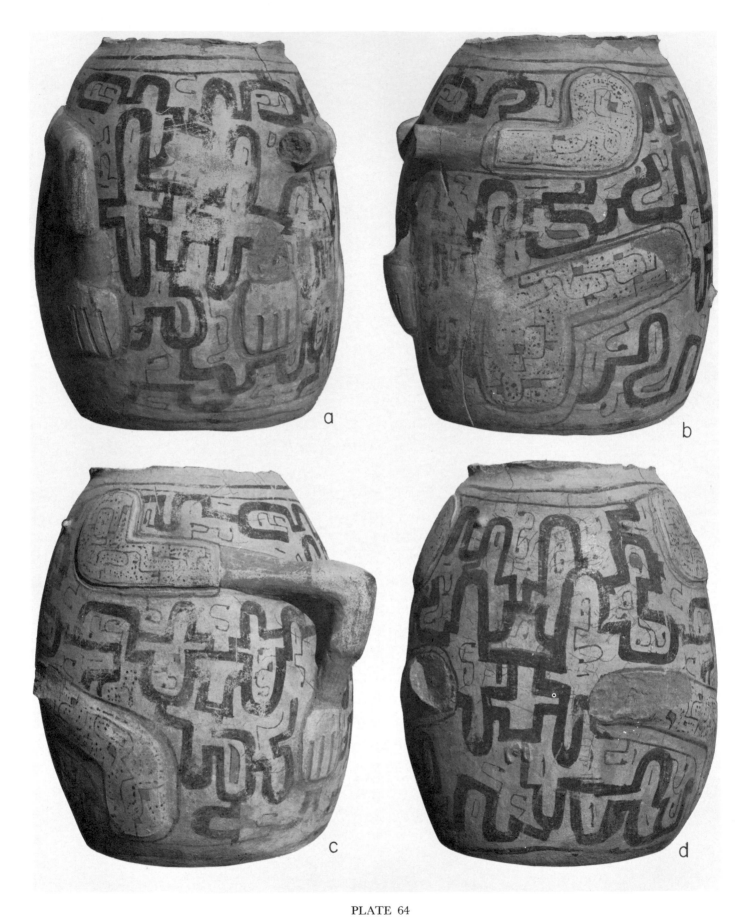

PLATE 64

Rocafuerte Painted anthropomorphic vessel Type C, painted red and black-on-white in Techniques 2 (body) and 3 (arm and legs). (Colegio Militar, Quito.)   See table A for detailed description.

PLATE 65

Rocafuerte Painted anthropomorphic vessel Type C, painted red and black-on-white in Techniques 2 (body) and 3 (arms and legs). (American Museum of Natural History.) See table A for detailed description.

PLATE 66

Tiputini Plain Excised bowl of Form 5; height 8 cm., exterior mouth diameters 23 by 25 cm. (U.S. National Museum).

PLATE 67
Type sherds of Tiputini Plain Excised.

PLATE 68
Type sherds of Tiputini Plain Excised.

PLATE 69
Type sherds of Tiputini Plain Excised with white retouch in incisions and excisions.

PLATE 70
Type sherds of Tiputini Plain Incised.

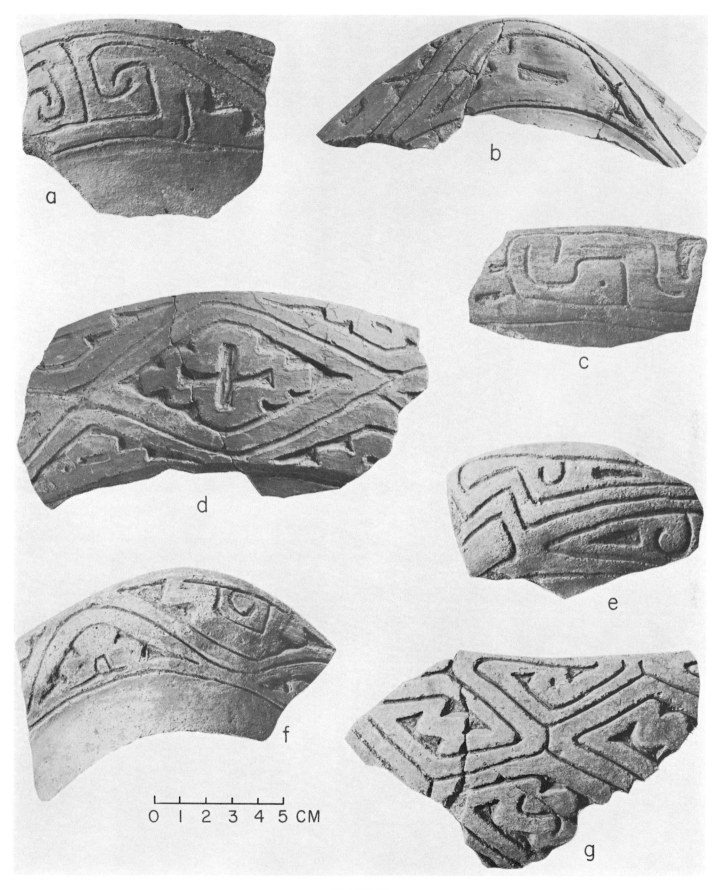

PLATE 71
Type sherds of Tiputini Red Excised.

PLATE 72
Type sherds of Tiputini Red Excised.

PLATE 73

Napo Phase pottery types. *a–l*, Tiputini Red Excised, White Retouched. *m–n*, Tiputini White Excised.

PLATE 74

Napo Phase pottery types. *a–i*, Type sherds of Tiputini Red Incised. *j–o*, Type sherds of Tiputini Red Incised, white retouched variety.

PLATE 75

Type sherds of Tiputini White Incised.

PLATE 76

Pottery from Napo Phase sites. *a–h, o,* Unclassified decorated. *i–n,* Sherds of probable trade origin.

PLATE 77

Cotacocha Phase pottery types. *a–e*, Cotacocha Plain. *f–l*, Latas Plain.

PLATE 78

Sherds from Peruvian complexes represented in the Zoned Hachure Horizon Style. *a–l*, Waira-jirca Phase (after Izumi and Sono, 1963, pl. 836). *m–t*, Tutishcainyo Phase.

PLATE 79

Decorated sherds from Coarí. *a*, White slipped after incision. *b–f*, *h–i*, Grooved, sometimes with a double-pointed or serrated tool. *g*, *j*, Red-on-white. *k*, Black-on-white. *l–m*, Single-line incised. (Courtesy Peter Paul Hilbert.)

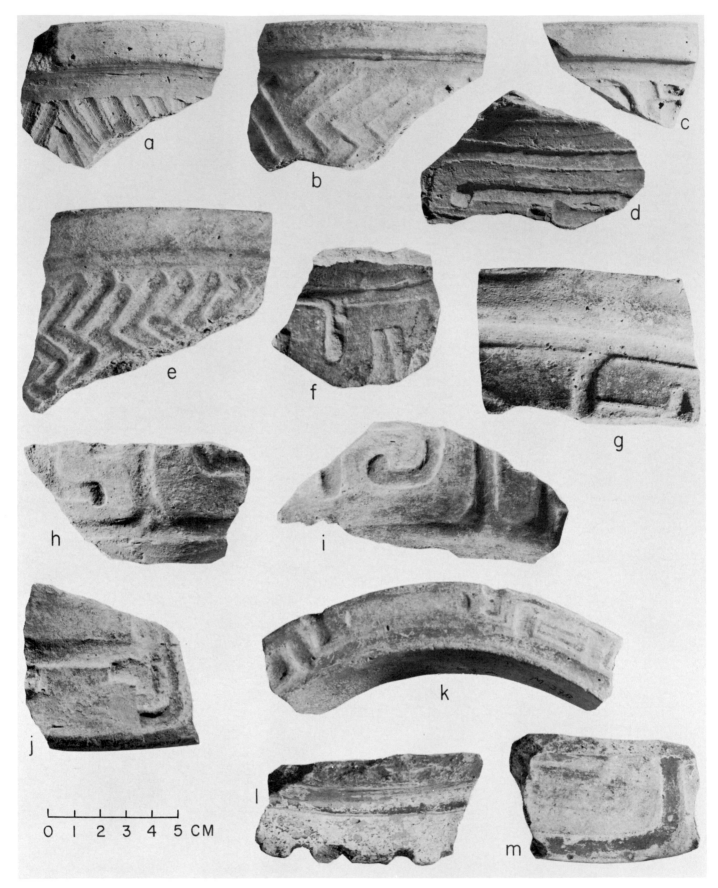

PLATE 80

Type sherds of the Guarita Phase from Refinaria Site, Manaus. *a–j*, Guarita Grooved. *k*, Everted rim with grooved and polychrome (red and black-on-white) decoration. *l–m*, Flanges with grooved and polychrome painted (red and black-on-white) decoration. (Courtesy Peter Paul Hilbert.)

PLATE 81

Decorated sherds from Itacoatiara. *a–f*, Excised. *g–i*, White slipped after incision. *j–k*, Single-line incision. *l–p*, Double-line incision. *q–r*, Grooved. (*a–b, d, f, i, k–m, p, r*, Courtesy Peter Paul Hilbert, Scale A; *c, e, g–h, j, n–o, q*, Museu Paulista, Scale B).

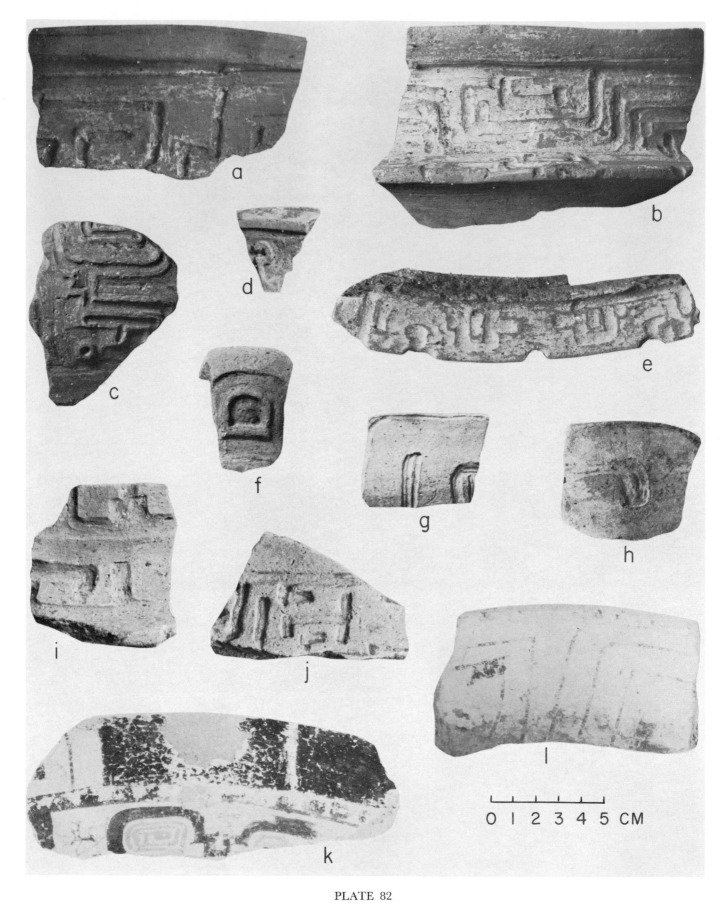

PLATE 82

Decorated sherds from Manacapurú. *a–b, e, i*, White-slipped after grooving. *c–d, f*, Excised. *g–h, j*, Double-line incised. *k*, Red and black-on-white. *l*, Black-on-white. (Museu Paulista.)

PLATE 83

Vessels from Manacapurú. *a*, Flanged vessel white slipped after grooving. *b*, White slipped vessel with tendency to square outline.
(Museu Paulista, São Paulo)

PLATE 84

Decorated sherds of Marajoara Phase pottery types. *a–c*, Ararí Plain Excised. *d*, Ararí Plain Excised, White Retouched. *e*, Ararí Red Excised. *f*, Ararí Double-slipped Excised. (American Museum of Natural History)

PLATE 85

Decorated sherds of Marajoara Phase pottery types. *a*, Ararí Plain Excised. *b*, Anajás White Incised. *c, e–f*, Pacoval Incised. *d*, Ararí Red Excised. (American Museum of Natural History)

PLATE 86

Marajoara Phase bowls with squarish form. *a–b*, Pacoval Incised. *c*, Ararí Red Excised, White Retouched. (*a*, Heye Foundation. *b–c*,
American Museum of Natural History)

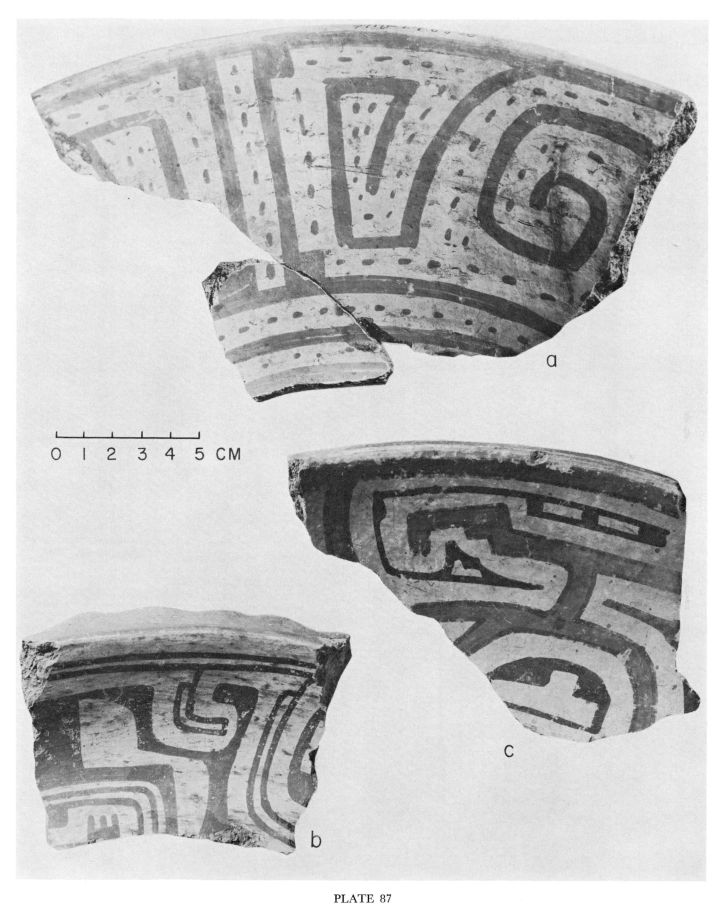

PLATE 87

Type sherds of Joannes Painted, Marajoara Phase. *a*, *c*, Red-on-white. *b*, Red and black-on-white. (American Museum of Natura
History)

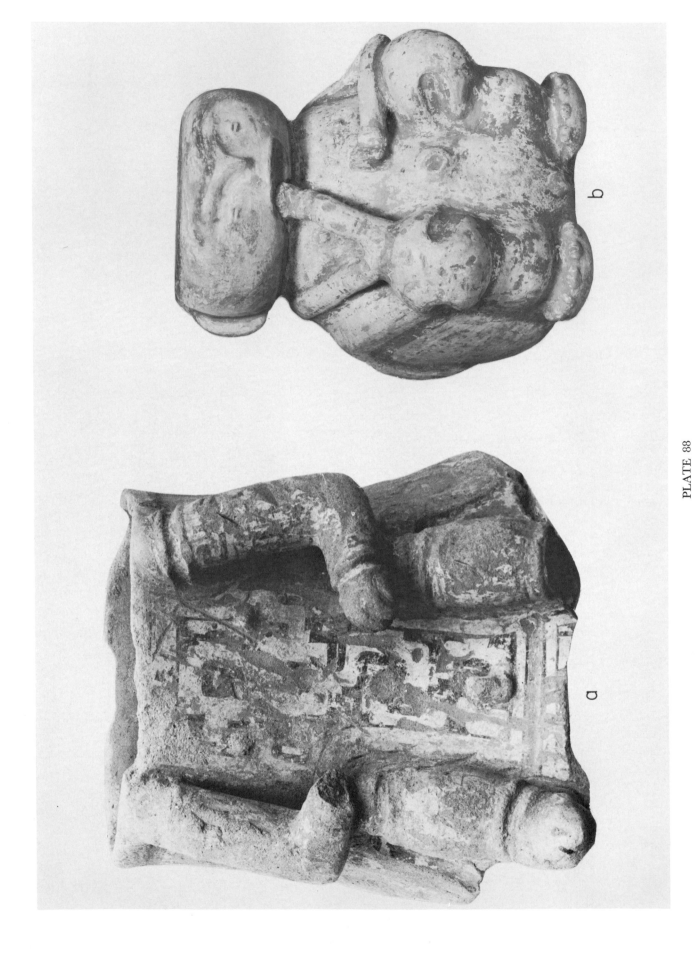

PLATE 88

Anthropomorphic vessels from middle and lower Amazon sites. *a*, Miracanguera (Museu Paulista, São Paulo). *b*, Marajoara Phase height 33 cm. (Courtesy Brooklyn Museum)

PLATE 89

Anthropomorphic vessels from middle Amazon sites. *a*, Miracanguera (Museu Paraense Emílio Goeldi). *b*, Nova Olinda, Rio Madeira. *c*, Rio Ipixuna. *d*, Provenience unknown. (*b–d*, Instituto Geográfico e Histórico, Manaus)

PLATE 90

Decorated sherds from Nazaré dos Patos. *a–h*, Grooved, typically with a double-pointed or serrated tool. *f, h*, White slipped after grooving. *i–j*, Excised. (Göteborg Museum, Sweden)

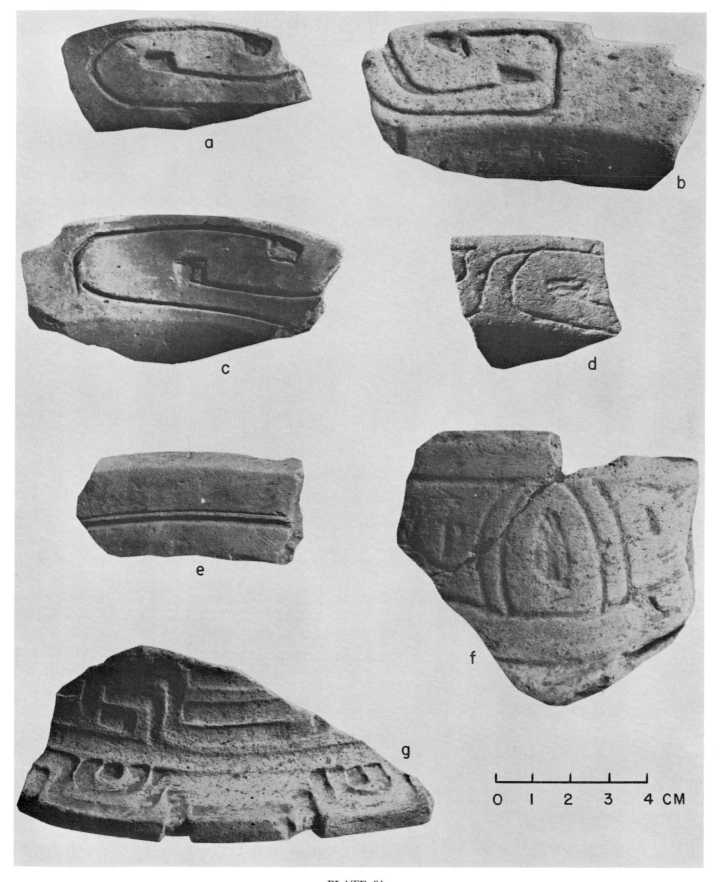

PLATE 91

Excised and incised sherds from middle Amazon sites. *a–c*, Paurá. *d*, Tauaquera. *e–g*, Pontão. (Göteborg Museum, Sweden)

PLATE 92

Decorated sherds from the vicinity of Santarem.   *a–g*, Double-line incised.   *h–l*, Single-line incised. (*a–b, d–e*, Göteborg Museum; *c, f–l*, Heye Foundation)

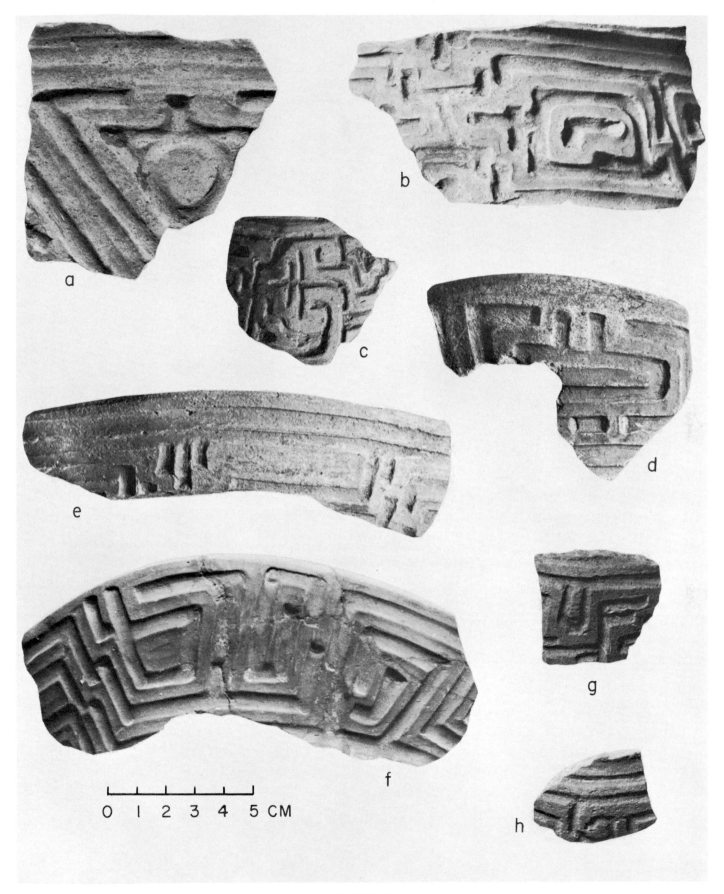

PLATE 93

Decorated sherds from the Tefé region. *a–c*, Excised. *d–h*, Broad grooved. (Museu Paulista)

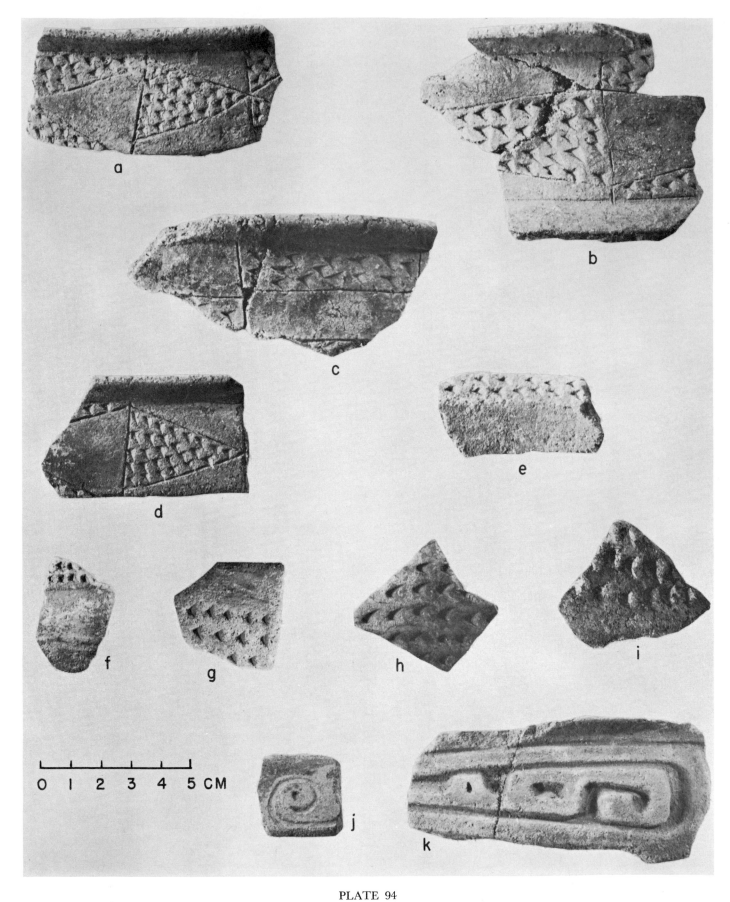

PLATE 94

Decorated sherds from Loreto, Rio Suno, Ecuador. *a–d*, Zoned punctate. *e–i*, Unzoned punctate. *j–k*, Possible Napo Phase trade.
(Courtesy Pedro I. Porras)